"As more systems integrators and computer resellers move to a "service and consulting" model, Freedman's advice, methodology, and insight will provide the necessary steps for building competent consultants and ensuring customer satisfaction. A copy of this book should be on the shelves of every IT consulting firm looking to move forward into the new millennium."

—Ron Layton, regional channel manager, Cisco Systems, Inc.

"Few consultants fail for lack of technical expertise, many fail for lack of relationship skills. This unique book is the cure for that problem."

—Dr. Peter C. Patton, chief technologist, Lawson Software

"Freedman shares his trade secrets to achieving a successful IT consulting career based on his vast personal experience. *The IT Consultant* offers a refreshing approach to the advisory relationship: understand your clients' business goals and develop a collaborative solution. A surefire strategy for success!"

—Elaine Biech, author, *The Business of Consulting*;
coauthor, *The Consultant's Legal Guide*

"A 'must-read' for any IT professional services manager attempting to upgrade the consultative skill set of their organization. Rick has done an exceptional job of articulating transformation areas and has provided real world examples that your staff can apply in the marketplace. The lessons learned here have a direct, linear relationship to the growth potential of your consulting practice or professional services organization."

—Peter N. Van Zant, senior vice president and managing principal,
ENTEX Consulting Services

"*The IT Consultant* is not only an excellent guide for individuals wishing to grow from skilled technicians to consultants, but it reminds today's practitioners that consultants are trusted business advisors to their clients. Rick Freedman has produced a well-flowing read that talks about required skills and considerations for consulting, gives "how-to" examples, and leads the readers through his suggested approaches."

—Mark Zemelman, regional consulting manager,
ENTEX Information Services

"*The IT Consultant* defines the skills necessary for IT consultants who want to launch their careers, while suggesting a framework for the IT consulting firm to adopt, evangelize, and practice for success. Rick recommends techniques and disciplines that I use to mentor and encourage my IT consulting team—disciplines that have helped make my career successful."

> —Jay A. Elder, regional network solutions manager,
> Colorado, Interlink Group Incorporated

"*The IT Consultant* is a complete playbook for any consultant interested in improving their game. It demonstrates how a consultant can become recognized for delivering what the client really needs—answers to business problems. The processes presented here build on each other to guide the consultant through to a successful engagement. As I begin to plan for my next consulting engagement I will definitely have a copy of *The IT Consultant* on my desk to use as a blueprint."

> —Howard Wilkens, senior project manager, Sprint Paranet

"Traditionally, those in the IT field have emphasized technical knowledge first and tend to reward these skills over the important communications that are really necessary. This is a refreshing and useful approach: business knowledge *before* technology. *The IT Consultant* provides valuable advice not only for those considering practicing IT consulting, but also for the IT industry as a whole."

> —Linda NeCastro-Pastel, software systems analyst, RS Information Systems;
> consultant, Office of Navel Research

"This book is a good primer for the novice or seasoned IT consultant. Rick Freedman clearly understands that the key attribute to building a successful consulting practice is developing an intimate relationship with your customer."

> —Matt Jones, president and CEO, Lipstream Networks, Inc.

The IT Consultant

A COMMONSENSE FRAMEWORK
FOR MANAGING THE
CLIENT RELATIONSHIP

Rick Freedman

Jossey-Bass
Pfeiffer

San Francisco

ISBN 0-7879-5173-0
Library of Congress Catalog Card Number 99-050574

Library of Congress Cataloging-in-Publication Data

Freedman, Rick.
    The IT consultant : a commonsense framework for managing the client
relationship / Rick Freedman.
      p. cm.
  Includes bibliographical references and index.
  ISBN 0-7879-5173-0
  1. Business consultants. 2. Electronic data processing consultants.
I. Title.
  HD69.C6 F74 2000
  004'.068'8—dc21   99-050574

Printed in the United States of America.

Published by

JOSSEY-BASS/PFEIFFER
A Wiley Company
350 Sansome St.
San Francisco, CA 94104-1342
415.433.1740; Fax 415.433.0499
800.274.4434; Fax 800.569.0443

www.pfeiffer.com

Printing 10 9 8 7 6 5 4 3 2

Acquiring Editor: Matthew Holt
Director of Development: Kathleen Dolan Davies
Developmental Editor: Susan Rachmeler
Editor: Rebecca Taff
Senior Production Editor: Dawn Kilgore
Manufacturing Manager: Becky Carreño
Interior Design: Claudia Smelser
Illustrations: Richard Sheppard

 This book is printed on acid-free, recycled stock that meets or exceeds the minimum GPO and EPA
requirements for recycled paper.

For Terri

Familiar acts are beautiful through love.

Percy Bysshe Shelley

ACKNOWLEDGMENTS

The IT Consultant is a compilation of wisdom handed down by the many teachers I've been lucky enought to encounter in my career:

Walter Sloan, my first (and still my best) mentor in consulting ethics and practices,

Tharyn Aiken at Citicorp: you were right—I'm not a banker!

Garry Hauxhurst, Marsha Hopkins and Ellen Clarke at D&B, my business school (of hard knocks),

Mike Gansl and the team at NetLan, where we learned together what it takes to migrate from products to services,

David White at Cap Gemini; a teacher of quality,

Dan Sullivan, Rick Nathanson, John Richardson, Joan Gaskins, Rebecca Braun, Chris Philpott, Gregg Klein, Jay Elder, and everyone at Entex; for teaching me courage under fire!

Matt Holt, editor and friend; thanks for the encouragement. You helped make a lifetime dream come true!

Susan Rachmeler, Dawn Kilgore, Adrienne Biggs, Ocean Howell, and everyone at Jossey-Bass Pfeiffer; this is your work as much as mine.

Clients past and future: the learning never ends.

Shawn, Leila, Danny, Dalia, Jeremy, Josh, Abby, Ellie, Patrick, Emily, Mikey: my best influences.

CONTENTS

Management theory and consulting practice are converging. Persuasion, interactive communication, and collaborative teamwork are replacing traditional command-and-control management styles. Even that bastion of command and control, the U.S. Marine Corps, is refocusing its leadership programs on consultative management. Both business and the military recognize the need for skills such as coaching, educating, consensus building, and cross-disciplinary teamwork. The most emulated role model for modern managers is the sports coach, who works with uniquely talented, highly paid, self-sufficient individuals and motivates them to achieve as a team. Consultative selling skills are also highly prized. Rare and treasured are salespeople who can build a trust relationship with their clients, guide them in the use of their product or service, and advise clients so they obtain the most value from the relationship. They have achieved the coveted "customer intimacy." They are sought by employers and customers because they build mutually beneficial relationships that last.

Businesses use these consulting practices because they work. Whatever the task at hand, teaming up, guiding, and advising one another, using coaching and mentoring skills, and emphasizing communication are tactics that produce results. Applying those practices to help clients obtain information technology (IT) results is the focus of this book.

There is no more customer-intimate business relationship than consulting. To excel in our profession, we must gain our clients' trust. Like doctors or lawyers, we must help our clients feel comfortable enough to confide in us, to tell us things that may not be easy to acknowledge or discuss. And, as in medicine or law, client and practitioner must work together to achieve results. Either one working on his or her own, no matter how expert and diligent, will fail. Only by forming a partnership, by heeding each other's advice and counsel, and by keeping each other focused on the goal, will we succeed.

This book is based on a few fundamental beliefs. I believe information technology consulting is a profession on a par with engineering and architecture. I believe in professional standards that must be applied once a consultant has accepted a consulting engagement. I believe that advisory skills, which enable us to develop relationships of trust and confidence with our clients, are as important to our success as mastery of technical disciplines. I believe there are proven practices and common sense techniques that help consultants deliver the benefits of information technology in a way that would be impossible without us.

I also contend that a structured methodology helps practitioners bring order from chaos. The structured programming methodologies of the 1970s, such as Wirth's (1971) "Stepwise Refinement" and Gane and Sarson's (1977) "Structured Systems Analysis," revolutionized the process of developing software systems by providing a clear path through the design process. I present here an organized approach to the client/consultant relationship, which I call the *IT Consulting Framework*. This framework is biased toward collaboration, communication, and results. Many IT development life cycles have phases, such as project definition, system analysis, design, development, implementation, and maintenance. Although these are descriptive, they seem to me mechanical and impersonal. Those methodologies and this framework have a similar goal—to provide a road map to help IT professionals deliver solutions consistently. The IT Consulting Framework, however, is designed to stress the human factor.

The phases of the IT Consulting Framework are as follows:

- Approach the Client,
- Negotiate the Relationship,
- Visualize Success,
- Understand the Client's Situation,
- Design Solution Options,
- Collaborate to Select the Solution, and
- Deliver Business Results.

These phases were titled to highlight the central premise of this book: *IT consulting engagements succeed or fail based not on the technology, but on the ability of the consultant to create a relationship with the client that encourages collaboration, communication, and results.*

By focusing on the relationship aspects of consulting, we keep in mind that each engagement is unique, because each person is unique and each situation is unique. We make a commitment to the success of our clients, with the unshakable intention of getting results together. Delivering "white papers" or "findings documents," or even installing functioning information technology, is not enough for us—we must share in the client's vision for success and collaborate to deliver it. We must also remember that to earn the customer's trust we must deserve it.

This book will present proven practices that IT consultants can use to define their role in the engagement, and to understand their clients' technical, organizational, and cultural environments. It will introduce creative design techniques, used by engineers and industrial designers, that can be adopted by IT professionals to stimulate innovation. It will emphasize the importance of providing a complete solution. Consultants who bring all the value-enhancing elements to the design table create superior solutions and build indestructible customer relationships. We'll review those additional services, such as training, documentation, and contingency planning, that differentiate the superior IT consultant and that allow the client to obtain the maximum impact from their IT investments.

WHO SHOULD READ THIS BOOK?

In this time of outsourcing and corporate downsizing, many IT professionals are considering consulting as a career. Others must apply consulting practices to their jobs within the corporation. Many computer technicians want to expand their career capabilities, to be more than a technician for hire. Unfortunately, for many, the skills they have learned as employees or technicians have not prepared them for the complexities of providing IT advisory services to clients. Additionally, the majority of books on the subject of consulting discuss the logistics and operational aspects of starting and running a consulting practice, but give little guidance on the techniques of giving advice for a living. *The IT Consultant* addresses the needs of both novice consultants seeking a blueprint for providing quality services and of experienced consulting professionals looking for direction in the development of their advisory skills.

HOW THIS BOOK IS ORGANIZED

I've tried to organize this book in the most accessible way possible. It is divided into three parts, each with a different theme. Part One is an overview of The Profession of Consulting, which outlines the basic principles for practicing consultants and the professional standards that consultants should apply. Part Two describes the IT Consulting Framework, the structured processes and techniques IT consultants can use to plan, design, and deliver IT systems. Part Three coaches IT consultants in the intricacies and nuances of Developing Superior Consulting Skills, with tips for dealing with resistance, inertia, sniping, and politics, and it provides guidance in retaining your customers by bringing added-value services such as training, securing, and documenting IT systems.

Also included is a case study that illustrates some of the principles presented. I've tried to imagine a scenario that would represent some of the real-life situations that we as practicing IT consultants will find ourselves in and to present that scenario in a manner that illustrates the principles I'm expounding in the text. The case study includes examples of a request for proposal, a proposal from a consulting firm, and a project plan as templates that consultants can use in their own practices and to show how the principles presented here are used in real life.

In a study published in May 1999, International Data Corporation projected that U.S. spending on consulting will reach $55 billion by the year 2003, a 14.5 percent annual growth rate. Clearly organizations have embraced the use of expert advisors as a method of achieving their business goals. By applying the diagnostic, analytical, and advisory techniques presented here, IT consultants can learn to help clients achieve the business benefits of modern information technologies.

The accompanying CD-ROM has been designed for use in conjunction with this book. It contains exhibits, figures, and appendices designated by the CD-ROM icon in the book. The files may be used as templates to be customized as needed. Further information on how to run the CD-ROM is located on the last page of this book.

August 1999   Rick Freedman

part one

The Profession of Consulting

The opposite of the word "professional" is not unprofessional, but rather technician.

David Maister

What qualities define a superior IT consultant? I always start my consulting seminars with that question. The answer typically depends on the technical specialty of the group I'm addressing. If my audience is a team of network designers, their answers center around expertise in firewalls, routers, and protocols. If the audience is composed of programmers, the qualifications include the ability to write a Java applet or to code in C.

My answer, and the philosophy presented in this book, is that IT consulting is most successful when advisory skills, rather than purely technical ones, are stressed. I want to expand the definition of IT consulting beyond the "technician-for-hire" model, which I call "IT contracting." A contractor fulfills a contract by bringing his or her technical competence to work every day, to be directed and managed by the client. A consultant counsels and advises. Technical competence is essential for professional IT consultants, but it is not sufficient. Technicians, to become consultants, must master communication, collaboration, and human relationship skills; in short, they must become skilled and trusted advisors.

As the profitability is squeezed out of the business of selling computer hardware, many resellers are trying to migrate to a services-based business model. These resellers and small consulting shops all have skilled systems engineers on their teams, with long experience and deep technical expertise. Yet these technicians struggle when expected to perform as consultants. Many of them have developed exceptional customer skills, yet few can engage with clients in discussions about business strategy or objectives. They are skilled at uncovering technical requirements, but inexperienced in unearthing business needs. These prospective consultants need to understand what it means to be a professional advisor; they need coaching in fundamental consulting skills; and they need a discipline for delivering consistent IT results.

When I begin training a team of prospective consultants, I start by reminding them that consulting is not mysterious; indeed, we consult with professionals all the time. When we talk to a doctor, lawyer, or accountant, we are consulting with a technical specialist. At the core, our consulting process as IT advisors is identical to the one followed by other professionals. Whether we are consulting our doctor about a runny nose or our accountant about a pending IRS audit, the consulting process consists of five steps (although each of these steps may be broken down into dozens more):

1. Understand the current state;
2. Define the desired state;
3. Analyze the gap between these states;
4. Recommend an action plan to move from the current state to the desired state; and
5. Partner with the client to implement the action plan.

When we visit our doctors, it's typically ill health that's the problem, and the doctor proceeds to perform an analysis of the current state by asking us our family history, our medical background, and our current ailment. The desired state is clearly a return to good health. The doctor performs a gap analysis, or diagnosis, based on technical expertise. Once he or she has decided on a diagnosis, a doctor prescribes a therapy that we, as patients, are responsible for following.

So, I tell prospective IT consultants, think of the basic steps your doctor follows, and you have a model of the process of consulting. By analyzing the patient's current situation, applying technical expertise to developing a diagnosis, and prescribing a cure, the doctor demonstrates how a professional advisor goes about business.

Yet the superior physician does more. He or she knows the patient well enough to decide how to communicate the diagnosis effectively. Based on a knowledge of the patient's lifestyle and character, a doctor weighs the treatment options and prescribes a therapy with the most likelihood of being followed. Doctors set up a monitoring program to ensure that the prescription is effective and develop an education and wellness program to help patients understand, maintain, and optimize their health. These same qualities, of intimate customer knowledge, thoughtful communication, careful selection of appropriate solutions, and partnering for results, characterize the superior consultant.

Consulting is more than expertise in a technical discipline or a craft. We all have had experience with the supremely qualified technician who cannot explain in plain English what's wrong or how to fix it. Who hasn't worked with a talented craftsman who had no understanding of working within a defined budget, or of the basic courtesies such as timeliness? In the IT world as well, there are plenty of technicians who can design and implement the most complex multi-site data networks, yet lack basic skills in communication, project management, time management, or human interaction.

Many IT organizations promote employees based on progressive achievement as a technician. A technical engineer proceeds from fixing PC's to installing desktop operating systems through setting up networks and corporate architectures, with promotions from technician to network engineer to system consultant along the way. Have these technicians become consultants, simply because they've reached a certain level of technical proficiency? I believe most clients, if asked that question, would answer "No." In the eyes of the client, engaging a consultant promises more than just renting competent technical skills. Clients want a technical expert they can trust to guide and advise them.

There is another area in which the doctor and the consultant must be successful: *achieving results.* Consultants whose only deliverable is a set of findings or a comparative white paper have not fulfilled their obligation to their clients. Part of what clients look for from a technical expert is help in designing a solution to their problem. Many clients, however, are unable to move from selecting a solution to implementing it; they need help translating their chosen strategy into a plan of action. Information technology consultants need a consistent, repeatable consulting process so they can help clients turn ideas into results. The superior IT consultant collaborates with the client to develop a solution, and then devotes just as much skill and creativity to building an operational business system.

The material in Part I outlines the fundamental advisory skills a consultant needs and presents some basic principles for counseling clients successfully. In Chapter One we'll discuss the five basic rules of the business advisor, rules that we will develop into a consulting framework in the second part of the book. In Chapter Two, we'll outline the fundamental skills that IT consultants must bring to each engagement, skills that go beyond the purely technical and that prepare us for our essential role, that of the counselor and advisor.

The Business of Advice

The greatest trust between man and man is the trust of giving counsel.

Sir Francis Bacon

It's widely acknowledged that doctors, lawyers, engineers, and architects are professionals. Their certifications by government and trade organizations proclaim it. The respect and admiration they receive from their communities demonstrates it. The pay scales they command confirm it. What is it about the work they do that characterizes these experts as professionals? It is their mastery of a specialized discipline, their role as personal advisors, their duty to the client, and the requirement to follow a set of professional standards that define these as professional callings.

Is IT consulting a profession? IT consultants also draw from a highly specialized body of knowledge that is sufficiently obscure so as to be understood only by a small cadre of specialists. Like doctors, lawyers, and engineers, we spend a significant part of our working lives explaining complex technical subject matter to clients. Our clients rely on the advice we give to be successful in their careers or businesses. We also have a responsibility to provide complete and correct advice. Yet the IT consultant is rarely thought of in the same context as the doctor or architect. Nor do most IT consultants think of themselves that way. The process of applying professional standards to the advising of clients is rarely the key skill IT workers think of when they consider becoming a consultant. We consider ourselves consultants because of our technical skills.

Clients also focus on the technical, rather than the advisory, aspects of a prospective consultant's skills. They often ask a consulting candidate, "Do you know UNIX?" or "Are you a Certified NetWare Engineer?," but rarely, "How do you overcome resistance to a new data system?" or "How do you ensure that the systems you design remain secure and operational after they are installed?"

Yet we know, from working with auto mechanics and plumbers, dentists and tax advisors, that technical expertise alone does not make one a good and trusted advisor. We've all had experiences with good and poor consultants. I've had doctors who walked in the room staring at a clipboard, asked a couple of questions in a mechanical tone, ticked off a checklist, and only then glanced up to see who the subject of the interview was. I often wonder whether these "advisors" cared whether I was a man, a woman, or a horse. I've also had experience with doctors who took the time to know me, my preferences, my personality, and the way I feel about my medical condition, and then prescribed therapies that I might actually implement. Good and poor advisors may be equally competent in their subject matter. It's their ability to give personalized advice that influences the client's perception of the experience, and the ultimate success of the relationship.

The similarities in the process of advising, whether used by a doctor, architect, or IT consultant, will be repeatedly emphasized in this book. Each of these professionals must use some process of interviewing, documenting, analyzing, recommending, and communicating to be an effective advisor. Many professionals have learned this process through trial and error, as it is not typically a subject covered in depth as part of their training and certification. For the skilled practitioner, advising becomes an ingrained and instinctual skill that is rarely thought of as a separate process.

For the less skilled, it is a hit-or-miss process that often leaves crucial factors undiscovered or critical decision criteria poorly understood by the client. I see in my practice, as an advisor to IT consulting firms, an epidemic of unstructured, inconsistent, uncoordinated activities that are called IT consulting. Both the IT professionals and their clients are often left wondering how a simple technical project could get so fouled up. Everyone understood the technology, but nobody managed the relationship or the delivery process.

There is very little in this section that is specific to the technical disciplines of IT. Instead, we are focused on setting forth the general principles of advising, which will then be expanded on with the specific practices that constitute an IT consulting framework. Just as the difficult game of chess has some simple rules such as "Develop the pieces early" or "Don't attack without a plan," the complex enterprise of advising clients on technology can also be better understood by reviewing a few guiding principles.

I believe there are five basic concepts that can serve as a foundation for the IT advisory process:

- *Focus on the Relationship.* Identifying who the client is and understanding the motivations, culture, history, fears, and goals of both the human being and the organization is one of the most difficult tasks in consulting. Your success in this task has much more bearing on the success or failure of your engagements than the technical discipline involved.

- *Clearly Define Your Role.* Setting the expectation with the client regarding exactly what you are there to accomplish, what tasks you are making a commitment to perform, what tasks you expect the client to perform, and where the boundaries of the relationship lie, is a key success factor.

- *Visualize Success.* It is the consultant's central role to help the client draw a mental picture of the desired result of the engagement. Failure to do so results in the dreaded scope creep, in which the engagement never concludes because the expectations keep changing. Visualizing a successful result creates a common goal that all participants can agree on and strive for together. Like the championship ring for a sports team, it is an unambiguous and motivational end point that clarifies the effort and helps clear away extraneous issues and barriers.

- *You Advise, They Decide.* One of the most difficult tasks for consultants is to cast aside emotional attachment to their own advice. Many technicians fall in love with a particular solution or technology and then lose interest in, or respect for, the client who decides to take another approach. We must always remember that the client understands the complexities of his or her own environment and lives with the result of the decision, while we move on to the next assignment.

- *Be Oriented Toward Results.* Consulting is more than advising: It is assisting clients to reach a goal. While some advisory relationships are strictly informational, most clients want us not only to recommend solutions, but to help implement them. Politics is often described as "the art of the possible," a good definition for results-oriented consulting as well. By considering implementation issues throughout the life of the engagement, we keep our eye on the realm of possibility, avoid getting sidetracked into the theoretical, and prepare the client throughout the process for the real-world issues of implementation and system operation.

FOCUS ON THE RELATIONSHIP

Like the impersonal doctor described above, some advisors believe that parachuting into a client situation, peeking around, making some profound pronouncements, and sending a bill constitutes an advisory relationship. This has been called the *oracle approach* to consulting. As with the Oracle of Delphi in ancient Greece, oracle consultants deliver obscure and mysterious declarations, which may or may not be pertinent to the subject at hand, and then leave it to the client to interpret and implement the advice. But success as a consultant is based on the ability to apply your technical specialty to the client's unique situation. Without focusing on the relationship and developing the trust and confidence that enable the client to reveal the problem, this is impossible to achieve.

The relationship with the client determines both the content of the advice and the manner in which it is given. The client will tell you how to give advice successfully, if you are alert enough to listen and observe. Obviously, the client knows the environment and corporate culture and the history and the personalities that have gotten the organization to the state it's in. And the client probably has an idea of where he or she wants to end up. Clients know their priorities. In this particular engagement, is schedule, cost, performance, ease of implementation, lack of disruption, data safety, or personal prestige at the top of the list? Get to know your client, because there will be many points in the engagement at which you'll need to make a judgment about what your client will prefer, how your client will react, and how to present problems or alternatives.

The successful advisor also alters the method of advising to fit the client. Many clients have constraints on the amount of time they can devote to meetings, interviews, and data-gathering tasks. Some clients may prefer a blunt, take-no-prisoners approach to the consulting relationship, while others may be extremely sensitive to their team's reaction to your advice. Some clients or stakeholders may be threatened or distracted by the consulting process. You may need to spend a significant amount of time educating the client in the consulting process, to set expectations, and to build in the assurance factors. Clients who are experienced in the use of consultants may be ready to engage fully in the process, prepared to give trust freely and to disclose fully the information required. For these clients, a monthly progress report may be sufficient to ensure that you are on track. For clients who are inexperienced in the consulting process, frequent assurances that you are remaining "on task" and producing the expected deliverables may be required. Weekly progress meetings and complete status reports may be necessary to reassure these clients continually that they are getting value for money. As an advisor, you must be mature enough to understand the client's need for assurance and not to interpret it as "the client breathing down my neck."

Focusing on the relationship aspect of advising will also help clarify one of the most problematic aspects of consulting, namely "Who is my client?" Information technology consultants are frequently engaged by managers to create systems for the departments they lead. Who is the client in these cases—the manager who hired you or the clerk or telemarketer who is the ultimate user of the system? In most cases the answer is "Both." The manager's requirements for schedule, budget, and reporting are driving factors that must be accounted for in the result, yet the user's need for functionality and convenience must be considered or the system will end up unused. All consultants should step back when entering into an engagement and ask themselves who the client is, who determines whether or not the engagement was a success, and who will pay the bill. The ability to keep multiple, and often conflicting, success criteria in mind is one of the hallmarks of the professional consultant.

As in any relationship, it is critical to "take the measure of the man." What is the personality of the individuals with whom you will be engaged? Some folks are naturally quiet, others are talkative. Some are slow to trust and reticent to reveal. Others will tell you more than you ever wanted to know. Some will act as though you're an intruder in their private domain, others will treat you like a long-lost friend. Human diversity is what makes the relationship aspect of consulting so challenging—and ultimately so rewarding. The most successful consultants develop strategies for dealing with both the reluctant and the cooperative client.

CLEARLY DEFINE YOUR ROLE

A clear understanding of the role of both the client and the consultant serves as a guide through the advisory process. It focuses the efforts of the consultant and the client. I've seen many relationships that could have been mutually beneficial go off the rails for lack of role definition. The client may believe, for instance, that, as a paid advisor, the consultant will be available for emergencies in his or her area of expertise. If a consultant is advising a client on a network design, does that mean the consultant will answer the phone in the middle of the night when the current network goes down? If that is not the expectation, client and consultant had better define that up-front. If it is part of the consultant's role, then the consultant must ensure that the client can get in touch when required and must negotiate a pay rate for that 3:00 AM call.

Clients' expectations of what you will deliver as an IT consultant are wide open to misinterpretation. Does the agreement to consult on the selection of new computer equipment imply assistance in procuring that gear? Does it imply installation? Does it imply ongoing support once implemented? Many clients assume that recommendation means implementation: "Why would I want you to recommend something if you're not going to install it?" In my work with system resellers, I've seen many cases of implied expectations that have poisoned otherwise healthy relationships. Some customers believe that if you recommend a $99 software package, you're committed to rectifying any bugs that arise for the rest of the customer's life! While this is an extreme case, when you recommend and implement complex technology, the client is justified in expecting some level of ongoing assistance. What is the appropriate expectation? It's the consultant's role to define that.

You must clearly determine the client's availability to work on the project. It's obviously going to be very difficult to make recommendations if the client and other organizational members are unavailable for work sessions to define their goals and objectives. Clients will often state in the negotiation phase that their internal team will take on a multitude of tasks to save money. Then, when the project is underway, these staffers are unavailable, and the assumption is that you will take on their commitments. So carefully consider and document any assumptions about client participation.

It may be clear to you, as a practicing consultant, what the roles and responsibilities of client and consultant are. The customer, however, may be a novice to the consulting process or may have had advisory relationships with very different ground rules. Especially with new clients, roles, availability, access, and disclosure should be negotiated with the same diligence as contracts and fees. Due to the importance of this part of the process, I've devoted an entire chapter to negotiating the relationship.

VISUALIZE SUCCESS

The visualization of a successful result is a technique that is frequently used in the world of sports. Many Olympic athletes and coaches believe that imagining themselves performing their event flawlessly, walking through the entire process in their minds, is a key factor in their success.

Like a good coach, a consultant must help the client see the end at the beginning. This technique is valuable for more than the confidence it inspires that the engagement can be successful, as important as that is. It also can be a method for controlling expectations, for ensuring that secondary, "wouldn't-it-be-nice-if" goals don't complicate and confuse the primary objectives of an engagement. In any project, the fear of scope creep should concern the consultant. Anyone who has attended a project management seminar has seen the statistics regarding the number of projects that fail to deliver their expected result. The blame for these failures is often placed on creeping specifications, the "moving target" of client expectations.

Working with clients to visualize success is the primary technique I recommend for managing scope and expectations. By creating a clear vision of what the client will have when the engagement is done, consultants can help focus the client's mind on the critical success factors. I often try to create a "tag line" for a project, a single sentence that characterizes the goal of the engagement. In Hollywood it's often said that a screenwriter who can't create a tag line for a script has not thought it through sufficiently. This is also true of consulting projects. Projects that require a two-page mission statement may be in need of refining—or may need to be divided into multiple projects.

A vision of success is also critical for communication. Most engagements require the participation of many representatives of the client organization, and often of many consultants or subcontractors. The clear and simple visualization of success creates a goal that concentrates the efforts of all involved. This is not a new-age meditation technique, but a process of mutual agreement on a clearly stated end point, so that all can agree when the engagement is complete.

YOU ADVISE, THEY DECIDE

There is an old saying that "When all you have is a hammer, everything looks like a nail." In IT consulting, this can be restated as "When all you have is NetWare, everything looks like a server."

One of the most prevalent problems I've encountered in my efforts to mentor consultants is the problem of the "technology bigot." I cannot count the number of times I've heard rookie consultants, and sometimes even veterans, proclaim that "The customer is too stubborn to admit that if they migrated to NetWare all their problems will be solved." In my experience, the consultants who make these statements just happen to be experts in the technologies they are touting. The predisposition to a specific solution is a real issue in our industry. I wonder how a firm can be, for instance, a Microsoft-centered reseller and also claim to be an independent consultant. Client-focused consulting requires vendor and solution neutrality. All problems do not have the same solution, for which we should be glad; if they did, IT consultants would not be needed.

Apart from the natural tendency to recommend a solution with which we have experience, there is also the entanglement of emotion to complicate the issue. Many consultants feel slighted if the recommendation they make is discounted or ignored. The ability to look beyond our own emotional need for status and validation—and to focus on the cultural, political, and prestige needs of the client—differentiates the professional from the amateur in consulting.

BE ORIENTED TOWARD RESULTS

There are many advisory relationships in which all the customer is buying is advice or research. I've been engaged many times in creating a "white paper" report that outlines various options and the pros and cons of each. When I delivered that paper, my task was done. I had no role in the ultimate decision or the implementation of the system, and often had no idea whether my work was utilized or stuck in a drawer and forgotten.

In the vast majority of engagements, however, the client wants more than advice. The client wants a *result*. And, while it's critical to keep an open mind and not pre-decide the solution before performing the analysis, there are certain techniques that pave the way for a successful implementation.

I'm continually amazed at how often consulting projects are done in complete isolation from the intended recipients of the new system. It's not an uncommon experience for system users to first be exposed to the new system when an installer shows up at their desk. This can be an outcome of some corporate cultures, in which decisions are made by managers in closed sessions and then sprung on the user community by management proclamation. In many cases, managers just are not used to considering the reaction of the troops when making technology deployment decisions. I believe it is in the best interest of the enterprise for the consultant to insist (diplomatically, of course) on communication with the user community. When users are sold on the benefits of the new technology, when they understand how it affects their duties, and when they are involved in scheduling the rollout, the odds for success are enhanced tremendously.

An orientation toward results also means designing training, support, and maintenance into your solutions from the beginning. When we talk about operational issues from the start, users are reassured that they won't be left "twisting in the wind." When we advise clients to announce the training program at the same time as they announce the creation of a new system, users feel that their welfare, effectiveness, and productivity matter to the organization and so are less inclined to resist or snipe at the new technology. By advising the client to consider these issues, consultants add value far above the purely technical. They help clients create an environment that is primed for success, and they demonstrate that they can participate at a strategic level, thus elevating their stature as a business advisor.

These five rules of advising will provide the foundation for the framework that will be presented throughout this book. These fundamental "good manners" of the advisory relationship prepare us to engage with our clients in a way that engenders trust and mutual respect—and that minimizes the chances for misunderstanding and unrealized expectations.

The IT Consulting Skill Set

Never fear the want of business. A man who qualifies himself well for his
calling never fails of employment.

Thomas Jefferson

What do we sell when we sell consulting? We may be selling technical skill, a project implementation, or a report comparing different technical options. For any consultant who has worked for a professional services firm, there's no question what the product is: Like a lawyer or an accountant, we're selling billable hours. When it comes to the profit-and-loss statement, the consultant's ability to sell enough billable hours to be profitable is, literally, the bottom line. In every management meeting at consulting firms worldwide, as the partners review results and make forecasts, the conversation inevitably turns to the utilization rates of the staff.

Among managing partners and team leaders, it is an axiom that some individuals are consistently able to keep their billable utilization high, while others, often with similar technical skills, can never seem to achieve their targets. Some consultants are so well-trusted that clients will wait for them to become available, even though other, similarly trained practitioners are unengaged. In some cases, clients will schedule their internal projects based on the availability of a particular consultant, or will actually kick off projects ahead of schedule rather than risk losing a certain consultant's services to another client.

What are the characteristics that allow some consultants to remain highly utilized, while others struggle month after month to meet their targets? As with most questions concerning the profession of consulting, a view from the client's chair is instructive. As we have done before in this book, let's gaze out from the point of view of a client we all can identify with, a doctor's patient.

Patients are typically not medical experts. They usually cannot judge, except by results, the quality of the medical advice they receive. As patients, we assume that the diplomas and board certifications hanging on the doctors' walls assure us that they are qualified to practice. Patients can, however, judge certain other attributes that doctors bring to the relationship. Because of the patients' lack of expertise with which to judge the doctors' technical mastery, these attributes often take on added weight in our evaluation process. These qualities are sometimes referred to as "bedside manner." We may not be able to define this precisely, but "We know it when we see it." It's typically a combination of personality, communication skills, qualities of empathy and caring, and a holistic approach—a focus on treating the patient rather than the disease.

This analogy to a doctor's bedside manner gives us some guidance about the qualities clients look for in an advisor. Obviously, technical expertise is a deciding factor. Without it the practitioner is clearly out of the running. The ability to communicate effectively is also key in both the doctor/patient and the consultant/client relationship. The doctor, or the consultant, who cannot ask the right questions, listen effectively to the responses, interpret what is said, and develop a dialogue based on trust is severely limited in the ability to diagnose and prescribe. The holistic approach in medicine is analogous to a business-centered approach in IT consulting. The consultant who focuses on the technological symptoms, without considering the business context, is in danger of offering a prescription that will never be filled.

Project management, like consulting, was once thought to be unteachable. One of the proverbs in the early days of project management was the idea that project managers are born, not made, and that success as a project manager was driven by personality, not methodology. Proponents of this school of thought stated that "You can't teach someone to ask the right questions, to resist scope changes, to be firm, to analyze the client's situation and come up with meaningful solutions, to estimate," etc. This opinion stands in sharp contrast to the disciplines and training that are now available for aspiring project managers. Organizations like the Project Management Institute and its "Project Management Body of Knowledge" and Project Management Professional certifications have shown that project management is in fact a system of thought and practice.

Certain character traits are important in the aspiring project manager or consultant. Success at these endeavors is largely based on a set of skills and methods that can be learned. I categorize the skills critical to a consultant as:

- Advisory,
- Technical,
- Business, and
- Communication.

We covered a basic outline of advisory skills in the previous chapter. We'll now review the other skills in turn.

TECHNICAL SKILLS

Successful professionals, whether accountants, doctors, or musicians, are typically strong in the technical discipline of their craft. These skills are the focus of all the training, certifications, and diplomas. Frankly, this is the endeavor that we are drawn to by our character and desire. Most professionals select and concentrate on a particular craft because they cannot help it, because it's the field where joy, talent, and aspiration converge. In the IT field especially, it's been my experience that most conversations about how folks get into the business usually boil down to "Once I was exposed to it, I knew I belonged."

When working with consultants on the development of their technical skills, the most important advice I can give is that *technical expertise is a process, not an event.* The technology changes so quickly that those who master a current skill set and stop there are doomed to obsolescence. Technical training in IT must be looked at as a lifetime learning experience, and one hopes curiosity and the joy of scholarship will motivate the consultant to stay current. In the real world of commercial consulting, it's critical to remember that clients become more sophisticated all the time, and they expect their highly paid consultants to be at least one step ahead of them. Five years ago, knowing how to install a PC and a printer was enough to generate consulting engagements. I started my consulting career teaching customers how to set up their new IBM PC's. Now I frequently walk into client's offices and find technical teams that could rebuild the Internet from scratch.

I've heard consultants say, "I don't need to know all about the subject, I just need to know more than the client." This is one school of thought, and even achieving this can be challenging. But the real value-adding consultant strives to do more, to gain depth as well as breadth in the technologies that drive competitive advantage for clients around the world. By subscribing to the IT trade magazines, scouring the bookstores, searching the Internet, attending vendor presentations and user-group meetings, and networking with your colleagues, you can ensure your ability to add insight to your client's decisions. In the professional world of doctors, lawyers, architects, and engineers, continuing education is a baseline requirement that is acknowledged and accepted as a cost of entry into the field. So must it be with IT consulting. The aspirant or ambitious veteran must come prepared to make the investment of continuous development in order to remain a viable player in the competitive world of commercial consulting.

As in all commercial enterprises, the market is the ultimate arbiter. If you find that your technical skill set is not bringing in the volume of business opportunities that you expect, perhaps you need to broaden your technical scope. Learning new skills and technologies can not only increase your value to the marketplace and to each client, but can also be a powerful antidote to boredom and to the "same-old, same-old" syndrome.

BUSINESS SKILLS

One of the common themes in the current business press is the shortage of IT professionals in the labor market. Articles in *PC Week* (Moad, 1997) and *Computer-World* (Hoffman, 1998) and studies by the Commerce Department's Office of Technology Policy (1998) bemoan the fact that hundreds of thousands of IT jobs go begging every year for the lack of qualified technical candidates.

How much rarer still is the technical candidate who also has an understanding of business issues. The cliché of the computer nerd who must be kept in the back room with a screwdriver in his hand is, like most clichés, based on a nugget of truth. Many talented IT practitioners have never mastered basic business skills, and many managers did not consider these skills relevant to the IT function. Salary surveys published by the computer press often state that the average tenure of IT professionals is eighteen months (Cone, 1998). This mobile labor market hardly encourages in-depth understanding of the employer's business.

When I train a cadre of technicians who aspire to become consultants, I often begin by asking a series of questions about the companies they work for. I ask if they understand:

- Their company's mission,

- Its competitive strategy and position,

- Its sales and profitability,

- Its key clients,

- Whether it is publicly or privately held,

- Its stock price and performance,

- Its organizational makeup and key managers,

- How managers are compensated and motivated,

- Its history, and

- Its strategic priorities for the coming year.

The answer is usually a roomful of blank stares. This deficiency, sad to say, is universal in teams of apprentice consultants I've trained in my career.

This is also the most glaring insufficiency that clients note when they work with rookies: "How can this person deliver a solution that contributes to my business without any business experience?" The client's desire for gray hair as an indicator of experience can be a stumbling block for novices. It's often unfair in terms of the business value and technical expertise that a particular consultant can bring to the table. Most clients, however, *are* prepared to be advised by youngsters if they can be convinced that the young man or woman brings an understanding of business context to the project. Obviously, experience is the best teacher. For many technical professionals, however, the opportunities to be exposed to business functions other than IT are limited. Here are some techniques for overcoming this difficulty and for expanding your understanding of business issues.

- *Read General Business Magazines.* Subscribe to *Business Week, Forbes, Fortune,* or *The Wall Street Journal.* If you aspire to specialize in a particular industry or are an in-house consultant, read the trade journals that cover that business. If you work in a consulting team, copy articles and pass them around. I've worked in consulting teams that form a Journal Club, trading off the task of reading magazines within the group and meeting periodically over lunch to report on what they've read.

- *Watch the Business News on TV.* CNN's *Moneyweek,* PBS's *Nightly Business Report* and *Wall Street Week,* CNBC, and Bloomberg News offer a valuable background in current business conditions. They provide an education on the factors that drive markets, on the state of the economy, and on business sectors that are doing well (or not so well). It's a common occurrence that a feature on the business news will have relevance to a customer engagement in which I'm involved, either due to direct coverage of the company or a mention of its industry or sector.

- *Use the Library and the Services of a Reference Librarian.* A competent reference librarian can work with you to put together a reading program that will help you develop into a formidable consulting asset. Learning to use the reference material, such as the *Business Periodicals Index, Gale's Encyclopedia of Associations,* the *U.S. Manufacturers Directory,* the *Thomas Register,* and others can give you research skills that set you apart from the multitude of technically focused consultants with whom you will compete.

- *Read the Fundamental Business Classics.* Any business person who has not read *Management* by Peter Drucker (1993) is as lacking in a classical education as an English major who has not read Shakespeare. A program of reading in management, sales, finance, marketing, and business strategy is an obvious place to begin discovering the inner mechanisms of business.

- *Use the Internet.* The astounding volume of business information, from SEC filings to Dun & Bradstreet directories to company and vendor websites, brings a worldwide reference library to your desktop. The simple act of reviewing a prospective client's website or annual report before a sales call has been the differentiating factor countless times in my career.

- *Include the Basic Business Questions Above in Every Consulting Engagement.* This is the most important way to illustrate to the client that you approach the consulting relationship as a business-savvy strategic partner, and not just as a technical "hired gun."

These suggestions are focused on general business understanding. In the context of an impending engagement, however, knowledge about the specific company, industry, and project issues for the client company are critical to success. I recommend that consultants develop strong research habits as they prepare to engage with a specific client. My experience is that nothing develops client confidence and assurance more potently than a bit of pre-project homework by the advisor. Consultants who walk in the door with some knowledge of the client's industry, company history, stock price, and competitive position create the image of an experienced and competent professional from the beginning of the relationship. I've constructed the Client Research Guidelines, Exhibit 2.1, to assist consultants in performing the basic business homework necessary to prepare for a client engagement.

Exhibit 2.1
Client Research Guidelines

Company name: _____

Primary business: _____

Industry: _____

❏ Publicly held?   If so, today's share price: _____

❏ Trending up?   ❏ Trending down?

Mission statement: (annual report or website)

_____

_____

Business objectives: _____

_____

Key clients: _____

Competitive position: _____

IT strategies: _____

Key managers: _____

Revenue growth over last year:_____

Profit growth over last year: _____

Key business drivers: _____

Key performance metrics: _____

Other comments: _____

_____

_____

COMMUNICATION SKILLS

Consulting is communication. If this book drives home no other point, I hope it clearly emphasizes this. Without clear, open, and effective communication between the parties, consultation cannot take place. The ability to help customers articulate their needs, understand the capabilities and constraints of technology, and create a clear and compelling project vision are tasks central to the advisory process.

Yet, the popular picture of an IT professional depicts the opposite. The cliché is that the IT staffer needs to be kept in the back room, that IT people are either going to talk in technical jargon that will put the CEO to sleep or compare the client's business strategy to an episode of Star Trek.

Most IT professionals are intelligent individuals, folks who have mastered a difficult and demanding craft that has required diligent study and training. The idea that they cannot also be trained to communicate well is nonsense. People develop those skills for which they are mentored, compensated, and judged. Superior communication skills have not, until recently, been a requirement of the IT profession. In the mainframe days, IT teams worked in the infamous "glass room," talking mostly among themselves, usually with a manager from the finance department to act as their interpreter. As computing moved to the desktop, however, and the ability to provide support and service to users in a language they could understand became a valuable skill, communication came to the forefront. Those technicians who could avoid jargon, who could communicate clearly with the secretary, clerk, salesperson, and manager, became valuable commodities. In short, the desktop PC revolution forced IT to become more consultative.

The IT consultant, in a typical day of practice, will need to interview a client to understand his requirements, to examine a candidate and assess her suitability for a spot on a project team, and to report on project activities to a manager or project sponsor. In between these oral communication tasks, the consultant will probably be sitting at a desk preparing a status report, a scope of work document, a proposal, or some operational documentation. The skill central to all of these tasks is the ability to communicate.

Communication *can* be taught and learned. It can be taught *by example:* by showing the novice consultant how it is done in a client situation. It can be taught *by practice:* by having consultants in a team setting deliver presentations on their technical specialties, by forming Journal Clubs to report on what was read, or by organizing facilitated work sessions to let teams review customer engagements and develop solutions together. I often say that no single consultant "owns" a project; the team owns all projects. This viewpoint encourages every consultant to bring problems and experiences to the team and to work them through as a group. There is no better communication training than this.

For the single practitioner without access to a supportive team of colleagues, these options are less viable. Even the solo consultant, however, can join local user groups and technical associations and make a habit of sharing ideas. In the final chapter of this book some of the fundamental techniques that consultants and advisors have developed over the years to improve their skills at interacting and communicating with their clients and teams are described in more detail.

The fundamental purpose of developing a consistent consulting methodology is to prepare IT professionals to excel in the central skill of consulting—communication. Business consulting has gone from an esoteric practice employed by a few experts to one of the fastest-growing job categories in our economy. During this period of explosive growth, practitioners have learned through experience some common-sense techniques that predispose consulting engagements toward success. Each of the steps of the IT Consulting Framework we will review in the chapters to follow is primarily an attempt to codify these communication practices into a system that consultants can follow to establish a clear, collaborative, and mutually beneficial relationship with their clients.

References

Cone, E. (1998, September 18). Rebirth of loyalty. *Information Week.*

Hoffman, T. (1998, January 9). U.S. facing IT skill shortage. *Computerworld.*

Moad, J. (1998, July 2). Study: Labor shortage to plague IT for years. *PC Week.*

Office of Technology Policy, U.S. Department of Commerce. (1998, January). *America's new deficit: The shortage of information technology workers.* Washington, DC: Author.

part two

The IT Consulting Framework

He that would perfect his work must first sharpen his tools.

Confucius

Methodologies, like "best practices," can be a double-edged sword. On the one hand, it's clearly an advantage to have a defined process for performing a complex task, whether it is a technology architecture design or a custom programming project. Most IT professionals would agree that the use of a structured development life cycle brings order and discipline to a potentially chaotic and enigmatic undertaking. On the other hand, however, methodologies and best practices, instead of being viewed as guideposts to steer the way through treacherous shoals, can become strictures that stifle innovation and force uniformity on what should be a creative endeavor. I've actually heard of IT professionals who have lost their jobs because they dared to undertake a project without consulting the corporate website and applying the "best practices" posted there. This, to my mind, is a misuse of the concept of best practices and an example of the triumph of bureaucracy over creativity.

I therefore use the term *framework* consciously. The process presented here is submitted to the reader as a *suggested approach* to the IT advisory relationship, not a strict recipe to follow by rote. The intent is to provide a touchstone to guide your thinking as you engage with your clients. Although the framework presented here will be organized according to the logical phases of a consulting relationship, I hope it will not be restrictive or dogmatic. Ultimately, consultants develop a method of working that suits their own personality, clientele, marketplace, specialty, and work style. This is as it should be, for consulting is a highly personal employment, one that often draws the best and brightest precisely due to its freedom from imposed regulation and approach.

This framework is focused on the advisory relationship, not on the technical disciplines required to design or implement IT solutions. I do not intend to discuss the advantages of client/server technology over mainframes, or the situations wherein you would select COBOL or Java for a particular programming project. Although I will give a substantial amount of advice on how to elicit requirements, define the current state of the IT enterprise, and analyze the situation to provide the best options possible to your client, I do not delve into specific IT disciplines. This framework is designed to be as appropriate to the designer of wide area networks as it is to the website designer or C++ programmer. Training in IT technical disciplines is well-handled in both certification programs and technical schools. It is the consultative relationship that has been neglected, and we focus on that here.

One final comment about the boundaries of the framework presented here. Although the sales activity that occurs prior to engagement is obviously critical (for without it there would be no engagement), this framework begins when the sale has been made and the client is ready to start the actual consulting process. It would take another book of this size to discuss the intricacies of selling consulting services. Additionally, the framework ends when the solution that is implemented goes into operational production. Although as part of the framework I discuss in detail the work a competent consultant must do to prepare a client to "go live," I assume that when the system is in normal operation, the consultant's role is done. I admit this is somewhat arbitrary, especially in this time of outsourcing, when many development projects can turn into opportunities to take on an operational and maintenance role. Outsourced support of IT systems is a fascinating and lucrative business niche, but it is a different kind of consulting than I am describing here.

The IT consulting framework consists of seven stages, as illustrated in Figure P2.1. As noted above, the sales process occurs outside of the framework, so it is

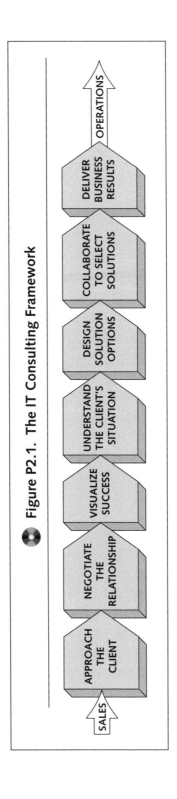

Figure P2.1. The IT Consulting Framework

SALES — APPROACH THE CLIENT — NEGOTIATE THE RELATIONSHIP — VISUALIZE SUCCESS — UNDERSTAND THE CLIENT'S SITUATION — DESIGN SOLUTION OPTIONS — COLLABORATE TO SELECT SOLUTIONS — DELIVER BUSINESS RESULTS — OPERATIONS

represented as an arrow leading into the process. Operational production, when the system is tested, accepted by the client, and then rolled out and integrated into the daily business processes of the organization, is indicated by an arrow pointing out of the diagram. Although some development life cycles are shown as a circle rather than a path, indicating that the consulting process can begin again with a "review and maintain" phase, my experience is that it is clearer and cleaner to consider each engagement separately, with its own separate deliverables and end point. The consultant can always be re-engaged, but my recommendation is that client acceptance of the original scope or deliverables be viewed as a perfect opportunity to reassess the relationship and to refine the deliverables and expectations for the next phase of the engagement formally.

The figure illustrates the following process:

1. *Approach the Client.* Although this initial contact can range from a short meeting that is little more than a handshake to a lengthy facilitated work session with a team of client representatives, it is a critical stage in the path to a working advisory relationship. In Chapter Three, which covers this stage of the framework, we will discuss both the formal agenda and the mutual assessment process that inevitably takes place.

2. *Negotiate the Relationship.* Although the assessment and discovery that takes place in the "approach" phase is to some extent informal and incomplete, in the negotiation phase we must solidify the objectives, roles, and deliverables of the engagement. Even in the most routine of engagements, these agreements on roles and responsibilities must be documented, in a Scope of Work Document, a letter of agreement, or both. The relationship may be based on a verbal understanding of expectations, but the complexities and risks of an advisory relationship require the precision and permanence of a written record.

3. *Visualize Success.* In the interest of approaching all engagements from a positive viewpoint, I use the concept of visualizing success rather than the more common "problem statement" terminology. It's all too easy to become bogged down in the "blame game" and the obstacles to change, in even the most proactive of organizations. By helping the client look beyond the problem to its ultimate solution, we stack the deck psychologically in favor of positive change.

4. *Understand the Client's Situation.* The mechanics of performing interviews, facilitating work sessions, designing surveys, and performing architecture in-

ventories are critical to success as a consultant, and we review them in detail in Chapter Six. More important, however, are the techniques of developing trust and cooperation in the holders of process knowledge in the organization, so that they are motivated to participate in the process.

5. *Design Solution Options.* The greatest degree of creativity in IT consulting resides in the development of solutions to business problems. Innovative consultants utilize their understanding of human, technological, business, and process elements to design strategies that address the problem, optimize the solution, fit the client's culture, are practical and affordable, are standards-based, and can be maintained and supported.

6. *Collaborate to Select Solutions.* Inexperienced advisors, whether lawyers, engineers, or IT professionals, will often make the error of assuming that, because the client is paying for expertise, the client wants the advisor to tell him or her what to do. Seasoned advisors understand that their role is to *help their clients discover the best solution for themselves.* By performing our consultative role with excellence, we present clients with the appropriate options and prepare them to make informed selections.

7. *Deliver Business Results.* The schedule, scope, and complexity of activities in this phase can vary widely, depending on the expectations set in the beginning of the relationship. Some consulting engagements are complete when the options are presented and when the client then takes ownership of the implementation and support of the selected solution. The orientation of this framework, however, is toward action, and so we will review in Chapter Nine the multitude of practices that the competent IT consultant will perform to ensure that the client organization achieves the expected result from the advisory relationship. Training skills, project skills, communications, business process understanding, and team motivational talents all come into play in this activity.

I think of this framework as an overlay of concepts and techniques with which to approach the client relationship. Engagements that include implementation of IT systems will likely require a disciplined project management methodology. Complex technical projects can also call for detailed specification and design documents, enterprise IT infrastructure plans, application and data architectures, and other discipline-specific tools for delivering quality IT solutions. Use this framework as a layer in the total blueprint for delivering quality services.

APPROACH
THE
CLIENT

- Why Is the Client Seeking Advice?
- What Is the Potential for Success?
- Engage with the Client as a Person
- Don't Prescribe Before Diagnosing
- Test Your Understanding
- Profile the Engagement

Approach the Client

A bad beginning makes a bad ending.

Euripides

WHY DO CLIENTS ENGAGE CONSULTANTS?

There is inherent tension in the initial meeting between any two people. No matter how self-assured, confident, and experienced an individual is, approaching an unknown person creates some degree of apprehension. Will this new acquaintance be friendly or cold, cordial or rude, open or reserved, wise or foolish? Will my ego be soothed, threatened, or bruised by this encounter?

Now imagine how this anxiety is magnified in a business setting, where livelihood, prestige, and power are at risk. By the time a client approaches a consultant for advice, that client has acknowledged some things which may not have been easy or flattering. The client may have recognized some or all of these deficiencies in his or her organization:

- They lack the technical expertise to solve their problem without outside help;

- They lack the business experience to apply whatever technical knowledge they do have;

- They lack confidence in their ability to evaluate the options;

- They cannot convince their management or team that a particular solution is valid, and so need independent verification;

- They do not have the staffing or the time to address the problem or opportunity; and/or

- They doubt their ability to implement the solution.

Information technology consultants must take care not to assume that lack of technical expertise is the only issue. As a technology consultant, it's easy to conclude that the client wants to buy your technical knowledge and advice. When developing a relationship with a new client, IT consultants need to keep in mind both the inherent anxiety of the initial human contact and the full range of deficiencies with which the client may need help.

ASSESSING THE POTENTIAL FOR SUCCESS

The initial client contact is an assessment session as well as a work session. The formal agenda for an initial client meeting is always focused on the project issues, such as objectives, scope, fee arrangements, and the like. But the client and the consultant are also evaluating one another. The client is seeking technical competence, of course, and questioning will typically center around that. But the client is also wondering, "Can I trust this individual? Will this person work well with me? Does the consultant understand what I need to get from this relationship? Will the person fit into my corporate culture?" Of course, the consultant is also stepping through a range of concerns: Does the client understand how to work with consultants? Does the client understand the technology well enough to make the necessary decisions? Is the person interested in partnering in this endeavor or will he or she come looking for a blame agent if things go wrong?

As expressed by Euripides in the opening aphorism, the outcome of the entire engagement can be tainted by poor handling of the initial contact. On the positive side, consultants can tip the scales significantly in favor of success through thoughtful treatment of the initial sessions. As consultants proceed through this dance of evaluation and counter-evaluation, they should consider the following questions:

- With which of the deficiencies described above is the client asking for help?

- What is the client's demeanor? Casual and open, or formal and restrained?

- Are there any clues to indicate the client's time pressures? A client who appears rushed and must run to the next meeting will participate in the project in a different way than a client who relaxes and wants to go into great detail.

- Is the client excited and enthusiastic about the possibilities of this engagement? Or does it seem like another burden that was dumped on the client?

- What are the physical clues? Does the client's office have a child's finger paintings on the wall, a fine art poster, or a picture of the local football team?

Using powers of observation effectively is one of the critical success factors for a consultant. Important clues can be gathered from observing the client's reaction to the simplest of questions, such as, "Where shall we meet next?" or "Who should be in our next meeting?" If the client wants to get out of the office to have your next conversation, how do you interpret that? Does it mean that the client wants to avoid interruptions and give complete attention to you? Or does the client want to make sure that others don't hear your conversation? Is the client including or excluding staff based on their need to participate, or to protect power and prestige? All of these questions demonstrate the nuances of human relationships that are at the heart of every engagement. And, as when you first meet your brother-in-law or your new auto mechanic, you must use your sum of experience and your own character to make these interpretations.

It's obvious that, if either the client's evaluation of the consultant is negative or vice versa, the relationship will never get off the ground. There are some simple rules a consultant can follow to positively influence the client's evaluation:

- *Give Confidence to Receive Confidence.* Tell your client about yourself and be forthcoming and engaging if you want your client to reciprocate. This refers not to the false backslapping of the huckster, but to a genuine attempt to connect as an individual with the client. Help the client understand the advisory process you are about to engage in. Help the client see the context of the questions you ask. Help him or her understand why you need to know and what you will do with the information. Give the client an opportunity to ask questions.

- *Don't Push the River.* Let the story either trickle or flow in a torrent, as the customer desires. At this stage of the relationship, don't be too concerned about getting the total picture. As we engage, we will follow a process for performing a full analysis. Don't budget too tight a time frame for these initial contacts, so you're not trying to push the client through the process. Listening, caring, and not taking undue control of the conversation are critical to building trust.

- *Don't Prescribe Before Diagnosing.* Inexperienced consultants want to assure their clients that they "get it" and that they have a solution on the tip of the tongue. Veterans have seen similar situations so many times before that they feel they know the answer by the time the first sentence is uttered. Both of these impulses must be resisted. Talking later and less, but talking judiciously and with complete knowledge of the situation, is the sign of a skilled advisor.

- *Test Your Understanding.* Repeat the client's goals and concerns in your own language to ensure that your interpretation and the client's are harmonious.

These human interaction issues are a key success factor in any advisory relationship. Information technology consulting, however, is still a technical discipline, and it requires not only rapport with the customer, but a clear understanding of the business situation. In many instances, the consultant is but one member of a team that will be addressing the client's needs. Additionally, if the consultant works for a professional services firm or inside a corporation, he or she must report to a management chain. For all of these reasons, it's critical to use a structured method of profiling the engagement during the initial contact. Don't confuse this task with the full analysis activities that come later in the process. We'll dig down into the nitty-gritty details then. This is the preliminary contact, but it must be fruitful and complete in its purpose, which is to take the initial measure of the engagement.

The Engagement Profile Form, Exhibit 3.1, shows one way of documenting your conversation with the customer. Some consultants will present a form like this to the customer before the meeting and ask that it be filled out. For me, this smacks too much of assigning homework to the client, so I present it right before our meeting and tell the client that this is the type of information I'll be looking for. It can then be used as an agenda to help lead the client through our initial meeting.

Many professional service firms provide their consultants with customer questionnaires that are much more detailed and extensive than Exhibit 3.1. However, by focusing on the baseline factors listed above, we assure that we're not turning

Exhibit 3.1
Engagement Profile Form

Company name: _____

Project sponsor: _____

Project sponsor's title: _____

Initial project statement: _____

_____

_____

Business objectives: _____

_____

Compelling event: _____

Preliminary schedule: _____

❏ Other major projects?   Comparative priority: _____

❏ Out to bid?   ❏ RFP?

Decision criteria: _____

Why us? _____

_____

❏ Existing relationship?

If existing relationship, describe: _____

_____

Other comments: _____

_____

this mutual evaluation meeting into an interrogation. We also assure that we're not trying to jam the entire analysis phase into one meeting. If the client is particularly cooperative or enthusiastic, these questions will naturally lead as deeply as the client wants to go.

The initial meeting is the place to request any additional data you'll need in later phases. Bring a list of documents you'll want to review, including technical data such as network diagrams, application manuals, policies and procedures, or contingency plans, as well as corporate data such as organization charts or annual reports.

It's also critical that the engagement be put into context of the client's overall business strategy from the start. I've always been amazed at the number of technical consultants who will meet with their customers, have detailed conversations about system requirements, data, and applications, but cannot tell me what business the client is in. Just as a patient would not be comforted by a doctor who only treated the injury and not the person, a consultant who only addresses the technology issues without understanding the business context will not gain the customer's confidence. Always remember that clients are applying technology to serve a business need. By gathering the data required to fill out the Engagement Profile Form, we demonstrate that we are business advisors, not just techs for hire. This elevates our value in the client's mind from the inception of the relationship.

Remember that the role of an advisor is a role of influence and power. Like any such role, there is the potential for harm as well as good. An IT consultant is a professional and must follow a professional code of conduct. In many cases the client is inexperienced in partnering with a consultant, is in immediate crisis and is reaching out desperately for help, or does not understand the technology. In each of these cases, the client's judgment can be clouded. It is up to you to advise your client well, not only within the technical disciplines, but also within the advisory relationship. If the client is engaging with unreasonable expectations, is clutching at straws to save a job, or is expecting magic instead of technology, you need to identify that. This meeting may not be the appropriate forum to raise those issues, but at least they must be recognized. Even if you merely "can't work with this person" for whatever reason, you need to take that impression seriously. The consultant's responsibility to assess the potential effectiveness of each engagement must be taken in earnest. Just as a scrupulous judge will recuse himself from trying a case in which he cannot render impartial justice, an ethical consultant will sometimes need to walk away from an engagement if there are factors that make it impossible or unethical to continue. It is an exercise in frustration to engage with a customer whom we cannot advise properly; it is also a breach of professionalism.

Your initial contacts with the client must result in a deliverable such as the Engagement Profile Form. You should have a record of the problem, opportunity, client's requested services, and all of the other basic information outlined in this chapter, and you should use it to open a project file. If you are a member of a consulting team, a team meeting should be held to review the information you've gathered and to begin the process of defining a scope of work, a task list, a schedule, and budget. Solo practitioners should also get into the discipline of preparing written records of their client interactions. In the next step of this framework, you will be negotiating your role with the client. To prepare for this process, you must analyze the client's needs and document your approach. A major part of your role is to assist the client in building an engagement that can be successful for both of you.

As I repeat throughout this book, clients will teach you how to best serve their needs. One thing my seminar clients have taught me is that a little bit of real-world story telling often goes further than lots of abstract conceptual description. Based on this knowledge, I've constructed an ongoing series of case studies that follows a fictional consulting firm through the phases of the IT Consulting Framework. Following each chapter in Part Two, you'll find a short vignette that illustrates the practices and activities that Superior Systems, a mythical IT firm, employs to define, negotiate, and deliver a consulting engagement. In the Appendices are the requests for proposals, proposals, project plans, and other deliverables mentioned in the case studies, and I recommend that the reader refer to them when working through the examples, as they depict some of the situations the practicing IT consultant will face daily. I hope that these case studies will clarify the real-world application of the principles presented in each chapter. I also hope that these sample documents will prove to be valuable as templates or guides when you need to construct your own proposals, scopes of work, or project plans.

Superior Systems is an IT consulting firm specializing in network integration, focusing on the technical universe of servers, network operating systems, and internetworking. Their motto is "Superior Systems for Superior Results."

The three sales executives and ten consultants at Superior Systems hold a joint meeting weekly to discuss upcoming projects and opportunities. At a recent meeting, John Ryan, a "relationship manager" at Superior, mentioned that one of his follow-up sales calls this week was at Capitol State Chemical, the largest employer in town: "I saw a notice in the local business journal a couple of weeks ago mentioning that they were consolidating all their workers into one new building. I guessed that they might need some consulting help to plan the IT part of the move, so I called one of my contacts over there and she got me in to see Ron Gimble, the director of network architecture. I had a 'getting to know you' meeting with him last week, and now he's invited us back."

Nick, the managing consultant, asked: "Who from the technical side should go with you? Sandy?"

Sandy, the network designer on the technical team, said: "Yeah, I want to go! They've got some cool stuff there!"

John told the team: "I want Sandy for the technical piece, but I also need someone who can dig in with the client and understand the politics and culture over there. This would be our first big services deal with these guys and we need to excel. Who has the best interviewing skills?"

Nick volunteered to go, saying: "I want to understand for myself what they think we can do to help them. Team, what do we know about this client? What hardware and software do they use? Do they use other IT consulting services now? What's their business, who are their customers?" They spent another ten minutes reviewing the background for this opportunity. Nick persuaded John and Sandy that it would be a good idea for them to do a bit of homework on this prospect, advising them to check out the CapState website and to do some research on the stock price and the chemical industry. Then the team moved on to the rest of the meeting.

On the day John, Sandy, and Nick were scheduled to meet the client, Nick requested a fifteen-minute preparation meeting, saying: "John, this is your show, so just review with us, what's my role in this meeting and what's Sandy's role?"

"I just hope you can probe the client a little bit," John replied. "Help me see if there's really a project here. I haven't been able to find out whether they're interviewing other consultants or whether we have a good shot at this deal. I want Sandy there just in case it gets technical."

"Sandy," said Nick, "please take notes of the meeting. I'm going to try to keep the conversation focused on the expectations rather than technical issues, so if you could scribe our conversation. . . ."

Ron Gimble's assistant walked John, Nick, and Sandy into Ron's office, saying: "Ron, these are the IT consultants."

Ron was standing over a large meeting table, looking at a sheaf of blueprints: "John, nice to see you again, thanks for stopping by." Ron gestured toward the drawings: "This is it, the CapState Tower. Did you know that CapState leases 18 percent of the office space in this city? Or that we have 14,000 employees in twelve locations just within the city limits and another 5,000 scattered around the suburbs? We got sick of paying rent and decided to build our own building. We just signed the financing package last week."

"You seem very proud," said John.

"Proud but nervous. Nineteen thousand employees means about 15,000 desktop PCs. Our R&D team uses a UNIX server and about fifty special graphic workstations for chemical design. We've got e-mail, groupware, Internet connectivity, a website, and a PC training lab for our customers, all in different buildings. We hired IBM to move the data center, but the network, servers, desktops . . . there's no way we can support our ongoing business activity and do this move ourselves. We need some outside assistance."

Nick noted that Ron expressed the problem as not having enough resources to keep the business running and do this project simultaneously. Nick feels that it's important to understand what motivates a client to seek outside help; he will use the information to choose consultants for this engagement. Plus it is an indicator of the client's view of the state of the internal IT organization.

John did the introductions and chatted briefly about Superior Systems. He described Nick's role as managing consultant and requested permission for Nick to ask a few questions.

"Ron," said Nick, "thanks for the opportunity to chat about this move. It seems like a challenge for your organization. I've done these before and they're not easy. When do you expect the building to be ready for your folks to move in?"

"We've already broken ground," replied Ron. "They're predicting sixteen months. It seems like a long way away, but. . . ."

"I understand your concern," Nick said. "In a large, technology-driven enterprise like yours, there are innumerable details that must be considered to guarantee the success of a complex project like this. Sandy is our network technology genius, and she'll work with your team to prepare a comprehensive technical move plan. But right now I'm very interested in understanding your business. I've never worked with a chemical design firm before."

As Ron had displayed pride in the new building, he now displayed pride in his organization. By giving Ron the opportunity to explain their product development cycle, Nick showed that he was interested in the business context, not just the technical aspects. He also mentored John and Sandy, teaching them that it's critical to understand the client's business and to give the client an opportunity to display feelings about his or her organization. Good or bad, Nick knew, the client's attitude is instructive for the consultant about to take on an engagement.

Nick reviewed with Ron some of the details of the CapState organization, asking questions:

- "What do you think an IT consulting firm like ours can do to help you?"
- "Which parts of this move project will your team handle?"
- "Are you looking for technical assistance, project management, or both?"
- "Will your team design the network infrastructure in the new building, or will the consultants you select assist?"
- "What other departments or managers will the consultant be working with?"
- "Are there other IT projects that are ongoing at the same time as the move?"
- "What concerns you about this move; what do you fear can go wrong?"

Nick gathered lots of important details in a short time. Even though Ron was interviewing them as technical consultants, all of Nick's questions were focused on the client's expectations, constraints, feelings, and business. Nick felt confident that, when the time came, the consulting team and CapState's technical crew could get together and work out the technical details. He wanted to be sure that he had a measure of the client and the project, that the client's expectations were reasonable, that the project was a good fit for Superior, and that he could deliver successfully. He counted as good signs that Ron had the blueprints there for their review, that he had set aside uninterrupted time to meet with them, and that he answered Nick's questions in a straightforward and open manner.

After Nick had asked questions, John asked Ron, "How will your selection process work?"

"We've been chatting with a couple of other consulting firms," said Ron. "We've sent out a short request for proposal to the firms we think are contenders. You should receive it today or tomorrow. We'll have a short lead time on the RFP, because we want to engage someone on this soon."

Finally, Nick asked Ron, "Would it be all right if Sandy got in touch with some of your network engineers, just so we could understand your environment a bit better, to write a bid that fits your needs?" Ron was obliging and gave Sandy his lead technician's number.

When they arrived back at the office, Nick spent a few minutes with Sandy and John to review the meeting. "So, what do you think? Is this a good fit for us?" Nick asked.

"Are you kidding?" asked John. "This could be huge!"

"Does any of it concern you?" asked Nick. "What about you, Sandy?"

"Well, yeah," she replied, "there are a few things. Fifteen thousand desktops is a lot! I guess we can get some college kids to help us with the inventory and disconnect, but it's going to need a lot of project management. Also those UNIX boxes and special workstations might be a challenge."

"Come on!" exclaimed John. "We can do this! This could be a great customer!"

"Yes, it could," Nick agreed, "but only if we do this one right. I just want to make sure that we think this through up front before we spend a lot of time proposing and planning for a project that we can't deliver."

"Okay," said John. "As soon as I get the RFP I'll schedule a planning session, and we can put a proposal together."

Nick asked Sandy to transcribe the notes from the meeting. Using Sandy's notes, he sat down with John and wrote a follow-up letter to Ron, thanking him for the time, reiterating in summary what the project was, and informing him that Superior Solutions would deliver to him by the following Friday a proposal to assist CapState with their move.

John rushed into Nick's office the next morning with the CapState RFP in hand (see Appendix A.) "Here it is! It looks like they've done a great job of outlining their needs. Let's pull the team together for a meeting and see how we need to respond."

"It's not quite that easy," Nick laughed. "The consultants are all out billing, thankfully! And hopefully the sales team is out with their customers as well. I'll have to figure out who we want in the room, and then schedule a meeting."

John interrupted: "I don't think you get it! This is a huge deal for us! There are three other firms in there that I know of, and they're all making this a high priority project! Let's get Liz to page everyone and have them take a break from their current assignments to come in here and. . . ."

"Okay, okay, John, just calm down for a second. I understand the importance of this, and I want this deal as much as you do. I can't just pull folks away from commitments we've already made to propose on a deal we haven't even scoped yet. Give me a little while to review the RFP, put together my initial list of questions and ideas, and I'll ask Liz to reach out to everyone and see when they can get in here. We'll get this done, I promise you."

Nick distributed a copy of the RFP and his initial notes to everyone that evening via e-mail and scheduled a lunch meeting to start developing a response. At the meeting, he began by saying, "I asked each of you to attend because I want everyone to agree on an approach to this project. CapState can be a great client, and this move has huge visibility in town. We can really shine if we win it and deliver well, but there's a huge risk if we take it on and can't execute. We've done some small server-room moves before, but nothing of this magnitude, and I want consensus from everyone in this room that we can do this before we even propose."

John spoke up immediately: "Nick, this list of concerns you published is really making me uncomfortable. You dig down into every little detail and make it seem like this project is just impossible. This is a move project, that's all. We're picking a bunch of stuff up and moving it across the street. We're not even moving the stuff; they've hired a moving company to do that. All we're doing is counting it, unplugging it, reconnecting it on the other side, and testing it. I don't understand why this has to be so complicated."

Sandy chimed in immediately: "Let's not trivialize this. There are a lot of unanswered questions here. They say their stuff is 'scattered through multiple departments and locations,' but they don't even list them. Are there five locations or fifty? Are they central or all over the place? They want to ensure no disruption. How do we ensure that? Do they mean they want us to build a whole parallel network, or just try our best to get everything running after the move?"

Adam, the firm's application specialist, spoke up next: "They say they have a complete asset management database. I've heard that one before! If it's so complete how come in the next line they say they have 'about' sixty servers, 'about' twenty-five jukeboxes, and 'about' fifteen scanners?"

Nick broke in: "Okay, let's do this in a structured way. John, I understand you want this deal, and so do we all. The client will appreciate that we've thought this through and that we're focusing on the successful delivery. That's our key selling point. Team, let's start at the top and put together our list of concerns."

Nick facilitated the team work session, leading them through the RFP and recording the questions and ideas that were generated. Some examples of the questions generated included:

- What does CapState mean by "scattered locations"? Would they provide a list?

- How did they define "no disruption"?

- What data does the asset management system capture? How current is it?

- How do they expect to move R&D without any interruption? Was this an example of unrealistic expectations?

- What special problems did the production department pose?

- CapState lists certain skills as being required, such as video conferencing, IP design, and voice communications. What are their expectations of services we'll provide in those areas?

- They state they want bidders to provide "hot spares." Does this imply that we're taking responsibility for hardware maintenance in the move?

- Will CapState assemble a steering committee for escalation of project issues?

- What are the specific roles and responsibilities of the selected vendor and of CapState's IT teams?

After working through the RFP in detail, Nick asked for a show of hands of those who thought the firm should bid on this project. Although a clear majority voted to bid, a couple of the consultants disagreed.

"I just think this is too amorphous to bid on now. Without answering some of these questions, I see a lot of risk here," said Tim, the desktop specialist.

"I agree," said Sara, the strongest project manager on the team. "Who here has ever dealt with UNIX molecular-modeling software before? Who has ever moved sixty servers? Who's relocated 15,000 desktops? With this many open questions, this thing makes me really nervous."

"How about if we bid this as an assessment and discovery project?" Nick suggested. "We could sell them on the idea that they'll need to do an assessment with whomever they select, and that they'll get a worthwhile deliverable out of it even if they decide to pick someone else for the move."

"I don't like it," said John. "The other firms are all going to bid a fixed price. Ron will see that and assume we don't have confidence in our ability to do this."

"I'll help you sell it to Ron," Nick replied. "I believe I can convince him that this approach shows that we're interested in delivering a quality engagement, not just selling the job."

Nick led the team to agreement that an assessment approach was the right thing and composed a rough draft that evening. He circulated it for comment and modification, and John and Nick presented the finished proposal to Ron Gimble at CapState the next day. Nick explained their concept of performing an assessment project in order to better understand the circumstances and requirements of the move. Ron was noncommittal, but accepted the proposal graciously and told them to expect a call within the week.

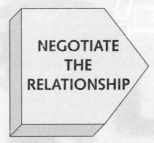

**NEGOTIATE
THE
RELATIONSHIP**

- Remember, Consulting Is Ambiguous
- Clarify Expectations Early
- Take the Emotion Out of Negotiations
- Negotiate All Elements of the Triple Constraint
- Document Your Agreement

Negotiate the Relationship

*Every human benefit and enjoyment, every virtue and every prudent act,
is founded on compromise and barter.*

Edmund Burke

CONSULTING IS AMBIGUOUS

When an IT manager hires a C++ programmer for an internal software development team, the manager has a clear idea of the role that employee will play and the skill set offered. The programmer has probably gone through a rigorous series of interviews with technical staff members, managers, and HR personnel. Credentials and references were reviewed. The IT manager's expectation is that, under the direction of the software development manager, this programmer will perform the tasks assigned with talent and skill. The relationship between manager and programmer is well understood by both, as are the remedies for poor performance.

When the same IT manager engages a consultant to design an Internet connectivity strategy for the organization, the roles and responsibilities are much less clear. Is the consultant going to deliver a strategic white paper or design and implement an intranet? How will the consultant learn about the organization in order to make the best recommendations? Who from the client's team will need to be involved, and for how long? How will the client know what kind of budget to set aside for the consultant's time or for the solutions recommended? When does the relationship begin ("When does the meter start running?") and when does it end? What is the consultant's responsibility to deliver a quality result, and how is that enforced? During the course of the engagement, how will the client know that they're on track? Does the client have any remedies if the consultant turns out to be unqualified, unprofessional, or just a poor fit with the client's organization?

The contrast between the clarity of an employer/employee relationship and the ambiguity of the client/consultant relationship should make it clear why negotiating is a skill every consultant must master. Consulting is vague and prone to misunderstanding; all consultants must grasp this baseline concept, for it forces us to take seriously our obligation to clarify our roles with clients. As the preceding litany of questions illustrates, the client approaches the advisory relationship in need of guidance and assurance from the consultant about the nature of the association. The most successful consultants are skilled in helping clients understand how the process will work, reassuring them that together they will reach the desired result, and ensuring that expectations on both sides are clearly delineated.

Clarifying Expectations

The client's expectation of the role you will play determines the style you bring to the engagement. A consultant who has negotiated a role as a strategic IT policy advisor to the CIO will engage differently than will a programmer for hire. If your role is to write a time-card module in Java, it's probably not a good idea to be spending your efforts (and the client's money) making recommendations on an e-commerce strategy. The client's style of engagement will also be affected by the roles negotiated. The IT manager should expect to engage more closely, and on a different level, with the strategic policy consultant than with the Java programmer. When defining roles, we must focus on the roles of both the consultant and the client. The client's expected contribution to the project effort, in availability, access, and resources, must be defined plainly if the consultation is to be successful.

It's also important to define the boundaries of the relationship. Does a recommendation for a particular brand of network router imply that, if it malfunctions at 3:00 AM, the client can expect the consultant to run by and fix it? This is one possible scenario, but if the relationship is not negotiated as such, one of the parties will be disappointed when that telephone rings. In an IT advisory situation, almost any assistance that the consultant agrees to provide can imply any of several different levels of service. Does the design of an accounts payable system imply a link to the client's existing general ledger program? This area of implied or "obvious" linkages is an area of IT consulting fraught with the danger of miscommunication. It's easy for the client to assume that if you're recommending hardware you can supply it, and if you're supplying hardware you can fix it. Consultants must dig into every service they're proposing to the customer and make sure that there are no implied tasks or results that could be misunderstood.

Ask the Client

Most of the questions I ask my clients focus on two points: (1) How I can help, and (2) What results are you looking for? I will ask, in different ways, "What can I do to help with that problem?" "What role would a consultant play in that effort?" or "What would be the best result of that project if all went perfectly?" If you're lucky, the client can clearly articulate the problem or opportunity, why the organization has decided to seek an advisor, and what the expected outcome is. In many cases, however, the client does not have a clear understanding of the problem, has never worked with a consultant before, and is not sure what you can do to help. Every practicing consultant will eventually be faced with an even stickier situation, in which the client does not really believe there is a problem, and does not believe an outsider can add anything, but has been instructed by a manager to bring in specialized help. Whether the client is an old hand at the use of consultants or is a reluctant participant in the process, the consultant's responsibility does not change: to gauge the client's expectations, to guide the client through the advisory process, and to focus on the best interests of the client and the client's organization throughout the engagement. Wherever on the spectrum a particular engagement may lie, listening to the client tell the story from his or her own perspective will help you formulate an appropriate strategy.

Just as it is important to evaluate who the client is when we consider taking on an engagement, it is also critical to understand who we must negotiate with to frame a successful outcome. Is it sufficient to negotiate our role with the project sponsor, who may be paying our bills, or do we also need to negotiate with representatives of the users or the IT staff? Remember that many unsuccessful systems are designed by managers behind closed doors, without team participation or support. Be sure in every engagement that you understand the other constituencies you will need to deal with, your access to them, and what role they will play in a successful rollout. In situations in which your negotiations include a large team of client representatives, like a selection committee or project team, observe carefully the team dynamics. Learn who the decision makers or thought leaders are, who may or may not be your advocate, and which interests are over-represented or under-represented. Be alert to the tone and atmosphere of your conversation with your client. If you sense that the client wants to keep you away from others for the wrong reasons, such as the fear that they may have a different idea of the problem or may disclose things that damage his or her prestige, you may need to negotiate contact with them in order to do justice to the advisory relationship.

With all these cautions about negotiations, we must not lose sight of the bottom line: The agreement we negotiate must result in a successful engagement. In living up to the standards of our profession, we must guide the customer toward an agreement that is attractive and motivating for us as consultants and that grants us the access, information, and authority to deliver the business results that the client expects. This sometimes requires us to push back a bit against the client's misapprehensions or unrealistic expectation.

THE SIX RULES OF NEGOTIATION

There are a few key points to remember when negotiating:

- *Avoid Imposing Your Role.* Attempting to unilaterally define the relationship by telling the client what role you're prepared to take, what the client must do, and how the work will be done is not an effective method of building cooperation, confidence, and trust. In any negotiation, trying to impose a settlement on the other party is bad form and as likely to elicit resistance as cooperation. Start with the attitude that everything is on the table, and then negotiate out the elements that you believe are not in the best interest of the engagement.

- *Avoid Having a Role Imposed on You.* The position of the consultant is that of a service provider, but that does not mean that the customer is always right. In fact, it is a key role of the consultant to protect a client from bad impulses or misperceptions. Usually, the client is expecting guidance on what is possible and appropriate. In some cases, the customer's expectations of what you can do may be dead wrong. Either way, firmness in steering the customer toward reasonable roles and a beneficial relationship requires diplomacy, determination, and mental toughness, but it's in your mutual best interest.

- *Take Out the Emotion and the Ego.* If you see every negotiation as a contest that you must win, your projects (and career) will lose. Focus on the best interest of the client and the engagement. That must be your only agenda whenever you engage as a consultant. Anything else is unprofessional.

- *Negotiate Creatively.* There are many approaches to the same goal. Reach for the unexpected compromise that shows your commitment to the project and demonstrates that you are more interested in professional success than in victories at the bargaining table. Some of the most effective negotiating tactics involve giving a concession to demonstrate confidence in your skills. For instance, offer to perform an assessment and deliver a design document that the customer can then "shop" to your competitors. You demonstrate your conviction that you are the best person to do this job and your confidence that the customer will be satisfied and will want you to continue. I'll often offer to perform services on a "try-before-you-buy" basis, especially if this is a client I've targeted or a project I'm particularly interested in. Show the client you want to figure out a way to make the engagement work.

- *Table Disagreements.* Don't turn negotiation into argument. If you sincerely disagree, back off and offer to sleep on the issue and see whether you can devise a compromise. Sincerely consider the sticking point issue and see what you really need to have. Then offer a compromise. If the issue is a "must have," develop a justification that the client will understand and appreciate.

- *Document Your Agreements.* Take notes, or have an assistant present who can "scribe" the negotiations. No agreement is final until it is documented, reviewed, and initialed.

THE DELIVERABLES

These points address the advisory skills you bring into the negotiation process. The next question is: "What exactly are we negotiating?" As discussed in the previous chapter, your preliminary meetings with the client should have resulted in your creation of an Engagement Profile, as well as some preliminary task, schedule, and budget estimates. Now you must review those with the client, to define in detail the services and results you're committing to deliver. The outcomes of the negotiating process must be, at a minimum, the following:

- *Preliminary Vision Statement.* The client's description of the "compelling event" for seeking an advisor and the benefits to be achieved by doing so are a vision statement. This will be refined later in the process, but it's important to test your understanding of the overall objective at the very beginning of negotiations.

- *Preliminary Scope of Work Document.* The Scope of Work Document is the crux of the agreement on the technical deliverables of the engagement. It must be complete enough to present a clear picture to the client team regarding exactly what they are buying from you. If you need to perform an assessment or a system inventory before you can know what the complete scope is, say so here.

- *Preliminary Schedule.* The expectations of completion dates for the phases of the project should be couched as a "preliminary schedule subject to significant modification based on the results of discovery and data collection activities."

- *Preliminary Budget.* This is an estimate of the billable fees the client will incur for engaging you and your associates. Obviously, this is closely tied to the scope and schedule. If you are only engaging for an assessment phase and will renegotiate based on the results of that, state so clearly and present a budget for that phase only. This number will stick indelibly in the client's mind, so make it undeniably clear what you are including in this budget and which deliverables, such as hardware, software, support services, or other additional services, are excluded.

- *Deliverables Document.* This is a description of the deliverables you are committing to produce. This will typically include project plans, communications or internal marketing plans, status or milestone reporting, as well as the technical deliverables you are contracting to render, such as an Internet strategic plan, an asset management database, or a LAN implementation plan.

  (*NOTE:* I want to emphasize here that all activities in a consulting relationship have deliverables! Verbal reports, conversations, work done on a server in the middle of the night, or other informal or intangible deliverables are unprofessional. In addition, they are extremely hard to display in case of disagreement at billing time. For clarity, for professionalism, and for your own protection, produce a tangible deliverable, such as a report, manual, or customer acceptance sign-off sheet, at every phase of the engagement.)

- *Roles and Responsibilities Statement.* A clear statement must be produced describing which tasks and deliverables the consultant is chartered to take ownership of and which the client and team will commit to producing.

- *Assumptions.* This defines some of the basic needs of both parties and will typically include the facilities the client will be providing as work space, access and a guest ID to the client's computer network if required, and expected review and approval turnaround time on documents submitted by the consultant. If you assume that the client will allow access to a data center or to payroll and billing records or to the source code for inventory software, say so here.

  See the sample proposal in Appendix B for some examples of the language I use for presenting these to the client.

TEST YOUR AGREEMENT

Even when you believe you have reached agreement, that agreement must be tested and confirmed. Present a first draft of a Scope of Work Document or Letter of Engagement, including the elements outlined above, to the customer for comment. This step is vital, for it tests your understanding of the deal you've negotiated and flushes out faulty assumptions and miscommunications. Communicate clearly that you are expecting the client's response to these deliverables and stress the importance of a critical review to ensure that you are still in agreement. Any misinterpretation of the client's expectations must be renegotiated, and the documents must be reissued, until they conform to your mutual understanding of the engagement. Once accepted, these documents form the contract you will work from. They may not be a legal contract, but the legal issues are not our focus here. The documents are a professional contract, a promise to perform at a professional level the tasks to which you have committed.

As with most components of the consulting relationship, we are negotiating both hard, factual elements, like the scope, budget, and schedule, as well as less tangible ones, such as executive sponsorship and support. Do not confuse what is tangible with what is important. The support and commitment issues are as critical to success as scope and schedule. The risks surrounding lack of support may be more dangerous than an ill-defined scope. Scope can always be refined if the commitment to success and partnership is there.

TIPS ON SCOPING A PROJECT

Scope refers to the total effort you will put forth to assist the client. A detailed Scope of Work Document between client and consultant is the most important element in determining success or failure of your engagement. No other component of your negotiation does more to set true or faulty expectations. The information technology consultant who can define a scope that addresses the clients' needs totally, and clearly documents the services and results expected, is protecting the client as well as himself or herself.

Scope can be determined in many ways. In engagements that result from an RFP, the client has documented objectives, and the consultant then needs to interpret those objectives into roles, tasks, and results. In cases in which the client is less sure of the problem or its possible solution, you must help the client shape a relationship that will achieve the objectives. By working in a top-down manner with the client, defining overall goals first and then focusing on specific tasks and results, you can work with the client to build a scope that will serve as a blueprint of the project.

Remember that scope also must address the boundaries of your enquiry. Consultants often get in trouble by being overly ambitious, like the Java programmer previously mentioned who wanted to design an e-commerce strategy. Remember that the customer is inviting you in, so—like any good guest—don't start going through the drawers. In the course of writing an accounts payable module, you may notice that the client's network infrastructure is token ring, and you believe they would be better off with ethernet. Unless evaluating the status of the network topology is in your scope, your comments will not be welcome, and the client will not relish paying you for the time you spend outside your mandate. Clearly understand not only your scope, but also its limits.

It is critical that you negotiate a scope that is neither too broad nor too narrow. Be sure that the expectations are not broader than the time and resources you, or the client, are prepared to invest. Also ensure that the scope is not so narrow that you cannot deliver a meaningful business benefit. I've had clients ask me to perform network design reviews, but been explicitly notified that cabling was off limits or that the network addressing scheme could not be changed. Boundaries that make it impossible to succeed must be exposed to the light of day and explicitly dealt with in negotiation.

Scope definition is an ongoing process. There are elements of scope that will be impossible to predict until you begin to assess the current state. At this point, you should aim to get a general sense of the client's objectives, the business goals of the project, the extent of the role the client is offering you, and the boundaries of your efforts. Consulting engagements must be properly scoped from the start, but, if the relationship is open and cooperative, scope can be refined as an organic part of the process.

The time to introduce the concept of scope changes or unexpected impacts to the project is at the beginning of the relationship. It is well known among consultants and project managers that "scope creep" is the virus that infects and kills engagements and relationships. Like most viruses, however, a little prevention is usually much more effective than after-the-fact attempts to cure the damage. Discussing the possibility that, as you work together, the vision that each of you had of the problem and its solution may change, and assuring the client that you have an orderly process for managing that event, is critical. We will discuss scope and impact management in more detail in Chapter 9, but for this phase, it is another assurance factor that will make the client feel you're a pro who has been through this before.

BUDGET

It is a proverb among salespeople that you must keep the customer focused on the value rather than on the cost. This is equally true for the consultant, where the client is buying service, an intangible, rather than, say, a piece of hardware that can be touched. Consultant fees are high, in many cases substantially more per hour than the client is paid. The client is not going to do the calculations required to understand that the consultant has to pay for downtime, research time, continuing education time, benefits, and marketing time with that $125 per hour fee. The client just sees a very expensive meter running as you work, chat, write, research, and communicate. Take the client's money seriously; you can be sure the client does.

Keeping the client focused on the value is a process that takes place throughout the relationship. During the negotiation phase, it's good practice to not only help the customer define the project's objective, but also its justification. While the objective states the function of the proposed new system or software, the justification describes, in financial terms, why it makes business sense to spend money on the project. How much faster does the client expect to get paid with the new accounts receivable system, and what is that worth in dollars? How much incremental revenue can be generated with the new e-commerce website?

The negotiation phase is not the right time to perform a detailed cost/benefit analysis, but it is the time to start the client thinking about the metrics that will be applied to the final product, to determine whether it delivers the benefits expected. Will it be enough that the new network is robust, reliable, fast, and secure, or will it also need to be 20 percent cheaper to maintain than the mainframe it replaces? If so, it's better to know that now than at the end, when your success as a consultant will be judged based on a measurement you had no part in defining.

The budget that will be presented as a deliverable of the negotiation phase should be preliminary—and must be clearly labeled and communicated as such. Without the benefit of the discovery process that you will perform in the "Understand the Client's Situation" phase (Chapter 6), it's impossible to know how much effort you will need to expend on subsequent phases. Obviously, different types of engagements will be more or less difficult to estimate. If you are engaged to do a revision of a software module for a customer you've worked with before in the same capacity, and you have good visibility into the systems, interfaces, and personalities you'll be dealing with, you can safely present an estimate. Doing so would not be prudent with a complex project utilizing cutting-edge technologies for a new customer. You need to honestly ask yourself how much you know, and how much you need to know, before you can put a budget in front of the client (where it will be remembered forever!).

My personal policy is to stay away from fixed-bid or not-to-exceed pricing engagements. The purpose of these price structures is to move the risk from the client to the consultant. By building in status reporting, regular budget and expenditure reviews, and other ongoing assurance factors, you can reassure the customer that you will advise continuously on how much is being spent and that you are prepared to make adjustments as you go. This seems to me a fair way to control client expenditures without putting yourself at an injudicious financial risk. Once I learned to build in the assurance factors and status reporting, I never had a client who would not accept a budget based on a good-faith estimate, with the provision that I would bill actual hours expended.

As with scope, define in your budget not only what is included, but what is excluded. Be sure the client understands how hardware, software, subcontracted labor, travel expenses, maintenance contracts, and any other projected expenditures are being represented in your budget. Financial surprises are the worst kind of surprises for the client/consultant relationship and are devastating to the trust and confidence you have worked diligently to build. Clearly categorize and document all projected costs and over-communicate so there are no missed expectations.

PRIORITIES

Scope, budget, and schedule are often called "the triple constraint" in project management literature. One of the important outcomes of the negotiating process is a sense of the client's priorities. A particularly vivid way of referring to scope, budget, and schedule in the context of prioritization is the question: "Does the client want it good, fast, or cheap?" *Good* refers to the project's performance specifications, *fast* refers to the speed of developing the solution, and *cheap* is obvious. Once we agree on the definitions, then the question is which of these is the higher priority, because you can only achieve two:

If the client wants it good and fast, it won't be cheap.

If the client wants it good and cheap, it won't be fast.

If the client wants it cheap and fast, it won't be good.

This is a cynical and glib way of looking at this (and I probably wouldn't share this with the client). I present it here because it clarifies the choices we consultants need to make when we help our clients prioritize the objectives of an engagement. Tactfully probe the client with questions such as "What would the impact be if this project could not be delivered in the time frame you envision?" or "How would you handle a situation in which the technology available could not deliver the functionality you expect?" I present these not as literal questions to ask verbatim, but as examples of diplomatic explorations of the client's priorities and expectations. The key is to get a flavor for the client's tolerance for risk and change and for the client's order of precedence of cost, schedule, and functionality.

Negotiation is not an incident that occurs and is done. As circumstances, understanding, and personnel change, and as trust and confidence grow (or diminish) between the advisor and client, the roles and responsibilities can shift—and shift again. Perhaps the Java programmer *will* gain the clients' trust to the degree that the programmer has an opportunity to devise an e-commerce solution after all. As the due diligence and discovery process moves forward, insight may be gained that sheds a new and different cast on the entire engagement. As hours are expended and the client sees the budget reserve diminishing, he or she may ask for a reduction in the consultant's efforts. As the options and recommendations start to take shape, the client may begin to realize that the technology was not what was expected. The skilled consultant is prepared to negotiate and renegotiate throughout the engagement. By remaining flexible, by having the maturity to resist personal disappointment or "ruffled feathers" due to the need to revisit expectations, by keeping everyone's eyes on the prize, the skilled consultant becomes a valued partner.

Let's return now to our case study, where we'll review some of the activities a typical consulting firm might make when preparing to negotiate an engagement. As illustrated in this example, approaching negotiations as a facilitated work session with a view toward helping the client define an achievable engagement is a winning strategy. Please review again the RFP in Appendix A and the proposal in Appendix B, so that you have a clear understanding of the details discussed in this case study.

"Well," said John to the team at the weekly meeting, "great news! CapState wants to begin negotiations with two of the firms immediately, and we're one of the two!"

"Wait a minute," said Nick. "They want to start negotiating before they've selected a partner? That doesn't make much sense!"

"Yeah," John said, "I know, but that's how they want to do it. I just got off the phone with Ron, and he said that since they're on such a short time line, they want to start two separate tracks of negotiation with the firms they're interested in and see where the talks go. They believe that they can learn who they want to do business with based on the atmosphere of the negotiations."

Nick thought about that for a minute. "I guess it's not so weird after all. Since neither vendor knows whether it has the business, CapState thinks we'll both be more willing to compromise. Not a bad ploy!"

"So what do we need to do to get ready?" John asked.

"Let's figure out who we want on our team for these meetings. Then we should all review the RFP and our response again to be sure we're in agreement on our position. Then let's just go into this as a facilitated work session and help Ron and his team define the project."

Ron Gimble of CapState met John, Nick, Sandy, and Sara in the lobby to escort them to the conference room. John introduced Sara as a possible candidate to manage the project for Superior.

"My team consists of myself," Ron explained, "our IT operations manager, one of our network technicians whom I see as a project manager candidate from our side, and an IT representative from the R&D group. We're looking forward to reviewing your proposal with you. We think your idea of performing the assessment as a separate project is interesting." Ron raised his eyebrows on the word "interesting."

When they entered the conference room, it was obvious to Nick that their competitor for this project had just left. The screen and data projector were still set up, and each of the CapState representatives had a big fancy binder in front of them with the competitor's logo imprinted on it.

Ron and John did their respective introductions; then Ron spoke to the group: "We've asked you to come back and begin a negotiating process with us for a couple of reasons. We've checked your references in town, and, although you really didn't have a reference for a move of this scale, one thing all your clients agree on is that you focus on the delivery aspects of your engagements, and you don't make commitments you can't keep. Frankly, the other vendor has more experience with projects of this size. But out of all the bidders, you were the only one who suggested breaking out the assessment as a separate phase. There's still some question on my team as to whether that makes sense for us, but it intrigued me enough to make me want to hear more, so go ahead and make your presentation."

Nick was sitting across from Ron. He went to the whiteboard and picked up one of the markers there. "Frankly, Ron, our approach to this process is a bit different from that of our competitors. Rather than reiterate the material in our proposal as a presentation, what I'd rather do is turn this into a working session. Let's figure out together what value a firm like ours can bring to this project, and let's be sure we have the same understanding of the expectations, priorities, and deliverables. Does that make sense to you?"

Ron smiled and relaxed in his chair. "That sounds great. We thought we had done a great job of building a comprehensive RFP until we saw your response. The questions you raised actually helped us go back and rethink some of our own assumptions about this project. Frankly, one of the reasons we picked you to go through this process was that we thought you could help us clarify our thoughts about how to approach this."

Rob Newell, CapState's IT operations manager, then said: "I like this approach. Can you believe the other guys brought their lawyer in here? For the first meeting! Can you imagine what that relationship would be like if things went south?"

Kelly, the CapState network technician, laughed. "Some people hear the word 'negotiate'. . . ."

John handed out the only material they had brought to the meeting, a bound copy of the Superior Systems proposal (see Appendix B). Nick picked it up and turned to the "Background" section. "The first thing I want to do is be sure that we correctly identified the services you want a consulting partner to provide. Let's take a look at the list of services in the Background section [p. 234] and see if we agree on the general scope." Nick walked through the services listed and gave the CapState team a chance to comment as he read each one.

When Nick reviewed the line regarding the disconnection of PC's, Ron remarked: "We haven't determined yet whether we want to outsource that or do it internally." Nick wrote "Open Issues" on the board and listed *disconnection outsourced or internal?*

"What about follow-up support?" John asked. He looked to Rob Newell for a response, as he knew from his research that PC support was one of Rob's duties.

"I see this as a joint activity," Rob said. "My team knows the applications and the associates well and can quickly identify which applications are business-critical and which are not. But I don't think we will have enough feet on the street to cover all the issues that will arise the morning after, so I see you guys adding a lot of value there."

"Great," Nick said. "We're starting to build some agreement on the broad scope of this. Are there any services that we neglected to include in this list?" He gave the CapState team a chance to look over the list and reflect for a moment. When no one commented, he went on: "Let's dig down a bit into the success criteria we identified in the proposal, and make sure that we've prioritized them the way you would." Nick reviewed the critical success factors. When he mentioned the need for special handling of the R&D group, the R&D IT representative nodded in agreement, but remained quiet.

Ron stopped Nick in the middle of the list and asked, "What about the requirement to do this over the Christmas break? Is this going to cause a problem for your team? Our folks have been preparing for this for a long time, and they're highly motivated to get into the new building. Will you be able to motivate your consultants to focus on this during the holidays?"

Sara spoke up: "A lot of our clients are in the financial and brokerage industry, and we often can't touch their systems until after hours or on weekends. We're used to working in the off hours. Also, I have a big enough crew that I can stagger the teams in and out so everyone gets some family time for the holidays. Are you planning to work on Christmas and New Year's Day?" Sara and Ron discussed the details of the holiday work schedules. They fell into an easy give-and-take, as if Superior had already been awarded the contract.

Nick started to probe a bit on another of the success criteria: "Ron, you mention in the RFP that you expect the vendor to provide spare systems and parts, but you don't detail your expectations regarding hardware maintenance as part of this project. I was a bit confused; are you expecting the selected vendor to take responsibility for the hardware that's being relocated?"

Rob Newell responded: "This was one of those things that your response made us think twice about. Also the next line, where we listed skills, like video and voice, but didn't describe how those services would be needed for the move."

Nick smiled: "So I'm hoping that our approach, of doing an assessment first so we can clarify these expectations, is starting to make sense."

Nick and John looked around the table at the CapState team, then glanced at each other. They were feeling more and more comfortable that, by focusing on the delivery criteria rather than making a slick sales pitch, they would be persuasive to this prospective client.

Nick and his team spent another hour with the CapState crew, reviewing the details and the deliverables of each phase. In some cases, such as when Sandy queried about the state of network documentation, Ron seemed to become quiet and reserved, which Nick interpreted as a sign that he needed to be diplomatic in exploring that area further. He made a note to warn Sandy to tread carefully there and to assume that there probably was not much existing documentation to rely on. Questions about the asset management database also seemed to touch a sensitive spot, so Nick quickly moved on.

When Nick mentioned the idea of performing facilitated sessions with the R&D group, their IT representative finally spoke up: "I don't think that's a good idea. These chemists are obsessed with security. They won't be very cooperative with someone they don't know poking around and asking questions."

"How do you recommend we clarify their requirements?" Nick asked.

"Oh, just talk to me. I'll tell you everything you need to know about them. I'm their primary IT support guy anyway. Our applications are so special we don't get much support from the regular IT ops guys."

Nick noted that there might be some tension between IT and R&D. He also made a note to coach Sandy and Sara about how to address these sensitive areas without being isolated from information they would need to be successful.

"Any questions about the fee structure?" John asked.

"Let's just the two of us take that off-line," Ron replied. "This team doesn't need to be involved in that conversation."

At the end of the session, Nick reviewed the open issues list with the joint team: "So, it looks like we still have some open questions regarding the responsibility for doing the actual disconnects and reconnects, and I still don't feel that we've reached a conclusion about the hardware maintenance piece."

"Yes, we need to review those in a meeting and see what our current consensus is," Ron replied. "I'm also still not sure that your idea of interviewing and meeting with associates from R&D and other areas is going to work. We may need to do that ourselves and get you the data."

"If we do it that way," Nick responded, "I'd like our team to be involved up front so we ensure that the data we need is captured."

"That could work," Ron said.

Alex, the R&D IT representative, spoke up: "I'm not hearing anything that makes me feel like you bring any special skills to the R&D part of this. How do you propose to deal with our special hardware and software?"

Nick responded: "Alex, I'm looking to you for guidance on how to ensure that your team's requirements are met. My typical process is to go through a few sessions like this one with the key technical and functional team members, and then put together a mutual plan that everyone feels comfortable with. You sound like you're not convinced that would work. Let's you and I sit down off-line and see if we can agree on a process for developing a plan that's specific to your needs."

Ron cut this dialogue short: "Alex, let's chat about this after this meeting. I've got a few ideas that I think can help. I'm satisfied that we can work this out and move forward." Ron asked John to call him back with some open slots for a follow-up meeting next week and then closed the meeting by gathering his materials and getting ready to leave.

As the meeting broke up, Nick, John, and their team walked around the room and shook hands, chatting with the CapState members for a few moments. In the elevator on the way down, Ron shook hands again, thanked them for coming and remarked: "That went well."

"So, what do you think?" John asked as they drove back to the office.

Nick looked at Sara and Sandy before answering, then asked: "What did you think?"

"I felt pretty good about it," Sara replied. "They obviously didn't like the fact that the other guys came in with a lawyer, and they sure were talking as if this was a done deal."

"The fact that they don't have a real inventory or any network documentation makes me nervous," Sandy said. "They were real defensive about it, which leads me to think that it's a sore spot internally. Maybe there's some kind of turf war about it or something."

"Yeah, and that R&D guy!" Sara continued. "What is he, James Bond or something? 'Obsessed with secrecy!' Give me a break!"

"I thought it went well," Nick finally responded. "They seem like a reasonable crew. They admitted that our reply made them think, which is always a good thing. They're a big, diverse company, so there are always going to be some politics and turf situations. That comes with the territory. But it seemed pretty clear that Ron has the authority, and he seems clearly in charge. Sara and Sandy, let's chat about some strategies for dealing with documentation and turf issues when we get back to the office." Nick started to walk through the list of open issues; they each volunteered to take ownership of some of them, and they agreed to meet again in a couple of days to review their strategy for moving forward.

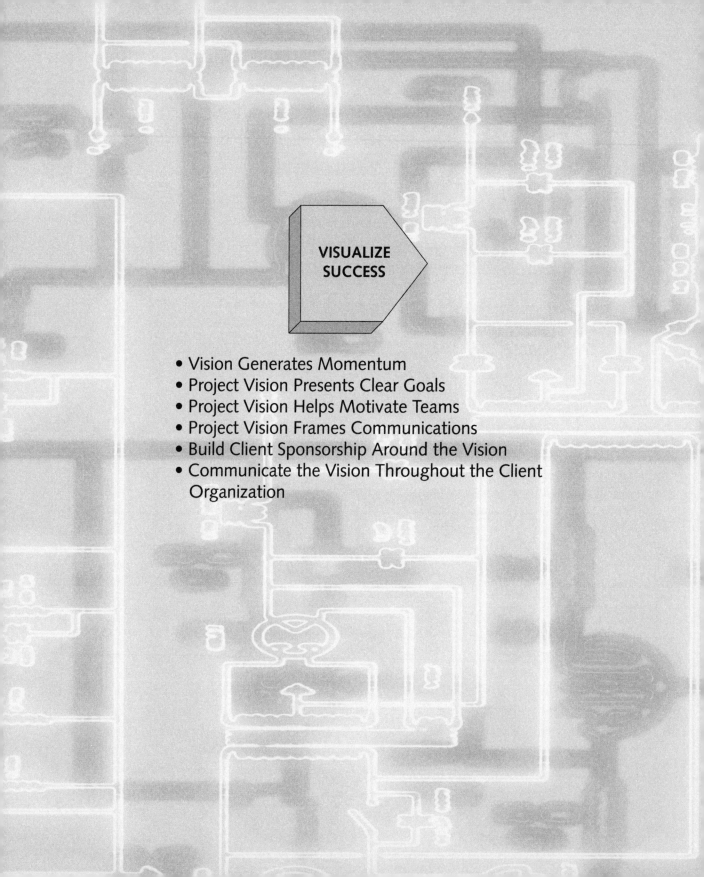

VISUALIZE SUCCESS

- Vision Generates Momentum
- Project Vision Presents Clear Goals
- Project Vision Helps Motivate Teams
- Project Vision Frames Communications
- Build Client Sponsorship Around the Vision
- Communicate the Vision Throughout the Client Organization

Visualize Success

Nothing great was ever achieved without enthusiasm.

Ralph Waldo Emerson

IT INERTIA

Question: "How was God able to create the world in six days?"

Answer: "He had no installed base!"

Conventional wisdom would suggest that having a base of dedicated users of your technology would be an advantage. Wouldn't it be easier to sell this captive audience upgrades to your systems? Wouldn't you have a database of registered users to whom you could market additional products and services? Couldn't you use an installed base to build an empire of supplementary products?

Well, yes and no. The advantage of having an installed base, especially if your system is proprietary or closed, is that the costs of switching to another technology can be so prohibitive that you essentially create a captive market. If you've done a reasonably good job of servicing and supporting your customers and have kept up with the current innovations in technology while maintaining compatibility throughout the old and new product line, you indeed can build an empire around your base products.

But there's the rub. Eventually your responsibility to protect your existing clients' investments, by maintaining compatibility and not forcing them to throw out their existing systems to benefit from new technologies, becomes a drag on innovation. How many programmer hours did Microsoft spend carrying DOS compatibility into the Windows universe? Anyone who recalls the slow migration from DOS-based personal computing to Windows will also remember the cry and protest from the installed base at every step of the way. The fact that users would need more memory and hard disk space was a scandal! The fact that Windows sometimes crashed was an outrage! The introduction of the local area network, while obvious and useful, was also cause for protest in the computer press. Whatever happened to the pure idea of "a computer for every person"? Wasn't that what the personal computer revolution was all about?

No matter what your opinion of Microsoft; there's now little doubt that graphical, network-enabled computing has brought huge benefits. People did not resist these benefits because they were stupid or short-sighted. They resisted them for a couple of very human reasons:

1. Existing systems represent a substantial investment in hardware, software, training, and hard-earned process knowledge.
2. People resist change.

Even technically sophisticated people cling to the familiar. Remember Ken Olsen of Digital Equipment and his famous comment that nobody would ever need a computer on the desktop, or Xerox's well-known failure to take advantage of in-house innovations like the graphical user interface and the mouse (known inside Xerox as "fumbling the future")? The combination of vested interest, hard-won expertise and experience, sunk investment in both hard and soft assets, and human resistance to change creates an inertia that any action-oriented consultant must learn to counteract.

PROJECT VISION

The opposite of inertia is momentum. So far in our process, we've typically been working with a single client or a small project team, reaching agreement on roles and goals. But the fact that the project sponsor, an executive committee, or the project team has reached a consensus does not automatically turn inertia into drive. A common vision, clearly articulated, of success and its benefits is what creates momentum in the organization. This chapter will help you help your client to develop and communicate a vision of what will be gained when your advice is followed.

Don't make the mistake of assuming that visualizing success is a "soft" goal, not on a par with "hard" deliverables like a project plan or network design. As former president George Bush can attest, "the vision thing" can be the difference between winning and losing. Barriers to change are significant, inertia is a powerful force, and the consultant's job is evolving from that of a technologist to that of a business strategist. As strategists, we must do more than devise systems in a roomful of managers. If the study of organizational change over the last twenty years has taught us anything, it is that vision, communication, and consensus regarding change are critical to success.

Because we believe that a project vision provides a central communication and motivation factor, we recommend that consultants help their clients to do the following:

- Create the "tag line" for the engagement;
- Build project sponsorship teams;
- Create a vision communication plan; and
- Cascade communications throughout the organization.

Create the "Tag Line" for the Engagement

Many books on consulting recommend creating a mission statement for every project. Although this can be a powerful technique, the downside is that these statements, rather than cutting to the heart of the client's requirements, end up being a compendium of primary and secondary goals, nice-to-have's, "feel good" objectives, and dreams and wishes. Your goal during the visualization process is to simplify, to get to the core objective that the client sees. I begin by asking my client or project team, "When this engagement is successful and we go our separate ways, what will we have delivered?" I like this phrasing because it calls on the client to use imagination, to see the moment when the completed system is up and running and all the benefits are delivered. In short, it forces the client to visualize.

The most important guidance you can give your client at this stage is to "make the vision statement compelling." The project's compelling event may be related to competition, customer service, comparative costs to other enterprises in the industry, the inability to enter new businesses due to insufficient systems infrastructure, or any other business-driven need. The vision of the end state must be compelling enough to build sponsorship, drive internal marketing, and create organizational enthusiasm. If the vision does not portray the benefit as greater than the pain of change, inertia will triumph over momentum. Help your client keep an eye on the ball, which is the need for a vision that can build impetus toward change in the enterprise.

The goal of this exercise is to help your client draft a tag line, a one or two sentence declaration of what the project will deliver. For example:

> "The X Corp E-Commerce Project will create a web-based platform to allow our clients to view our complete catalog, order our products, and gain access to expert assistance using our products."

Try to refine your client's definition of project success into a concise and persuasive statement, then repeat and polish it together until the client feels it expresses a vision of the project's success. The key is, when you have flushed out the core success factor, and phrased it in a compelling way, you have the basis for the communication and consensus building to follow. You also have a "light at the end of the tunnel" to point to, when the client decides it would be nice if the system also brewed coffee and mowed the lawn.

Build Project Sponsorship Teams

Change doesn't just happen; it must be lead. Executives cannot lead change unless they are committed to it themselves. Once they are on board, they must then gain the commitment of the troops. As Jack Welch, CEO of General Electric, has said, "The job of the leader is to . . . articulate the vision to employees." Information technology consultants can differentiate themselves from their colleagues by helping clients obtain the executive sponsorship they need.

Every IT project that crosses departmental lines or is visible at an executive level should include the creation of a project sponsorship committee. For instance, consultants implementing enterprise resource planning software or other technologies that require business-process reengineering need the support and authority of a senior project committee to make decisions that transcend the departmental. This committee should be recommended during the project negotiation period, and should be composed of departmental management from the functional areas involved, senior company management, and client IT specialists. Most companies can be sold on bringing a committee together to periodically review the status of important IT projects. By bringing the committee to consensus on the project vision, the committee can then help broadcast to the organization a consistent, persuasive project message. Assisting clients to utilize structures like the project sponsorship committee creates an opportunity for the IT consultant to operate at the level of a true management consultant.

Large organizations can have dozens of departments that could be affected by a project. A hospital relocation project, for instance, can involve office workers, sales teams, research and development scientists, clinical lab workers, and radiology technicians. Participants from internal IT departments could include desktop support, the data center team, the telecom group, and the network architecture team. Each of these constituencies can have a sharply dissimilar view of what's important in planning the move. In these situations I recommend the creation of an integration team, whose role is to ensure that all share a common goal and that project planning and activities are coordinated and working together. This team is a crucial component of any organizational communication plan, bringing together all stakeholders in a forum that allows interaction, debate, and knowledge sharing. Consultants should ensure that not only the senior executives, but also the local departmental managers and IT "thought leaders" are involved in sponsoring and communicating the vision. By creating an integration team and scheduling regular integration meetings, we assure that the vision of the project is received in the same way by each group and project lead, and that the overall enterprise goal does not become consumed in conflicting departmental agendas.

Create a Vision Communication Plan

At this stage of the engagement, it is your role to help lead the steering committee and the integration team to agreement on the core success factors of the project. Your client has engaged you because he or she believes you can help clarify expectations. The members of these teams and committees expect you to bring experience with the technology and its implementation, with the "gotcha's" and pitfalls as well as the benefits. You must use these teams, and your facilitation and leadership skills, to carry the vision of what can be achieved to this level of stakeholder. By asking the question posed earlier (What will have been achieved when this is over?) and facilitating a discussion about the inevitable differences in conception, you can assist these teams in developing a shared vision of a successful conclusion.

When agreement has been reached, it is again important to distill that to a tag line. This may be exactly the same as the tag line you developed with the project sponsor, or it may differ significantly. It's important that these teams understand that this tag line will be a key component of your communication program. That fact will influence the phrasing and emphasis. This is a process of incremental refinement, by which we help the client arrive at a vision of success that can be a banner throughout the engagement.

When project sponsors, executives, and team leaders all agree on a vision of success for the engagement, it's time to cascade that vision to the next level of stakeholder, the population of employees. If I were to rank the causes of project failure I've seen in my career, *ineffective communication* would top the list. Poor or absent communication directly causes rumor, gossip, fear, division, confusion, and ultimately resistance. Conversely, nothing can have such a positive influence on the chances for success as a well thought out, clear, targeted, consistent, and continual communication strategy. In consultant teams I work within or lead, I absolutely insist that one of our deliverables be a communication plan. Any engagement that lacks this element is setting the stage for defeat.

Cascade Communications Throughout the Organization

Every communication plan must contain a number of fundamental components. Foremost is linkage to the guiding strategy. Simply stating that we are, for instance, migrating from a mainframe-based to a client/server-based accounting system tells people what we're doing but not why. The benefits, goals, and objectives must be declared and marketed to those affected. Note the key word *"marketed."* The point of this exercise is to build enthusiasm for the result we've visualized. This requires more than just a statement of fact. As in any marketing effort, it requires the building of demand.

Communication must be consistent. If we merely recommend that all team leaders let their teams know that we're going to perform a migration, we're exercising no guidance over the form and content of the message. Competent consultants will instead advise clients to compose a uniform message that is designed not just to inform, but also to persuade. By uniform I don't mean that the R&D group, for instance, will receive the same message as the production workers, word-for-word. Rather, the underlying linkage to strategy should be consistent. Inconsistent communication of the vision is as bad as no communication at all, as it confuses people and fosters resistance rather than momentum. ("If they can't even get the message straight, how are they going to implement a complex system?") Consistent communications do not happen by accident. They are the result of agreement by all the parties that communication is a key success factor, worthy of planning and coordination. Communication should be a recurring agenda item for the teams that control the engagement.

Honesty is central to effective communications. It is a common conceit of managers that they can "spin" the negative aspects of a project so that the disturbing elements won't be noticed. The fact is that people are not stupid, and they will draw their own conclusions. It will be obvious to folks that a massive outsourcing effort will result in some job loss. Denying or ignoring this fact in your communication will just shed doubt on your entire message. It is only fair to prepare people for the results of your initiative, both good and bad. Competent consultants help their clients frame their messages so they are truthful without being demoralizing.

Communication should be constant and should be transmitted through many mediums. I cannot count the number of project sponsors I've known who send out a memo and think their communication tasks are complete. One of the key adages of communication is that rumor fills a vacuum. If communication is not kept up throughout the life of the engagement, gossip and hearsay will take the place of fact. When planning communication, plan for the message to be sent by memo, e-mail, poster, meeting, video, "lunch and learn," and whatever other medium is available in the organization. With the availability of intranet technology, a project website can be an effective medium for both message transmission and group interaction. Ongoing updates, chat sessions, frequently asked questions (FAQs), interviews with managers, and Q&A e-mail boxes can create an interactive community focused on the progressing changes.

Finally, communication is not a solo exercise. A memo that falls in the forest with no one to hear it makes no sound. Without the opportunity to respond, ask questions, make comments, and complain, the employees will not feel as if they have been communicated with. Consensus, enthusiasm, and momentum toward change cannot be decreed. Build opportunities for feedback and interactivity into your communication plans.

LESSONS IN CHANGE

Organizational change has become a discipline in its own right, gaining the focus of top business minds such as Michael Porter, Peter Drucker, and Michael Hammer. The Business Process Reengineering (BPR) movement has emphasized that managing change is a fundamental business skill. One of the fundamental tenets of BPR is the requirement to apply information technology to the correct processes. "Turning cow paths into superhighways" is the disparaging term used by BPR consultants to describe companies that automate inefficient and unproductive processes. Reviewing the underlying processes themselves, ensuring that they add value and are not redundant or unnecessary is a central element of any effort to improve efficiency and quality. The lessons of the BPR movement must be understood by IT consultants. We do our clients a disservice if we do not question (at least in our own minds or with our teammates) the value and productivity of the processes we are computerizing.

Another lesson of the BPR movement is that technology is an enabler, not a driver, of competitive advantage. When the case for change is made based on business justification rather than the availability of new technology, communication is easier, gaining consensus is simpler, and the results are better.

The introduction of Enterprise Resource Planning (ERP) software, including products by SAP, Baan, JD Edwards, Peoplesoft, and others, creates an environment in which it is no longer advisable to create pockets of incompatible and isolated systems within departments of the organization. Enterprise resource planning software, and its cousin customer relationship management (CRM), require the technology consultant to apply significant business analysis skills. These modern classes of enterprise software focus on the entire operation and its complete chain of business processes, and so require deep understanding of the following:

- The business integration points, where functions and processes meet and interact,

- The boundaries, where functional, political, and cultural divisions exist, and

- The details of current financial, organizational, system, and product strategies and tactics.

Not all IT consulting projects will require this level of complexity or strategic analysis. Many, perhaps most, IT consultants are focused on a technical specialty and are engaged to bring that specialty to bear on a discrete problem or opportunity. The expert in HTML requires some basic business background, as we've discussed, but is usually task-focused. The network infrastructure designer may need to grasp a broader scope of enterprise issues, as the network will probably cross internal departmental borders. The expert in groupware and messaging systems must delve still deeper, as the issue is not just network "plumbing," but also issues regarding team interaction and human communication needs, as well as the mapping of existing processes onto a new technology. The consultant who tackles major change projects such as ERP implementation must also understand underlying political and human issues that will affect the ability to integrate functions and cultures successfully. These are not judgments on the worthiness or importance of these specialties. Each is meaningful and delivers benefits within its own scope. But the mix of technical and business skills required are driven by the engagements we take on, and vice versa.

Information technology consultants are well-trained and certified in their technical specialties. They are typically not as well-versed in advisory skills. The clients with whom you will engage as a consultant are, in many ways, in the same boat. They have historically been proficient in the financial analysis, organizational, and marketing skills that are emphasized in the typical MBA program. The "softer" skills of motivating people, dealing with the ambiguity of human emotion and fear, and of communicating a common vision may be outside of their comfort zone. The practice of visualizing success, of agreeing on a clear goal, and creating organizational momentum toward fulfilling it is a value-added service, outside of the strictly technical, that the effective consultant can learn and then teach clients, leaving them with a valuable skill that will endure beyond the engagement at hand.

Let's return to our case study. In the last chapter, I attempted to illustrate that even in a competitive situation, the consultant who adds value has the advantage. By turning a negotiating session into a facilitated work session and helping the client clarify an approach to the project, our Superior Systems team has persuaded the CapState relocation project team to select them for the engagement. In this vignette, we'll peek into a session focused on the development of a communication plan. Please review Appendix C, the Superior Systems Communication Plan for CapState Relocation Project, to prepare for this case study.

Ron introduced Nick and Sara to Jane Darian, the director of corporate communications for CapState. "I thought it would make sense for Jane to be part of this conversation," Ron explained.

Jane shook hands and sat down. She referred to the communication plan that Nick had distributed to the CapState project team: "I had a chance to review your communications proposal, and I appreciate the chance to walk through it with you. I'll tell you frankly that it's unusual for an IT vendor to participate in our internal communications. We feel that we do a pretty decent job of getting the word out to our associates. You do make a couple of interesting points, though."

"We certainly had no intention of implying that you don't know how to communicate internally," Nick replied. "I've seen your website, and Ron showed me the world headquarters newsletter that you've put together. I'm impressed by both. I will tell you that we have done some major projects, including some relocations, where the communications to the users affected were much less complete. My real goal is to ensure that everyone on my team understands the message, and that we're stating it consistently. The last thing I want to happen is for anyone on my team to undermine or confuse the message."

"Thanks again for joining us," Ron told Jane. "I wanted to have this session to make sure we're on the same page as far as the message. I'll confess that there have been times when my technical team has been accused of lacking communication skills, and I want to make sure that, at least on the IT part of this, we're covering all the bases. So, Nick, how do you want to start?"

"Let's just walk through the proposal," Nick suggested. "As we stated on page 1, I'm interested in ensuring that we manage expectations, that we present a plan for educating users, and that we build a consensus of business unit managers. Do these broad goals make sense?"

"As far as expectations go, I feel that we have that pretty well covered," Jane remarked. "We've had a scale model of the new building on display in the lobby of the main building for about a month, and there's a kiosk next to it that lets our associates take a virtual tour through the building."

"May I just ask a question? Are there any associates who don't have a chance to visit the main building?" Ron asked. "I know that there are some staff members who work in the suburbs, and I was wondering whether they would come into town to see the display."

"I'm sure that's true," Jane replied. "There probably are some folks who don't come into the main building often."

"As far as the education piece goes, I'm not really clear on what we would be educating them about," Ron continued. "Frankly, some of this read as if it was directed at an implementation of totally new technology. We're really just moving the same stuff from one building to another. I'm not expecting a big re-education effort here."

"Again, may I just ask a couple of questions?" Nick responded. "I would guess that there are some associates who were accustomed to working in the same building with other departments, and who may have developed some informal methods of interaction that may be disrupted based on their new locations. I also recall that we planned to consolidate some of the network printers, scanners, and CD towers, and that some users may have to access those devices in a different way than they are used to."

Jane replied: "That does make sense. In a move like this, there probably are some folks whose regular work patterns are going to be disrupted. We should probably get the Corporate Training Department involved in putting together a little program for retraining users on some of those details."

"Just letting associates know that we're developing a program for these things is a big part of a positive communications effort," Nick said. "We probably have some time before we need to design and execute a training program; I just want to recommend that we let the associates know that that is part of our plan."

"I did like your point regarding the communication to the IT staff themselves," Ron said. "It hit home, because when we did our ERP rollout last year, we actually lost some good folks. In their exit interviews, a couple of them said that they didn't feel we valued them, because we never announced any plan to train them or bring them up to speed on the new software."

"As a technical consultant, I really feel it's critical to include a specific plan for involving and retaining IT team members," Sara inserted. "Lots of technical specialists are really motivated by the opportunity to experience new technology, so giving them some training and some attention is a great strategy for keeping them interested and committed to the project. Even though the technology isn't changing much, the support needs will be different with all the new associates in the building and the changes to the network design."

"How did you feel about the types of events and media I mentioned?" Nick asked Jane.

"One thing I wouldn't have thought of is the lunch and learn trade show idea. We have computer vendors come in and do those with us all the time, but it didn't occur to me to use that technique for this project. I think that one makes a lot of sense," Jane responded.

"I agree," said Ron. "I can really see where that would attract some positive attention in the organization, and I see it as a motivator to the project team as well, to have a chance to receive some recognition for the work they're doing on the project."

"One other idea I really liked was the electronic suggestion box," Jane added. "We have a general mailbox that people can send comments and suggestions to, but it really doesn't get a lot of action. I would want to really publicize this, and let the associates know that we're listening."

"I would incorporate some of the comments and suggestions you get into the newsletter," Nick suggested. "That would demonstrate that the mailbox isn't just a black hole, but that the comments really are reviewed."

"Let's talk a bit about the remarks you made in the last section of your plan," Ron said. "You talk about a project vision. Help me understand what you're getting at there."

"I would guess that you're talking about a sort of features and benefits statement, like the fact that we're moving into the new building to save on costs, to foster better communication and interaction among the teams, to gain the prestige of a world class headquarters building, and so on," Jane inserted.

"Exactly!" Nick responded. "My experience with teams of programmers and developers taught me that a focused vision of the endpoint really helped me keep a team together—and keep them motivated toward the goal."

"Yeah, I guess 'We'll save lots of money on rent' is probably not the rallying cry of the century," Ron laughed.

"Yes, but a tag line that said something like 'One team, one vision, one company' or something like that could be powerful," Jane responded.

"So where do we go from here?" Ron asked.

"I'll get with the training group and see what we can put together for the associates whose access to network services is changing," Jane said.

"One thing we've used that worked really well is a little leave-behind card, like a tent card, that users can refer to after the move," Sara offered.

"I'll work with you on that," Jane offered.

"And I'll help you put together a program for the IT team," said Nick.

"I'll make the communication program an agenda item in the next relocation team meeting," Ron said. "Jane, maybe you could join us for a little while and chat with the team about the message we want to send."

"Okay," said Nick. "I feel like we all are looking at this the same way."

"Yes," agreed Ron. "I appreciate your including this in your project planning. I feel that it really gives us a head start on building some enthusiasm in the associate community."

> **UNDERSTAND THE CLIENT'S SITUATION**

- Better Understanding Equals Better Advice
- Discovery Process Must Be Designed for Each Engagement
- Base Discovery Process on Enterprise IT Model
- Consultants Have Due Diligence Responsibilities
- Create an As-Is Model

chapter SIX

Understand the Client's Situation

If I have ever made any valuable discoveries, it has been owing more to patient attention, than to any other talent.

Sir Isaac Newton

THEORIES INTO FACTS

Sherlock Holmes, the timeless literary creation of Arthur Conan Doyle, has been called the father of fictional detectives. But, if you believe the master detective's own words, he considered himself a consultant. In fact he remarks, in *A Study in Scarlet*: "I'm a *consulting* detective, if you can understand what that is."

To the practicing consultant, however, there is a more instructive quote from Holmes: "It is a capital mistake to theorize before one has data. One begins to twist facts to suit theories, instead of theories to suit facts" (from *A Scandal in Bohemia*). Unfortunately, until now we have been committing Holmes' "capital mistake." We have been proceeding based on conjecture. Our client has given us theories about the cause and probable solution to a problem. We have applied theories, usually based on the biases we bring into the engagement, about the technology that might be used to solve those theoretical problems. We have hypothesized with our client about what the organization might look like when we are done with our project and what benefits might accrue.

All this speculation is an integral part of the consulting process. Beside the obvious fact that we have to start somewhere, each of these theories is in its own way a fact. It is a fact that the client perceives the problem to be as described. It is a fact that the sponsors have individual visions of the end point. The fact that these perceptions and preconceived notions exist will be an important factor for us to consider as we progress. More importantly, the trust, confidence, and sense of shared mission we have created during negotiation of our role and visualization of a successful conclusion will be critical to the more intrusive activities we are about to begin.

We as consultants have an important role to play in turning theories into facts. We can, if we are skilled, perform a detection process that will guide us, and the client, to the best choices for solving the problem at hand.

I use the terms "data collection," "discovery," and "due diligence" interchangeably to describe the activities in this section, but I want to bring special attention to the concept of *due diligence*. Accountants or bankers can be held legally liable for actions that are in conflict with their professional duty to act in the best interest of their clients. As I've emphasized, consulting is a profession, like accountancy, with a similar responsibility to act in the best interest of our clients, to protect them from their lack of knowledge about our specialty, and to inform them of risks that we uncover in the performance of our tasks. There have been cases of consultants being sued by clients for not informing them of Year 2000 risks that the consultant should reasonably have uncovered, even though the consultant was not hired to do Y2K work. You must perform due diligence, well, *diligently*. Include enough time in your estimate and project plan to uncover and analyze the data, so you can make an informed decision about risks and special situations in the client's environment. Have the courage to dig a bit deeper and to be the bearer of bad news if you discover situations that threaten the project. Develop a relationship of mutual trust by being truthful and thorough in your investigations. Protect yourself, your consulting firm, and your client by communicating risks with diplomacy, but with urgency.

AN APPROACH TO THE DISCOVERY PROCESS

Before we begin to develop an organized framework for collecting the necessary data and gaining an understanding of the "as-is" state, I want to again clarify the goals of this framework as they relate to this phase. There are libraries of books that present methodologies for discovering and understanding the complex interactions of systems in the enterprise. "Structured Systems Analysis," "Business System Planning," "Information Movement and Management," "System Architecture and Investment Planning," "Enterprise Information Management," and many others have added insight and process to the task of understanding information systems. I am not bold enough to try to restate or improve on the extensive literature available. For those consultants who need a detailed procedure for creating process maps or data dictionaries, refer to the bibliography. This framework, however, is not designed for that.

My intent is to offer an approach to the tasks of due diligence and discovery. Although I do present an outline of techniques for collecting and analyzing the required information, the questions I hope to answer here are:

- How do I gain a better understanding of the client's culture and norms of behavior, so that my diagnosis is correct and my recommendations are followed?

- How do I develop a holistic view of the as-is state, so I can make recommendations that are in their proper business context?

- How do I set the client up for successful project results by the actions I take during the data-collection process?

This is not to slight the formal disciplines. For most IT professionals, our specialties require that we apply a rigorous and precise process to the collection of current state data. As I have said, this framework is a layer, to which the consultant must add the project management, data collection, analytical, and technical tools pertinent to the field.

THE ENTERPRISE IT MODEL

One of the most instructive experiences of my professional career was my engagement as a technical project manager by a large pharmaceutical firm. My objective was to advise the IT Steering Committee on the consolidation of the firm's employees from multiple offices scattered around town to their newly constructed corporate headquarters. While planning the data cabling routes through the building, I negotiated with everyone—from facilities managers designing electrical power and air-conditioning ducts, to architects trying to squeeze wiring closets onto each floor, to cabling contractors trying to figure out where to put their cable trays in the ceiling between sprinkler systems and ventilation ducts. I saw architects dissecting every inch of available space and negotiating to ensure that every need was served. The architects' blueprints were organized in layers, with one layer for ventilation, one for power, one for sprinkler systems, and one for data cable. The point of these comments is that, like architects, consultants need to think in layers.

Most structured programming methodologies recommend that complex problems be divided into smaller and simpler parts, so they can be conquered more easily. It may be overwhelming to think of designing an integrated accounting application, but writing a module to print checks may not seem so intimidating. Those of us who have been exposed to networking technology are familiar with another "divide and conquer" reference model, the Open Systems Interconnect (OSI) model. This common illustration of network functionality is based on a layered approach, with the physical medium of communication—the wire and the network interface card—at the bottom, successively higher layers representing more abstract functions, and the application that the end user works with at the top. This way of partitioning an intricate system into successive layers is a potent aid to understanding.

Deconstruction also makes sense when trying to understand an organization's data systems. Before any data collection begins, I recommend thinking about the client's business systems in their component layers. The bottom-up assembly of elements that I apply to my discovery process, and which I teach to consultant teams, is the Enterprise IT Model:

- *Technology infrastructure* is the bottom layer, succeeded by
- *Data,*
- *Applications,*
- *Processes,* and
- *Business.*

Figure 6.1 is a graphical representation of this concept, which is described in the following text.

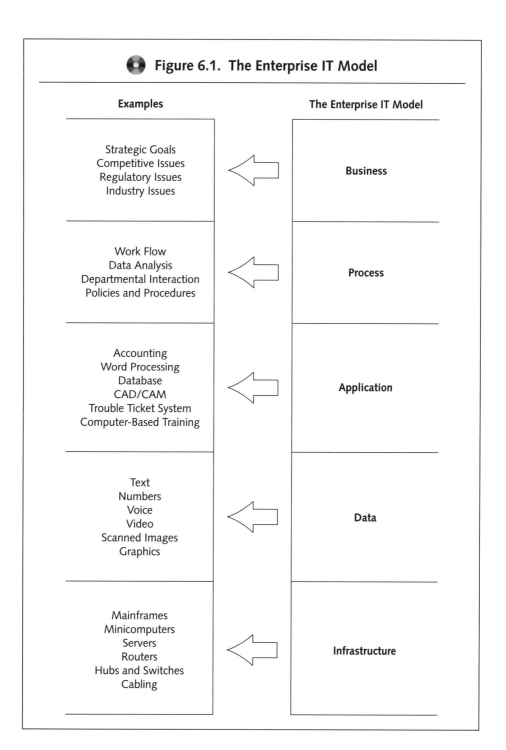

Figure 6.1. The Enterprise IT Model

Examples	The Enterprise IT Model
Strategic Goals Competitive Issues Regulatory Issues Industry Issues	Business
Work Flow Data Analysis Departmental Interaction Policies and Procedures	Process
Accounting Word Processing Database CAD/CAM Trouble Ticket System Computer-Based Training	Application
Text Numbers Voice Video Scanned Images Graphics	Data
Mainframes Minicomputers Servers Routers Hubs and Switches Cabling	Infrastructure

- *Technology Infrastructure.* For those businesses that are not automated, only the process and the business layer are pertinent to this discovery phase. For the majority of our clients, however, some systems will be in place. Whether it's an IBM mainframe, with channel-attached cluster controllers and CRTs or a multi-site, multi-domain wide area network, each business has an infrastructure, its IT plumbing.

- *Data.* The next component is the data that is transported through these pipes. For those of us, such as network designers, who are primarily concerned with data connectivity and throughput issues, the infrastructure and data levels are the most relevant.

- *Application.* The applications that the client uses to run the business are a level up in this model. For the consultant engaged in software design and programming, the implementation of new programs, or the migration to a new release, understanding this level is crucial.

- *Processes.* The processes and procedures that control use of the systems and their information is the next level we need to understand. For the business process consultant, the ERP specialist, the groupware and messaging expert, and the intranet or website designer, the work flows, rules, and culture under which work is done must be analyzed, documented, and understood.

- *Business.* Finally, for the strategic IT consultant and the management consultant, an in-depth analysis of the enterprise, its strategic vision, and its business model is central to the task. As emphasized previously, even the IT contractor, such as a programmer for hire, should not implement IT in a vacuum. No matter what layer of the systems architecture you are primarily focused on, it is your duty to the client to understand the business context within which you operate, to ensure that your recommendations and finished systems address the right need in the right way.

The more you understand all these layers, both those above and below the one at which you perform your role, the better a partner you will be for your client. This does not contradict the earlier assertion that you should stay focused on the tasks for which you have been contracted. It is part of the art of consulting to make a judgment about how much investigation and discovery your role calls for. Always keep the client's wallet in mind, and make sure you don't put yourself in a position in which you have to justify investigations into areas that were outside your scope. It's just as important, however, to be prepared to negotiate for access to data that is clearly pertinent to the project. If the client, or any participant, is trying to manipulate the outcome by building barriers, this is a cause for alarm, for diplomacy, and possibly for renegotiation.

DATA-COLLECTION METHODS

There are some basic data-gathering methods that apply at each layer of the Enterprise IT Model:

- *Review of Existing Documentation.* This includes analyzing existing reports, output, plans, diagrams, manuals, procedures, forms, flow charts, and other documents related to the system.
- *Observation.* Watching the flow of activities that make up the systems and processes under discovery.
- *Inventory.* Counting and documenting the physical components of the IT architecture.
- *Surveys.* Questionnaires that are sent to a representative sampling or the entire community for information on the system under discovery.
- *Facilitated Work Sessions.* Group working meetings, led by a facilitator, to discuss and uncover required information about the systems under review.
- *Interviews.* One-on-one conversations relating to the engagement.

I've ordered these deliberately. I believe that the less intrusive activities should take place at the beginning, when you are first building an understanding of the client organization. Once you have performed the early phases of your due diligence process and the relationships and processes start to take shape in your mind, you can engage more interactively with individuals and teams. My experience has been that clients and work teams consider it unprofessional and distracting for you to ask them basic questions about things that could be learned from documentation, surveys, and inventories. By performing our basic discovery procedures up front, and then using our "face time" to clarify and amplify, each conversation and team session is efficient—and a further display of our professionalism. Remember also that each of these data-collection methods is better applied to certain parts of the enterprise, and each is inappropriate in some circumstances.

Review of Existing Documentation

Clearly this part of the discovery process touches all of the enterprise layers described above. For engagements that involve the physical plant itself, such as the move of a data center from one building to another, power and HVAC diagrams may be meaningful. For the design of a reporting module, the review of building blueprints is obviously deeper than we need to go. Following is a list of some of the existing documents that might be collected, depending on the engagement, when reviewing each layer of the enterprise IT architecture:

Infrastructure

- Product standards lists,
- Asset management or purchasing data,
- Network diagrams,
- Network addressing schemes (such as IP schemas and subnets),
- Domain and directory structures,
- Building blueprints and schematics,
- Cabling plant diagrams,
- Wiring closet blueprints and port diagrams, and
- Facilities documents, such as power and HVAC schematics.

Data

- Data dictionaries or schemas,
- Data warehouse documents,
- Standard reports, and
- Network analysis ("sniffer") dumps.

Applications

- Standard application lists,
- Manuals or training materials,

- List of nonstandard applications in use, and

- Asset management reports.

Process

- Process or procedures manuals,

- Flow charts,

- Forms,

- Backup and recovery procedures, and

- Contingency plans.

Business

- Annual reports,

- Strategic plans,

- Competitive analyses,

- Organization charts,

- Team rosters,

- Job descriptions,

- Training materials, and

- Marketing materials.

This is a comprehensive list that will be overkill for many engagements. The purpose of this list is to guide your thinking. Ask for and review the relevant materials before you begin to interview and survey. You will avoid looking unprepared and asking redundant questions, thus annoying and unnerving your client. The trust, confidence, and vision aspects of the data-collection process must always be included in your calculations. By doing your homework, you elevate your services in the eyes of the client.

Observation

This is a good place to quote Yogi Berra, who remarked that "You can observe a lot just by watching." It's also a good spot to mention one of the most effective management techniques in use today, MBWA, which stands for "Management by

Walking Around." As I've mentioned before, the great consultants I have met had one thing in common: a keen power of observation. More can be learned about the strengths and challenges of a company, or a team, by observing the atmosphere and environment than by poring over flow charts all day.

Any reader who has a background in physics will recognize Heisenberg's "uncertainty principle," one tenet of which is that systems are modified by the act of observation. You don't need to be a physicist, however, to know that if the boss tells the team that a consultant will be watching them work, what that consultant sees will be different from the norm. This makes observation a difficult practice to structure.

Care must be taken not to disturb the patterns of work you're trying to observe. Rather than walking through the workplace taking notes on a clipboard, which will surely influence the outcome, observation should be a casual and unobtrusive exercise. Try to observe:

- *The Environment.* Is it a noisy shop floor or a dignified office? Can the teams communicate normally or do they need to shout?

- *The Atmosphere.* Is work done in an informal, collegial way? Are workers self-directed, or is a shop supervisor monitoring the activity?

- *The Work Flow.* Is it automated and process-driven, or manual and relationship-driven? Is there a high level of interruption or does work flow smoothly?

- *The Attitudes.* Is there a team atmosphere with everyone chipping in to assist their mates, or is there a contentious atmosphere, with everyone keeping track of how long their co-workers take for lunch?

One of the first questions I ask consultants on my teams when they return from working on an engagement is: "What's the atmosphere?" This may seem like a less-than-rigorous method of analysis, but the attitudes toward consultants, toward IT in general, toward the company, the team, and the work are indicators of the potential for success. As we discussed in the opening chapters, advice must always be adjusted to suit the audience, and our observations of attitude and atmosphere will influence the content and style of our counsel. Organizations with a formal atmosphere, where everyone wears a business suit and all communication flows from the top down, will be less than tolerant of informal grooming, dress, or expression. In a contentious atmosphere, where co-workers are checking each other to assure that nobody takes too long a break, formal time accounting and justification of tasks are a critical component of the consulting relationship. If, on the other hand, the atmosphere is collegial and trusting, and the client is an old hand at partnering with consultants, interaction can be less rigid and "covering your back" may not be an appropriate use of your time. Your assessment of atmosphere will also influence the formality of the processes and procedures you design into your systems. By heeding your observations on organizational culture, you can build the appropriate amount of system checks, balances, and status reporting into your work flow and processes to suit the client's requirements.

Inventory

Performing an enterprise inventory can be the most frustrating exercise in an IT consultant's life. When we start the process, we know that as we complete each section, it becomes outdated. When we try to convince the clients that an inventory is necessary, they will reply that they have complete records in their asset management database. When you review the asset management database, it will consist of furniture and typewriters, plus four Apple IIs and an Atari 800. Network documentation will be superficial or incorrect. Standards enforcement, especially in the realm of distributed computing, is lax or nonexistent. Employees will consider it a disruption to have to allow a technician to crawl under their desk and start noting serial numbers or data ports. When your team shows up to inventory a PC, that user will have a report due to the CEO in an hour.

With these inefficiencies and frustrations acknowledged, let's also concede that there are circumstances under which an inventory is indispensable. When performing a workstation standardization project that requires us to replace any workstation not capable of running Windows 98, for example, we need to know which ones fit into that category, exactly how many there are, where they are, and who owns them. The level of complexity increases if an upgrade of existing systems is an option, because rather than simply replacing all noncompliant machines, we now need to understand them at a component level to determine whether they're worth upgrading. In either case, we also need to know what applications are running on them all, so we can ensure that the user retains access to programs and data. We need to know whether the data resides on the local hard disk or on the network, so we can migrate data to the new or upgraded machine. This information will not be collectible from a survey, because most users won't know the answers to the questions.

There are some organizations that have implemented asset management and can supply a reasonably accurate report on their installed base of hardware and software. In these lucky cases, I still recommend at least a random representative sampling to ensure the accuracy of the data. Asset management will not record whether data storage is local or networked, for example, so some follow-up will still be required, if the project needs those details.

Each consultant will need to determine the level of detail required based on the engagement at hand. When a detailed inventory is required, the fundamental questions to consider before setting out are:

- "Exactly what do we need to capture, and at what level of detail?" As shown in the previous example, an upgrade project may require that data to the component level be captured, while a move project may just need a system count.

- "What level of application data do we need?" A migration between different operating systems at each desktop may need more data than an application upgrade.

- "Do we need to understand how data is flowing and where it resides?"

Once we've answered these questions, the design of an inventory project will typically have these components:

- *A Schedule.* This outlines when inventory teams will collect data on each department, work group, or geography. Remember to consider business timing issues. Don't plan to inventory the tax department in April, for instance. Also have a plan for those times when you arrive as scheduled and the user has a priority task that cannot be interrupted.

- *A Communication Plan.* This is used to inform users that an inventory is about to take place. Performing an inventory is intrusive. Be sure that users are informed and persuaded that this is a meaningful activity so they cooperate with the process.

- *A Database to Collect the Information.* There are several commercially available inventory programs, such as Tally Systems, that have pre-designed database schemas to capture PC-based data. If your inventory project is not PC-based, you will need to create a schema and select a database system for managing this data.

- *A Collection Form or Program.* Systems like Tally can create a "walk-around diskette" that allows technicians to visit each PC and collect its data on a diskette. Other systems collect data on log-in or over the network. For older systems or non-PC environments, a checklist or form may be required.

- *An Inventory Strategy.* Will this be an ongoing process during business hours or a "SWAT team" approach with a large team descending overnight to collect data?

- *A Reporting Structure.* Who needs to see the output of this data and in what format? Web-based output can be quite useful, especially if the client is the audience for the data collected.

- *An Update Mechanism.* In projects for which the data will become out-of-date during the course of the discovery, it may be necessary to plan a procedure for revisiting some sites to confirm findings. When it is critical that the data be accurate, I recommend negotiating a moratorium on new hardware and software installations during discovery.

Information technology advisory services, such as The Gartner Group, that analyze and report on efficient use of computing resources, have established that asset management enables organizations to save money and to more effectively manage their technology assets (Vargo & Frink, 1998). By advising your clients to take the long view and look at inventory activities not as a one-time event tied to a specific project, but as an opportunity to consider implementing an asset management strategy and so gain control of their systems architecture, you can add significant value. If the climate is right for this discussion, you can help your client move from a tactical to a strategic model of IT management. The benefits that a comprehensive asset management system can add are discussed in more detail in Chapter Ten.

Surveys

Surveys are typically questionnaires pertinent to the environment under review. For instance, when I'm preparing to do a large desktop operating system migration, my team needs to know what applications are in use to prepare for compatibility and data-migration issues. It would be another complete project to do a desk-by-desk inventory, and in many organizations users are scattered all over the globe. The use of a targeted questionnaire can elicit a response inexpensively and quickly. Surveys are useful in situations in which:

- A knowledge holder can respond. Although it makes sense to survey users about the applications at their desktops, who would you survey to ask about the age and status of the cabling plant? Different elements need different collection techniques.

- Knowledge holders are scattered.

- The time to perform an inventory or interviews is not reasonable based on the schedule.

- The budget to perform an inventory or interviews is not available.

- A wide statistical overview is required.

- Opinion and comment are invited. Besides the obvious fact that those on the front lines have the most knowledge about how processes really work, the chance to submit anonymous comments can build an atmosphere of give-and-take, communicating that those affected have a voice.

Some of the advantages and disadvantages of using surveys are listed below:

Advantages of Surveys	Disadvantages of Surveys
Inexpensive	Questions can be misinterpreted
Unobtrusive	Data is reviewed in a vacuum, without the chance to meet and observe the individual and the workplace
Can be reviewed and tabulated by administrative staff, saving client money	Low response rates
No interviewer bias to distort the analysis	Low interaction
	Little opportunity for clarification or amplification
	Little opportunity to influence attitudes by explaining or marketing the project vision.

Designing surveys would seem to be a simple exercise. If you need to know what application the subject is using, just ask. If you want to know what role the person has in the process, just put in a questions that asks: "What role do you have in the work flow?" Unfortunately, most employees don't think of their jobs as part of a work flow and may not know what happens to the reports they produce, or whether Microsoft Word is an application, an operating system, or data. This is not to imply that they are not bright. They just think of their jobs in a different language and context than we, as IT analysts, would.

When designing surveys, we need to think through the following points:

- Who are the subjects of this survey? Is it everyone, a sampling by department, a random sampling of the whole enterprise, managers or production workers only? How do we decide?

- What is the use of the data we collect?

- Exactly what are we trying to discover?

- How will we communicate to the subjects of the survey what we are trying to accomplish and why they should care? (For instance, in most cases a cover letter from the president of the company will get a better response than a letter from some consultant no one knows.)

- How do we ensure that the questions are clear, direct, unbiased, inoffensive, and jargon-free?

- How do we arrange the questionnaire so the data collected can be easily analyzed?

- How do we make it as convenient as possible for the subject to respond? This can mean multiple-choice questions, check offs, pre-addressed forms and response envelopes, and so on.

Surveys can be valuable tools in the data-collection kit, but they should be applied under the right circumstances, with the understanding that they are impersonal and that a majority of those contacted will never respond. Also consider that, unless there has been substantial communication, the appearance of surveys makes people nervous and can set off the rumor mill. Never neglect to take into account the facts that gossip fills a vacuum and that people are naturally nervous about and resistant to change. If a survey arrives out of the blue with no previous discussion, there will be a contingent of folks who interpret the question "What is your job function?" to mean that they are about to lose their jobs.

Exhibit 6.1 is an example of what a survey form should look like. As I mentioned, effective survey forms are designed specifically for each particular engagement, but this example can give you a starting point for creating your own forms.

Exhibit 6.1
Sample Survey Form

Associate name: _____ Date: _____

Title: _____ Department: _____

Location and office number: _____ Phone: _____

Please select your primary computer:
❏ Windows PC ❏ Macintosh ❏ CRT

Is this device a ❏ Desktop? ❏ Laptop? ❏ Laptop with docking station?

What is the primary application? (word processing, spreadsheet, accounting, etc.) _____

_____

_____

What other applications do you use? _____

_____

_____

What is the output of this computer? (documents, reports, spreadsheets, forms, etc.) _____

_____

_____

Do you print to a ❏ network printer? ❏ printer directly attached to your PC?

Do you have your own ❏ CD-ROM drive? ❏ scanner? other device? _____

To access corporate systems, do you have
❏ a single password? ❏ multiple passwords?

E-mail address: _____

Other comments: _____

_____

Facilitated Work Sessions

When we have reviewed any existing documentation, done some management by walking around, and analyzed survey results, we should be starting to develop a mental picture of the client's business and work flow. Typically at this point, we will start to recognize the gaps in our understanding, where only a meeting with the client teams will help us grasp the nuances of culture, the undocumented processes, and the shadow hierarchies that exist in every company. Looking at a company flow chart of the PC procurement cycle, for instance, may not tell us why it takes three months to get a PC on a user's desk.

As an example, I was contracted by a large Midwestern bank to help them optimize their PC acquisition process. Although their purchasing process followed a documented procedure and should have taken a couple of weeks from order to delivery, it was taking them up to one hundred and twenty days. Their acquisition and configuration process looked clean, and after some review it seemed that the purchase orders were becoming bogged down somewhere between the department manager's approval and their arrival in purchasing. During a work session with a group from the purchasing department, one of the agents told me, "Mr. VanKamp (the bank president) fancies himself a technology buff. He likes to look at every PC order to see what kind of hardware people are buying." So purchase orders for less than $2,000 were piling up on the bank president's desk while users waited for their PC's. This is the sort of out-of-process hang-up that never makes it to the flow chart.

Whether in interviews or group work sessions, the consultant will eventually reach the point in the discovery process at which it's time to test his or her understanding and move beyond the official, documented procedure to uncover how work is really done in this organization. The consultant will need to meet with employees, teams, and managers—in short, with the knowledge-holders. The facilitated work session is the ideal forum for exploring the reality behind the organization chart and the procedures manual.

Facilitation skills will also be important when we move to the creative process of solution design. Facilitated work sessions will be an important tool as we work with our design team to create a solution, and as we partner with the client to select and implement technology.

I use the term *facilitated work session* here, instead of simply *meeting,* advisedly. Before facilitation techniques became well-known, meetings were prone to unproductive behaviors such as:

- Poor or late attendance,

- Lack of clear goals,

- Lack of consensus,

- Lack of direction,

- Dominance of strong attendees or of managers,

- Interruptions,

- Hidden agendas,

- Lack of clear resulting action items, and

- Undocumented results,

to name a few. All business people have had the experience of walking out of a two-hour meeting with the question, "What was the point of *that*?" With no leadership and no methods, meetings don't achieve results.

Facilitation is the practice of structuring and managing meetings with the aim of achieving a goal. By following some basic, common-sense techniques, meetings can be conducted in a way that is more likely to:

- Obtain agreement on the objective of the meeting,

- Encourage dialogue,

- Discourage hidden agendas or rank from sabotaging group objectives,

- Involve all members,

- Clearly document the issues raised,

- Record the outcome,

- Provide concrete action items, and

- Facilitate the achievement of the best results possible.

I emphasize the fact that most facilitation techniques are based on common sense. Although expert facilitation is an art and the accomplished facilitator has mastery of complex methods and tools such as multi-voting, force-field analysis, and decision matrices, in this discussion we'll stick to the basics like listening, probing, questioning, and recording. For those who wish to further develop their skills in facilitation, refer to the bibliography.

A hallmark of the professional is preparation. Every meeting called with the client's team is an imposition on their time and productivity. This project may be your only mission, but most of the people you engage from within the client company have other jobs that are probably of higher priority. Therefore, use their time respectfully.

Some Hints on Meeting Preparedness

- *Do Your Homework.* Know your goal, how you intend to get there, and why these people are involved.

- *Prepare Your Team.* Make sure that all representatives of the consulting organization are on the same page so you don't have embarrassing disagreements or gaffes in front of the client.

- *Provide Pre-Reading.* Distribute agendas and background materials ahead of time so that everyone is prepared and understands the purpose of the meeting.

- *Adhere to a Time Contract.* Estimate the time you will need, inform the participants up front so they can plan their time, and respect the contract.

- *Set Reasonable Goals.* "Divide and conquer" so that meetings are focused and so that everyone leaves with a sense of accomplishment instead of frustration. Five focused meetings with the right goals and attendees are more productive than one marathon session with unreasonable expectations.

- *Prepare the Meeting Space.* Get your flip charts, markers, pads and pencils, audiovisuals, and other materials in place so you don't waste your client's time searching for an eraser.

- *Bring in an SME.* If you're dealing with technical material, have a subject matter expert ready to drive that part of the conversation.

- *Be a Gracious Host.* Provide food, drinks, bathroom breaks, phone breaks, and so on. Allow participants some informal moments to chat and bond.

When the meeting is underway, the facilitator will focus on ensuring that everyone understands and agrees on the goal and on managing the process of achieving that goal. Easier said than done, of course, so let's review some of the skills that aid us in facilitation.

- *Questioning.* Asking questions is the basic method for fostering participation. Open-ended questions such as: "Why do you think we have a bottleneck here?" or "What does the team think about this application?" encourage opinions, feelings, and reactions. Open-ended questions such as: "Why is that?" or "Could you give me an example?" allow you to probe more deeply and to challenge assumptions by requesting specifics. Closed questions such as: "Have we covered this in depth?" or "Does everyone agree on the goal?" allow us to bring closure to a topic and test the group's willingness to move on.

- *Summarizing.* Restating and consolidating remarks and ideas gives you the chance to test your understanding and to direct the group to the next agenda item.

- *Inclusion.* To ensure that everyone participates and that stronger personalities or ranking figures don't dominate, use techniques such as directly asking quiet members for their opinions or going around the room so all have a chance to contribute.

- *Impartiality.* Be sure to keep your facilitation pure by not telegraphing your acceptance or disapproval of suggestions and by preventing your biases or preconceptions from censoring the team's direction.

- *Listen Actively.* Don't allow the demanding role of facilitator to dilute your focus on the messages being conveyed. Don't interrupt, and don't think ahead to your response. Demonstrate by your attitude and body language that you are receiving the communication.

- *Record Diligently.* The flip charts and whiteboard are the official record of the meeting. The facilitator must ensure that open issues, decisions, and action items are documented. I prefer using a "scribe" to manage the recording process, although this is a matter of style. Some facilitators choose to do the recording themselves and use this function as a potent technique for managing the meeting. Keep a "parking lot" of unresolved issues, and be sure to agree on a method for revisiting them, whether it's another meeting, a memo, a vote, or assignment of issues for follow-up.

Structure the meeting in phases, with a defined beginning, middle, and end. In fact, a meeting is a microcosm of an engagement, with an approach, a negotiation, the joint creation of a vision, and the use of a framework for driving to a result. As in an engagement, focus on the relationship and the human interaction aspect, as well as on the content.

As the meeting gets started, perform the following tasks:

1. *Go around the room and do introductions.* Even if all the participants know one another, they probably don't all know you and will be interested in how you describe your role.

2. *Agree on the agenda.* You have informed the participants of your purpose for calling this meeting, but let them restate it so you are sure they understand. Stop and work through any misunderstandings or disagreements. It's as important to start the process with clarity as it is to reach a predetermined schedule or end point.

3. *Explain the role of the facilitator and the scribe.*

4. *Review logistics.* Explain details such as meals, bathroom breaks, phone breaks, pager and cell-phone etiquette, and so on.

When I am reviewing work flow in a discovery session, I will usually ask questions such as: "What triggers this action?" and "When you've completed your tasks on this, where does it go next?" The purpose is to get a picture of both the official and unofficial work flows and relationships. As the meeting progresses, it is your role as the facilitator to keep the group focused on the goal and to use your judgment regarding when to let conversation flow and when to move on. This is the art of facilitation: knowing when the creativity and value has been exhausted from a topic. By watching the body language, the flow of ideas and interaction, and by making some value judgments, you will learn from practice how to focus the discussion.

Before a facilitated session wraps up, ensure that the following tasks have been completed:

- Consensus on and documentation of all decisions;

- Agreement on action items (action items must be assigned and scheduled, not just listed);

- Schedule for next meeting, if appropriate;

- A brief feedback session (for example, ask: "Did this go as you expected it to?" and "Were there issues you thought we should have discussed that were neglected?").

Each meeting, like each engagement, has an atmosphere and a flow of its own. Some teams will instantly gel and work together cooperatively and freely to achieve superior results. Some will congeal like sludge and spend an hour sullenly staring at their hands. Beginning facilitators will be nervous or experience stage fright when managing a large team gathering. As your skill as a facilitator grows, you will develop strategies for dealing with different meeting situations. The key is to relax and let the flow be what it is. Don't take it personally when meetings are unproductive; some mixtures of personalities just don't "take." By remaining alert, focused, and compassionate, you will evolve into a skilled facilitator and learn to help teams contribute at their highest potential.

Interviews

Interviews are the most intrusive and intimate encounters of all. They should be used to obtain final clarification from key knowledge holders or final decisions from executives or sponsors. Interviews should be the final step in the discovery process, after all data from the other sources mentioned above have been tabulated, analyzed, and digested. Interviews are critical in filling any gaps in your understanding of any of the layers of the Enterprise IT Model. Interview front-line "doers" as well as supervisors, to get a real-world understanding of the informal as well as the official work flow. Try to select the best representative of the function you are examining, someone who has experience in the function and can articulate its meaning and boundaries.

As with all data-collection activities, prepare thoroughly. Interview preparation should include the following steps:

- *Make a Roster and Schedule.* Create a roster of interviewees, then set up a schedule.
- *Assign Interviewers.* If working in a consulting team, assign interviewers who have familiarity with the functional area or subject matter that is the focus of the interview.
- *Be Clear.* Have a clear idea of the objective for the interview and communicate that to the subject and the interviewer. If this session is to clarify or amplify a particular topic, communicate that as well so the subject can be prepared. If appropriate, design an interview form for data collection.
- *Be Prepared.* Gather any materials, such as organization charts, flow charts, forms, reports, or other material that may be needed in the interview session.
- *Use Good Meeting Etiquette.* Of course, follow the good meeting behaviors described earlier.

Facilitation skills are as valuable in a one-on-one encounter as they are in a group. The ability to set the expectations for the interview clearly, to manage the interaction toward an agreed objective, to reach consensus on the outcome, and to record that outcome requires some of the same listening, questioning, and probing skills we have just reviewed. Many of the techniques discussed in previous chapters, when we outlined methods of approaching the client and negotiating roles, apply in a fact-finding interview as well. The advisory, human relationship, and preparation skills are again the deciding factor in building trust and cooperation.

Each interview should result in a record, either a form that is filled in or a narrative transcription of the session. Remember that conversation is subjective and subject to interpretation, so be sure that you allow the interviewee to review your record of the session and to confirm or deny its accuracy.

THE AS-IS MODEL

The final activity in the discovery process is the creation of the as-is model, a compilation of the data that you've been collecting into a detailed description of the enterprise that corresponds to the Enterprise IT Model. The extent of your engagement will dictate the depth of your modeling.

Your team size will also prescribe the process for compiling this data. If you are working as a solo consultant, you will spend some hours working through the data you've collected and ensuring that you have an understanding of the issues that are pertinent to your project. If you are part of a consulting team on this engagement, then the facilitation skills we reviewed earlier should be applied to the creation of an as-is model. Bring your team together and facilitate a session wherein you review the material, put all the flows, processes, and systems on the board or flip charts, and come to a consensus on your findings.

One popular method of doing this is the "brown-paper" session, where a roll of brown butcher paper is tacked to the wall and team members can either write directly on it or stick Post-it® Notes to it, depicting the major systems, their interactions, and any open questions or concerns. This is a particularly open and involving type of facilitated session, and it can be a creative expression and a team-building experience. The natural tendency will be to try to move to the "to-be" model, so focus the group on documenting what they have found before they start to fix it. Remember what Sherlock Holmes said, and don't try to fit the facts to the theories!

The client deliverable to come out of these deliberations should be a "findings report" with diagrams, flow charts, and descriptive material about your discoveries and how they relate to the project at hand. You may want to assign different parts of the deliverable to different team members. Each IT consultant or team will apply specialized disciplines to this activity, whether it's the network design team using a graphic design tool to depict the current network architecture, or a software designer using structured system analysis tools to prepare diagrams of the process and logic of a customer order-processing application. The element that differentiates the technical craftsman from the consultant is the focus on communicating to the client in the client's own language. While you as the software designer may need data flow diagrams to visualize the interactions between systems, your client needs clear, business-oriented language in order to feel included in the design and decision-making process.

Be sure to review the deliverable for accuracy, pertinence to the engagement, and for correct expression. If you have found processes that are not working, say so directly but diplomatically. If you want to say that only an idiot would run an accounts payable operation like this, please review your language carefully! Remember again that you are a guest in the client's house, so don't call the baby ugly! Take your emotion and ego out of the process. Have humility and compassion for the history and personalities that have brought your client to the current state. Review, and then review again, the document that you are preparing to submit. Consider the total potential audience for your findings, from clerks to CEOs, and make sure that each of them would find it accurate, dispassionate, inoffensive, and helpful.

The discovery process is difficult and rigorous. It can be intrusive and contentious. Consultants who can master the arts of facilitation, surveying, and interviewing will have developed advisory skills that will place them ahead of their competition. The successful completion of the due diligence process sets us up for the next phase, the most creative activity in consulting, the design of IT solutions.

In our previous case study segment, we eavesdropped on a communications planning meeting for the CapState relocation project. This time, I present a session that takes place within the Superior Systems consulting firm, in which the consultants work together to design a discovery process. They'll make decisions about the information they will need in order to successfully prepare CapState for its move, and they'll decide on the best combination of discovery techniques to capture that data.

Reference

Vargo, M., & Frink, L. (1998, January 19). *Desktop outsourcing: The benefits of asset management.* Stamford, CT: The Gartner Group.

"Okay," said Sara, "I know we went through this exercise before when we wrote the bid, but now that we have the job we really need to dig down. Let's work through the RFP again from the top, mix in what we've learned so far from our sessions with the CapState team, and come up with a discovery plan."

"Well, to start with," Adam responded, "their asset management database is pretty weak. It's not totally useless, but the last time they did a review of the data it was about 25 percent inaccurate. That's going to make it pretty hard to meet their goal of minimum disruption to users."

"Their network diagrams are pretty sad too," added Sandy. "They show a very general picture of the network topology, and they don't reflect the upgrade from shared to switched ethernet at all. That tells me that they haven't modified them in at least nine months. That's a bad sign."

"And," Tim offered, "their workstation standards are ignored more than they're adhered to. I went to a few sites and spot-checked some desktops, and they have everything from super high-end workstations to 386 clones."

"So, where does that leave us?" asked Sara.

"We need to start with the physical layer," said Sandy. "I've scheduled some walk-throughs of all the data centers in the different locations, and I have the network architecture team ready to give me a 'tech talk' about their network technology."

"Do we need to do a network audit?" Sara asked.

"I don't think we need to go that far," Sandy replied, "although I will want to put a sniffer on some of the building links just to be sure I have a good picture of the departmental interconnections."

"Okay," said Sara. "Let's start to put a plan together. If we begin with the infrastructure, it sounds like we need to look at the network topology, the servers, and the inter-building links. Are there any mainframes or mini's we need to worry about?"

Sara walked the team through the design of an infrastructure discovery plan. They agreed that meetings with the network architecture team and the data center group were required. They planned to survey the network operating system setup and to inventory the server hardware. Tim, the desktop expert, agreed that he would do a spot check on the desktops in each location and match his findings to the asset management database.

"What about their use of data?" Sara asked. "Are there any special situations we should be aware of?"

"I assume we're looking at the R&D UNIX situation as a separate project?" Adam asked.

"Yes, let's address that separately. We don't really have the UNIX experience in-house, so Nick and I talked about subcontracting that piece out to a firm we know. What about any other special data needs?"

"Well, I know that they keep the records of their chemical compounds in a special database that has some heavy security on it," said Adam. "I also know that they scan in the FDA clinical trial data for the pharmaceutical compounds."

"So we need to talk to some directors and users in the document management group. Let's schedule some interviews and work sessions for those teams," said Sara.

They worked through the data and application layers, reviewing their need to understand how the data flowed from department to department, who used the information for what purpose, and how the users in departments interacted. In the end, they developed a plan that included surveys of the associates to gather information about the applications they used on the desktop and to understand which data resided on the servers and which was local. They planned to hold some work sessions with managers of the various departments and to validate those findings with some targeted interviews. Sara agreed that she would request a process review, so that she could assure herself that they had a backup and recovery plan, because she knew that would be critical in case a server was damaged or data was lost or corrupted during the move.

As they prepared to wrap up, Sara thanked the team for their participation and then reviewed the open items list to be sure that tasks were assigned to the right subject-matter experts. She took responsibility for writing the discovery project plan and for distributing it to the team.

DESIGN SOLUTION OPTIONS

- IT Design Has Standards of Quality
- Creativity Can Be Learned
- Utilize Design Techniques to Stimulate Creativity
- Base Design on the Enterprise IT Model
- Give the Client Options
- Help the Client Select the Best Options

Design Solution Options

*I never did anything worth doing by accident, nor did any of my
inventions come by accident; they came by work.*

Thomas Edison

CREATIVITY AND THE DESIGN PROCESS

"Genius," to use another quote from Edison, "is one per cent inspiration and
ninety-nine per cent perspiration." Although this quote is often used to illustrate
the importance of hard work and perseverance, I use it here to raise a different
question: Where does the 1 percent come from? Most consultants and IT professionals are quite prepared to provide the determination and persistence needed to
work through to a solution; were this not true, Jolt® cola would be out of business!
But, in the effort to provide creative solutions to technology problems, resolve is
not enough. We need to spark our creativity, to bring "genius" to the consulting
relationship. After all, if inventiveness and innovation were not required, the answers would be obvious and consultants would not be needed.

Is creativity a trait that you either have or lack, or are there methods of trigger-
ing our creative instincts so that we can bring the best and most ingenious solutions to bear for our clients? The technological insights that have brought us the
PC, the data network, and the Internet demonstrate a degree of ingenuity that has
changed our world. The organizations that bring these technologies to an intensely

competitive marketplace need strategies for keeping ideas flowing. How do they foster imaginative design?

To answer this question, let's look at the case of a creative design workshop in which methods of fostering innovation are taught. IDEO Product Design Services in California's Silicon Valley describes itself as "a professional services firm helping clients achieve strategic competitive advantage through product development and innovation." Famous for their design of such products as the Apple mouse and the 3Com Palm V hand-held organizer, IDEO has created more than three thousand products for Fortune 500 clients. When some of these clients asked IDEO to help them develop the in-house skills to design creative solutions, IDEO created a workshop series they call IDEO University.

The techniques that are taught at IDEO U encompass a core portfolio of methods proven to encourage creative thinking. Many of them were actually first developed in the world of data processing and systems design! IDEO's core processes include:

- *Brainstorming.* This is a group technique for encouraging the generation of many ideas without judgment or evaluation.

- *Prototyping.* This is the creation of a rough model of a design or device, under the theory that it's easier to discuss and improve on a model of something, even if primitive, than on an intangible idea.

- *Cannonball Run.* This is a competitive rapid design contest in which teams work against each other to develop a solution to a pre-designed engineering problem, in this case the creation of an accurate catapult, with a few simple materials.

In IDEO's one-day design and innovation workshop, teams of professionals, typically from Silicon Valley companies that rely on competitive creativity and engineering, are immersed in these techniques, refined by IDEO during years of designing products. Working together, they brainstorm, prototype, and design their way through an intense and competitive day, ending with a team being selected as the winner for the most efficient and innovative design. Whether they win or lose, however, attendees typically are overwhelmingly positive on the experience, with special praise for the emphasis on teamwork and on producing a working prototype that can be refined incrementally. Many IDEO clients credit immediate gains in team-design skills to techniques learned at IDEO U.

The reason for reviewing the IDEO training program is to demonstrate that creativity and inspiration are not ephemeral qualities that are possessed only by a lucky, gifted few. The ability to analyze a problem or opportunity, to apply some well-known methods for generating, testing, and refining ideas, and to then shape the best of those ideas into proposed solutions can be learned. The goal of this chapter is to review some proven design techniques and to discuss their application to the IT consulting process.

WHAT MAKES A DESIGN "GOOD"?

Before we begin to review the techniques of design, let's agree on some of the qualities for which we should strive in IT design. The key defining factor in determining the "goodness" or quality of an IT solution is its appropriateness for the client's situation. Defining a good design must take into account issues of cost, training, culture, support, and existing environment, in addition to technical elegance and efficiency.

When I ask consultants to define good design, I receive a series of responses that vary from the obvious to the bizarre. Some of the reasonable definitions of good design I typically hear are:

- It solves the problem;
- It fits client requirements;
- It is robust;
- It is secure;
- It is maintainable;
- It is documented;
- It is understood;
- It is flexible;
- It is standards-based; and
- It is proven.

Other responses, such as, "It uses this new technology that I really wanted to learn" or "It takes a really long time, so we can keep our billable hours up" don't fit into our discussion here.

What follows are a discussion of these characteristics of good IT design and some suggestions on ways to determine whether a design measures up to these standards.

It Solves the Problem

It would seem obvious that the core measurement of good design is that it directly and efficiently solves the stated problem. In our world of competing technologies and choices, however, there are many roads to a solution. Novell NetWare and Microsoft NT may both be viable solutions to the problem of sharing data and services among various users and teams. Cisco, Bay, or 3Com routers and switches are among the hundreds of choices available for building a network architecture. Hewlett-Packard, IBM, Dell, or Compaq servers all provide similar basic hardware platforms for building distributed computing environments. COBOL, C++, Java or Visual Basic can all be used to write an accounts payable module. Clearly, then, we need better criteria for describing the "goodness" of a solution.

As in all of our endeavors as IT consultants, the judgment is in the hands of the client. Each of the choices outlined above may be viable in a pristine environment, where there are no existing technologies with which to interface, no budgetary constraints to drive our selection, and no schedules to be enforced. In the real business world, however, budget, schedule, and compatibility issues must be considered. In a NetWare shop, NT may not be the best solution, regardless of its technical attributes. Nor in loyal Cisco or Compaq environments. Existing support relationships, purchasing arrangements, and staff expertise issues must be considered when weighing the options available. So, while many different permutations and combinations of technology may solve the problem, it's clear we need to dig a bit further if we want to achieve our goal of advising the client of the best options available for a special situation.

It Fits Client Requirements

When a prospective client approaches an IT consultant and declares, "I need to promote communication among my remote teams," the consultant may be tempted to come back with the recommendation to "implement a multi-domain IP-based wide area network to ensure universal distributed access, and design a web-based collaborative groupware solution to optimize existing work flows while creating a repository for corporate best practices," to which the customer may reply,

"That sounds great, but I was thinking of an e-mail package." Consultants often have difficulty distinguishing between what the customer wants and what they think the customer should want.

It is, of course, our obligation as professionals to inform the client of the options available and to help him or her understand the possible outcomes, both good and bad, of the decision. Once we have discharged that professional responsibility, however, it is then our job to allow the customer to decide which option fits best with the needs and to assist in getting the maximum benefit from that choice.

The point is that good design is not defined by what may be the most state-of-the-art technical solution, but by what option conforms with the client's requirements based on understanding of the nuances and subtleties of the client's environment.

It Is Robust

I first encountered the concept of system robustness as a programmer, when the term was used to describe programs that were "bulletproof"; that is, no matter what wacky inputs the client entered or what creative ways the customer thought up for corrupting the database, the program would deal with those anomalies and keep on running. The converse side of robustness was the program that, if the customer did not use it exactly as the programmer envisioned, would crash and burn, leaving the programmer cursing: "How was I supposed to know that the #$%!* user would do *that*?!"

Robustness is a quality that is built into a system during the design stages as a result of diligent risk planning. By thinking about what can go wrong as we design our solutions, what abusive and uninformed uses a client may make of a system once it is installed, we can design safeguards and fallbacks to ensure that services will not be interrupted. This concept of "boundary testing" is well-known in software engineering. Programmers try to think of unusual and extraordinary inputs that a user might try, and then they design routines to deal with those situations gracefully. I recommend that, whatever the technical discipline, every IT consultant should go through a similar process of mental review of the uses to which a recommended system might be put, sanctioned or unsanctioned, and to ensure that it is robust enough to handle those scenarios without disruption. This is simple risk mitigation at the system level, and it is a baseline requirement of professional systems development.

It Is Secure

As I write this, the IT world is abuzz with news about the arrest of the hacker responsible for the Melissa virus, a virus that multiplies by automatically sending infected e-mail messages to all users in a global address book. This may be old news by the time you read this, but it's safe to bet that some other worldwide virus scare or website penetration will be in the news. A community of hackers, with their own websites, software tools, magazines, and conferences, consider it an intellectual challenge to infiltrate corporate systems. Lawsuits proliferate regarding the subversion of key corporate data by disgruntled or disloyal employees. Stories of the corruption of websites, from the *New York Times* to the Pentagon, are common. In short, data security is as important an element in system design as robustness and appropriateness.

Security takes different forms depending on the IT discipline involved. For network designers, not only is "hack proofing" important, but the physical security of the servers and other network gear must be maintained. Any consultant who advises on the use of Internet technologies should have an understanding of firewall and proxy technologies. The procedures for backing up and restoring data in the case of contingency is also a security matter, as is disaster planning. By thinking of security in an integrated sense and by assisting your client to plan for physical and logical security, backup and restoration, disaster planning, and offsite storage of data, as well as policies and procedures for keeping passwords and user rights current, you become a strategic IT advisor rather than a technology-focused contractor. For applications such as electronic commerce or public access websites, or any technology that exposes client data on the public Internet, consultation with a data security specialist is prudent.

It Is Maintainable

Whatever the outcome of the feared Y2K transition (at this writing it is still ahead of us), one thing that it clearly demonstrates is that IT systems have longevity. Programs and applications that were expected to be long obsolete by the millennium have become ingrained into many companies' core processes, and replacing them causes major disruption. Studies show that the average IT organization spends 50 percent of its application development efforts on the maintenance of existing programs (*EDP Analyzer*, 1972). Whether we're designing programs, networks, websites, or migration procedures, we need to ensure that the client can maintain and support the systems we implement. To improve the maintainability of your recommended solutions:

- Use structured design procedures (like those we'll review later in this chapter);
- Design systems using industry-standard components;
- Document the design process and the results of that process;
- Perform comprehensive testing on systems before they are put into production; and
- Ensure that the client's IT staff is trained in the use and support of the system.

In my career as a consultant, I estimate that about 40 percent of my engagements have been based on the cleanup of IT efforts that were deemed unsatisfactory by the client. In the great majority of these cases, the problem was not that the previous consultant lacked the technical skill to deliver a working system. Rather, that consultant lacked the discipline and foresight to test, document, and explain the design to the customer.

Other sins against maintainability include:

- The use of bleeding-edge technologies for technology's sake, leaving the client with systems that are difficult to support because the talent to maintain them is unavailable or because competing standards have prevailed and the technology is orphaned;
- Systems that are rushed into production, so they still contain bugs that must be fixed while the system performs its business function;
- Systems that are designed to use nonstandard or undocumented features of the operating system (OS) or hardware, thus making them impossible to migrate to the next revision of the OS or platform; and
- Unproductive efficiency (the Y2K problem is an example of this; for the benefit of saving a couple of digits of memory, billions of dollars will be spent to revise and replace systems worldwide).

Any architect or engineer will have pride in the fact that a design will stand the test of time. Conversely, an architect who designed a building that could not be serviced, no matter its elegance, would be a failure. Information technology consultants, although we are dealing with bytes instead of bricks, should design and build with the same sense of permanence and serviceability.

It Is Documented

Ed Yourdon (1975, p. 9) states that "There is nothing in the programming field more despicable than an uncommented program." I agree with this and apply it to all fields of IT work. An undocumented program or system is a slap in the face to clients and support staff. It is often a display of arrogance, as I have heard countless programmers and designers state that "My work is obvious. Any competent IT person will understand it without documentation."

No consultant who has ever tried to maintain an undocumented system will disagree with Yourdon's comments. Diligent IT consultants document all phases of the client engagement process, from the contract and expectations they've negotiated, to the project vision they've committed to deliver, to the current state of the client's IT environment, to the steps of the design process that produced the options presented, through the selection and implementation process. As mentioned in the previous section, IT systems persist. Generations of programmers and support staff come and go—and the knowledge of systems goes with them. Only competent and complete documentation allows clients to maintain systems through their useful lifetime.

There are a multitude of diagramming and documenting methods, from Gane and Sarson's DataFlow Diagrams to James Martin's Decomposition and Dependency Diagrams. Modern software-based tools such as Visio and NetViz assist the network designer in recording technology infrastructure schematics. Infrastructure discovery tools, like those included with HP OpenView or IBM's Tivoli, automate the creation of network maps.

The point is, each IT consultant must find a tool and technique that fits his or her specialty, and then must use that technique consistently and effectively to leave behind a clear record of the system for the benefit of fellow IT professionals who must support this creation.

It Is Understood

Systems need to be understood, not just by the technical staff, but by the users. Any design that does not include a communication and training plan is incomplete.

Communication is necessary to impart the vision and to place the system in the context of its business processes. It is also a marketing tool, used to build enthusiasm and consensus for the new system, to get out ahead of sniping and resistance with a positive message that preaches the benefits of your design.

Considering training up-front is good design and good business. Why shouldn't you, as the system's designer, also be the trainer? Who understands better than you, after all this due diligence and system planning, how the system works and how it is meant to be used? Counsel your clients during the early phases of the project to create a comprehensive training program, both for the users and the support staff. This is one of the methods of delivering more complete business value, which we will discuss in Chapter Ten. It's a "win-win" situation, ensuring that the client uses and benefits from the advice you give and giving you an opportunity to sell more services.

It Is Flexible

As we've said, IT systems persist. They do not, however, remain unchanged. Businesses grow and shrink. Technologies change. Opportunities arise. Systems break down. For all these reasons, the "quick-and-dirty" approach has no place in the world of professional consulting. Building systems that last means building in the ability to respond to changes in circumstance.

Consider the following questions in each design effort:

- "What if you need to support more users?"

- "What if you need to change data structures?"

- "What if you need new reports or other output?"

- "What if the form of input changes?" (for instance, from terminal to web-based input)

- "What if the company changes or expands locations?"

This is just a short list, meant to be an example. In fact, every element of the system you design should be subject to this questioning process, with the philosophy that everything changes. There are obvious practical constraints on the amount of flexibility that can be built in, but by approaching design with these considerations in mind, we can avoid building in obsolescence.

It Is Standards-Based

Information technology consultants like technology. We like new technology. New technology is "cool." It's challenging. It gives us something new to learn, against which to test our technical skills.

Client engagements, however, may not be the best venue for trying out new technology. Due to their uniqueness, nonstandard technologies are difficult to support, simply because IT professionals have not learned them yet. They are subject to changing specifications in the standards bodies that populate our industry. They are unproven.

Some customers or situations will cry out for new technology. In an IT shop with a full contingent of "propeller heads" who can dedicate the time and energy to learning and supporting them, new technologies can add tremendous value. For companies that live and die by technical superiority, such as data carriers or Internet service providers, having the latest and greatest is a competitive necessity.

For other businesses, however, without the staff to maintain them, nonstandard systems can become a burden that buries support teams and sets back IT projects for years to come. Using our test of appropriateness, you need to determine whether there is an overriding business justification for applying cutting-edge technology to a customer problem.

It Is Proven

There is an old IT adage, "Never buy low serial numbers." Version 1.0 of a new technical product, whether software or hardware, is notoriously prone to bugs and breakdowns. Even with all the alpha and beta testing that goes on in our industry, technology is never proven until it has been sent out into the marketplace, to live among the various environments and businesses, and to be used in ways no programmer or hardware engineer ever dreamed of.

Protect your clients by advising them to utilize standards-based, proven technologies. This relates not just to proven in the technical environment, but in the business realm as well. It's not enough to ask: "Has this database ever worked on this hardware?" It's also pertinent to ask: "Have this database and this hardware ever been used by this type of company to do this type of processing?"

This brings us to two cornerstones of design, *pilot testing* and *reference checking*. Every IT project should include a pilot phase, in which the recommended technology is tested in the client's environment. This is typically done in a small section or department, or in a test group. This pilot process will be described in more detail as we discuss implementation, but it is worth mentioning here as a key element of good design. Let's not discover when we roll out a system into production that it doesn't work as advertised.

Standards-based technologies are standard because they are in wide use. With that being the case, let's get the vendors or suppliers of these technologies to introduce us to satisfied users of the technology so that we can ensure that it works as described. In my engagements, I often put the burden on the vendor to supply the names of satisfied users who will agree to be reference accounts, so I can arrange for my clients to talk with them or visit their sites. Seeing the system in action helps the client determine whether it's a good fit.

Some Final Thoughts on Good IT Design

Throughout this book I have compared system design with other design disciplines, such as engineering and architecture. These analogies emphasize the point that IT consultants should plan systems that fit the intended use, that can be kept up, and that last. Unfortunately, however, this analogy only goes so far. When a team of engineers designs a car, the results are easily quantifiable. Does it get forty miles per gallon of gas, or eight? Does it survive a ten-mile-per-hour crash, or does it crumple? Does it need a tune-up every fifteen thousand miles, or every hundred thousand? The same types of metrics can be applied to most other engineering practices.

Information technology is more nebulous by its nature. We can create standards based on qualities such as flexibility and robustness, but we cannot measure those qualities. How many units of flexibility or quantities of robustness are enough, and how do we know when we've achieved them? Unfortunately, this lack of metrics is often used to justify "quick-and-dirty" design in the IT world. "Because we can't measure goodness, and since any system we design will be modified or replaced soon, let's just come up with a quick fix and move on to the next technical challenge."

The opposite should be true. The dearth of metrics should force us to be *more* diligent in our efforts to understand the customer's requirements and to design a system that meets them exhaustively. Our clients engage us because they know they don't have the background to work through all the issues I've addressed above. We owe it to them to act in their place, to help them design the system they would design if they knew what we know. The difficulty of quantifying our results forces us to be sure we address all their needs, both spoken and implied, so we don't have to justify or defend our work product.

Now that we have reviewed some of the characteristics of a good IT system, the next logical question is: How do we design one?

DESIGNING SOLUTIONS

Before we begin to discuss a design process, I want to mention a technique acknowledged by good designers worldwide: stealing. Dennis Boyle, one of IDEO U's instructors, tells his classes, "Good design is to borrow, genius design is to steal." If we are following our guidelines of good design, we are using proven, standards-based technologies. This implies that those technologies are in use successfully in other installations. It therefore follows that we should seek out this existing knowledge and use it to our advantage.

For example, let's suppose we are contemplating a network design based on off-the-shelf components such as Compaq servers and Novell NetWare. There is no doubt that both Compaq and Novell would be glad to work with us to find an installation that is similar to our client's, to help us find pertinent white papers and design documents, and even to provide their own engineering talent to assist us in our design efforts. I'm amazed how often I need to tell consultants in my teams to go out to the vendor's website and look through the online documentation to find design pointers pertaining to the exact design objectives they're struggling with. Novell's website, for instance, has white papers describing in detail the manner of designing, implementing, and supporting their products in a wide variety of circumstances. The same is true of most major vendors. I have used these white papers and online manuals, and the assistance of vendor engineering staff, to design and implement technologies in which I had limited expertise.

I've also found assistance by reviewing the case studies presented by the IT trade magazines. I especially recommend *Network Computing* and *Data Communications* magazines, for the detailed case studies that describe in-depth the issues and benefits of implementing new technologies. Programmers can learn innovative techniques from journals such as *Visual Basic Programmer,* for example. There are abundant choices in technical journals for the IT professional, and each of these trade magazines has a website that can be searched for specific information.

Finally, I recommend that IT consultants become members of professional organizations in their field of specialization. Apart from the career benefits of such memberships, it's great to have other consultants or professionals to go to when stuck on a particularly thorny technical problem. Bringing a design problem to a discussion group can benefit both you and your association colleagues.

What We Can Learn from Product Engineering Disciplines

Information technology consultants are not the first technicians who have been faced with the challenge of turning a problem into a solution. From hydroelectric engineers building a dam to consumer product engineers designing an electric toothbrush, technicians face that blank sheet of paper every day. Where do we begin? How do we find the right balance of discipline and creativity required to devise the most appropriate solution?

The Massachusetts Institute of Technology, at its Center for Advanced Engineering Study, teaches that design itself can be treated as a process whereby the input is a problem and the output is a solution. By presenting a model of the design process, engineers can be sure that they are following a discipline. By including "ideation" as part of that discipline, we institute creativity as an integral part of that process. *Ideation* refers to the process of creating alternatives based on the objectives and specifications. This is obviously the central creative activity, and we'll review in detail the techniques, like those used at IDEO U, that allow for the development of creative solutions. The steps of a basic design work flow follow:

- Analyze needs,
- Set objectives,
- Develop specifications,
- Perform ideation,
- Filter for feasibility,
- Select the solution, and
- Document the solution.

These steps are illustrated in Figure 7.1.

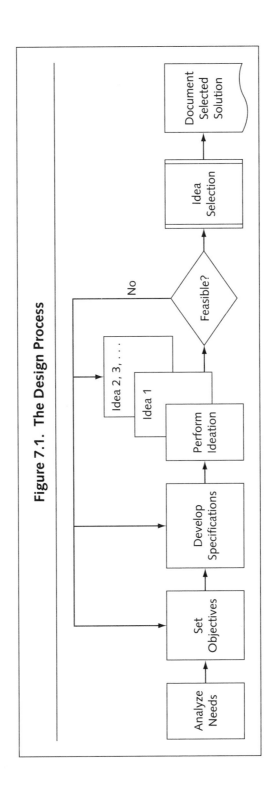

Figure 7.1. The Design Process

One note on this process: Some of the activities may need to be repeated as you move closer to a solution. For example, when designing the electric toothbrush we may find out that the amount of voltage required to run the toothbrush also gives the user a nasty shock. This would naturally cause us to rethink the design specifications! This iterative process of setting objectives, thinking about possible solutions, thereby better understanding the constraints and technical feasibility issues, and then going back to revisit the specifications based on that clearer understanding, is at the heart of modern engineering design philosophy. Building iteration into the process allows us to improve our design continuously, instead of becoming "married" to a design too early.

When boiled down to this basic framework, the design process becomes less mysterious and more systematic. This is not to say that it becomes easy, but at least we now have a framework for approaching the task.

What We Can Learn from Structured Programming Disciplines

Ed Yourdon, one of the prophets of structured programming techniques, called programming, "That advanced state of witchcraft" (Yourdon, 1975). In the early days of information technology, programming was an arcane and mysterious practice that lacked rules, methodologies, or measurements. Many of the negative stereotypes of IT professionals as incommunicative members of a secret priesthood who speak in cryptic tongues began in those times. Just to give you a flavor of some of the attitudes regarding programming in those days, here are a few quotations from recognized authorities of that time:

> "We build systems like the Wright Brothers built airplanes—build the whole thing, push it off a cliff, let it crash, and start over again." (R.M. Graham, as quoted in Naur & Randell, 1969)

> "I think it is inevitable that people program poorly. Training will not substantially help matters. We have to learn to live with it." (A.J. Perlis, as quoted in Buxton & Randell, 1970)

The programming languages of that day, like Fortran and RPG, were mostly symbol-based and numeric codes that, unlike the structured languages of today, had few English-language components and were unintelligible to the layman. There were no guidelines defining good programming, so systems were prone to poor practices such as uncommented code, GOTO statements that created convoluted and undecipherable logic, misuse of instructions to get results by "brute force," self-modifying programs, and other nightmares. In order to bring some order to this chaos, a philosophy of good programming and design techniques was developed and circulated by teachers such as Ed Yourdon, Edsger Dijkstra, Larry Constantine, and Niklaus Wirth. The theories that these mentors developed, such as Structured Program Design, Modular Programming, and Top-Down Design, are now axioms of system development and are built into many of the programming languages in use today. A language like C, with its inherent use of pre-built, reusable functions that perform standard tasks, is based on the concepts of modularity introduced by Dijkstra and Wirth.

I go into this depth regarding software design philosophies because they can teach us a lot, no matter what our IT specialty is. Some of you may have started as programmers, as I did. Many, however, are network designers, website developers, system administrators, server OS experts, or other IT specialists who have never written a program or been exposed to these design philosophies. As IT professionals, these techniques have relevance for all of us.

Top-Down Design

Top-down design is the foundation discipline underlying these programming techniques, and its basic concept is simple and fits nicely with the Enterprise IT Model that we've developed previously. The idea is to identify the system's major (top level) functions and to proceed from those to the lesser functions that derive from them. To write an accounting program, for instance, we can first visualize a system that allows us to input numbers and output formatted balance sheets, income statements, checks, and reports. This is obviously an absurd level of abstraction, but it serves the purpose of allowing us to think through the required inputs and outputs without getting dragged down into the implementation details. We can then deconstruct the system to its component parts and specify those in increasing detail as we go.

Whether we are programmers or not, using this top-down approach provides some real benefits to our design efforts. We can focus on the business need. We can work our way through the Enterprise IT Model without becoming bogged down in the technical details before we've created an overall system plan. We can mentally test the appropriateness of our overall conception, and only then start to devote our energy to decomposing it further and creating the more granular subsystems and components.

This process of abstract thinking is a key benefit. Most technicians want to proceed to the nitty-gritty technical details immediately. I can recount dozens of experiences with consultants who spent days creating detailed technical specifications for systems that were completely inappropriate for the customer. Just as programmers will lose patience with the design effort and want to start writing code, so too will other IT technicians want to start designing the network, or the database, or the website, without a clear idea of what the end product is supposed to look like.

Information technology consultants should follow this top-down process, based on the Enterprise IT Model, when designing a system:

- Recalling all you've learned about the customer's business, problem, and environment, develop a high-level conception of the system, as I did with the accounting system I used as an example earlier. As we learned with the vision statement, a simple tag line or solution statement can help us articulate our design. A solution statement for a global corporate e-mail system, for instance, might be something like:

  "A system that allows users throughout the company to create, address, and send secure e-mail messages to their co-workers."

  Start with the most general and top-level definition. We will refine it incrementally later in the design process.

- Develop a process statement, describing how the users would interact with the system, what they would put into it, what they would get out of it, and what they would expect it to do to turn their input into output. The input does not have to be data input as in a mainframe-based online transaction system. Their input could be an e-mail to a friend in another department, and the output could be a confirmation that the e-mail was delivered. For another example, their input could be a user ID and password, and the result could be secure access to the corporate network.

- Move down the Enterprise IT Model to the application level. Create a specification for the application that would allow these functions to take place. Start at a high level of abstraction, describing, for instance, an application that "provides the ability to enter an e-mail note, find a recipient's address from an online directory, lets the user send the completed e-mail to a selected list of recipients, delivers the message securely, and delivers to the sender a confirmation that the message was received."

- Consider the data implications of the application you've defined. In our e-mail example, for instance, think through what the data will look like. Is it all text, or are there pictures, diagrams, audio or video files? This thought process will eventually lead to the creation of a database schema, if you are designing a database application, but it is way too early to start to think about those implementation details. At this stage, create a data statement that describes what the data needs of your solution will be.

- Finally, consider the infrastructure, or IT plumbing, requirements that are implied by your decisions so far. Do they imply that all users in the organization have online access to the network? What about remote, home, or traveling users? What about speed and continuity issues? Design an infrastructure statement that simply describes what the basic requirements of your systems delivery mechanism will be.

This process of incrementally increasing specificity is referred to by programmers as step-wise refinement, a very descriptive way to think about this process. Designers should strive to visualize each function, for instance the function that allows an e-mail user to look up an address, as a module. In the beginning phases of the design process, these modules are simply "black boxes." We don't care what happens inside that box at this point; we just want to identify the required function. By focusing on the functional requirements of the major system components, and then digging in to them more and more deeply, we begin to develop a picture of the inputs, outputs, data, processes, and infrastructure required to deliver a solution.

What we've really been doing in this top-down design process is creating a system specification and then dividing that specification into manageable components that we can tackle piece by piece. This is another example of the "divide and conquer" method. Once the overall conception of the system becomes defined, most IT designers do not have much problem creating the inner workings of each module or element. This, after all, is what we are trained for and what we love to do.

This is not to say that the detailed design is easy. It is a normal part of the process to start developing the details of a module and to discover that it's not going to work as expected, which then requires us to revisit the overall design and modify the "black box" to make it fit the reality of what the technology can do. This "two steps forward, one step back" element of design is natural and healthy, allowing us to fix design problems while they are still fluid, thus getting away from the Wright Brothers' method of system design described by Professor Graham earlier.

Although this top-down design process provides a framework for developing creative IT solutions, we still need to come up with the ideas somehow. After all, every challenge is not going to be as straightforward as the e-mail system in my example. In most cases, the solution is not clear or obvious. This is where some of the creativity-enhancing techniques I described at the beginning of this chapter become critical. Let's explore some of these techniques in more depth here.

Ideation Techniques

In the MIT design process described earlier, *ideation* is at the center of the engineering process. This is the 1 percent inspiration referred to by Edison. Many of the basic techniques now used for idea generation were presented in the classic work by Alex Osborne (1993). Osborne described brainstorming as the generation of ideas by *deferred judgment.* Osborne had a key insight: social barriers, like ridicule, scorn, and fear, are the enemies of creative ideas. By expressing ideas in a group that has agreed to defer judgment, ideas can be brought to light freely and without internal censorship. Then the ideas generated can be reviewed for feasibility and appropriateness in a later phase of the design process.

Brainstorming

Brainstorming is one of the cornerstone techniques of any group's creative process. Even solo practitioners, however, can use the concepts of brainstorming to generate ideas. The brainstorming process is often misunderstood as a free-for-all, with everyone shouting out ideas, pertinent or not, and then following those ideas wherever they lead in a free-ranging group work session. Brainstorming, to be most effective, should follow some simple rules:

- *Focus on a Specific Goal.* If you are trying to develop the details of a module specified in a top-down design specification, concentrate on that. Avoid going off on tangents or digressions. Brainstorming should be structured to be productive.

- *Defer Judgment During Brainstorming.* Aim for quantity, and leave the evaluation process for later. Even bizarre ideas can lead to innovative avenues for discussion. IDEO University attendees are encouraged to try for 150 ideas in a thirty-minute session.

- *Build on the Ideas of Others.* Don't become emotionally attached to your own ideas, try to defend them, or get into a contest of best or worst ideas. Instead, build on the creativity of your teammates.

- *Record Well, and Record Visually.* Sketching out ideas is particularly helpful in the IT world. In many cases a simple block diagram can help people understand your concept better than an hour of conversation.

Brainstorming should be run as a facilitated session, using the facilitation techniques discussed previously. Ensure that everyone understands the process and the topic at hand. You can utilize a free-form approach, where everyone volunteers ideas at any time, or you can go around the room until the flow begins to ebb. The facilitator, when paraphrasing or rewording ideas, should be careful not to influence or manipulate the outcome.

Brainstorming can be a fun and intellectually stimulating exercise. It should be used when the team is enthusiastic and fresh, not at the end of a day-long top-down design session.

Structured Round

One of the problems with brainstorming, especially with the free-form approach, is that more aggressive team members can dominate the activity. Less assertive members, of course, may have ideas that are creative and useful. The structured round is useful to ensure that everyone has a chance to voice an opinion on a topic under discussion. It helps the team come to consensus, so a topic can be closed and the team can move on. This is a basic "round-robin" technique, using the following approach:

- Focus on a specific topic or issue;
- Move in order around the room, allowing each individual to express an idea, an objection, a clarification, or an amplification;
- Record this material as in brainstorming;
- Go around as many times as needed (this is a good example of the iterative approach discussed earlier, as it allows members to elaborate on the ideas expressed, and to refine and revise statements already on the table); and
- When the flow abates, summarize the ideas or issues generated.

This technique is good for dealing with disagreement, as it allows members to discuss the issue and not the personalities.

Flow Charting

When designing processes or functions, a flow chart can assist by displaying key steps and their relationships. It can be used both to ensure that everyone understands an existing process and to create a new process of function. For consulting teams in which different subject-matter experts are taking ownership of various pieces of the project, a flow chart can clarify the boundaries and handoffs required. A flow chart is a basic block diagram designed to show major processes, decision or approval points, handoffs, and end points. Figure 7.2 provides an example.

Figure 7.2. Sample Flow Chart

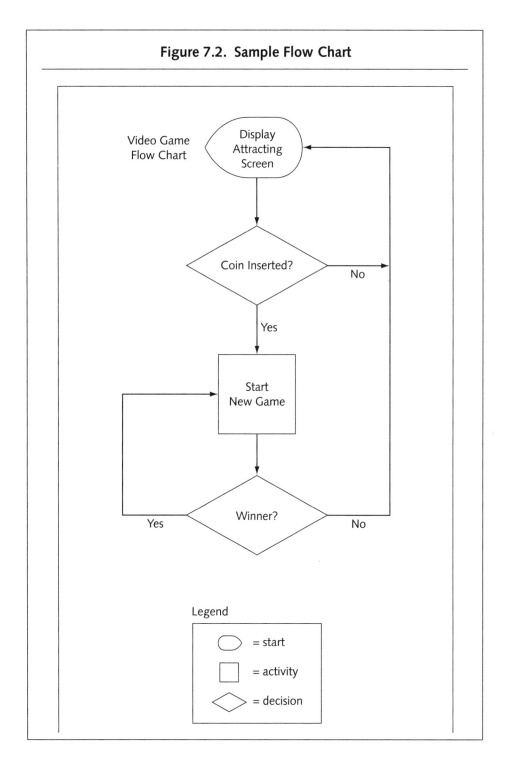

Filtering Ideas

Once ideas are on the table and some basic summarization has taken place, it's time to assess the material, to structure it into coherent solutions, and to develop the best options for presentation to the client. As with brainstorming, there are some techniques acknowledged to assist in the evaluation of ideas, so we can choose the solutions that achieve the highest satisfaction of the objectives. A couple of methods that I use in design sessions with consulting teams are described below.

Multi-voting is a group facilitation technique that is a natural follow-up to brainstorming. Because we intentionally defer judgment as part of the brainstorming process, multi-voting is our chance to eliminate ideas with limited support or merit and to start selecting those ideas that make the most sense, so we can explore those in depth.

To Use Multi-Voting

- Post the record of the brainstorming session, so all ideas generated are visible;
- Work with the group to combine or summarize any ideas that everyone agrees are redundant;
- Assign a letter to each remaining idea;
- Allow each person a number of votes that is equal to one-third of the items on the list, for instance, if there are thirty items, give each member ten votes;
- Have members vote for ideas, that is, each member should list the letter of the idea voted for and the number of allotted votes being cast for that idea (members can cast any or all votes for any number of ideas, until they run out of votes);
- Tally the votes;
- Discuss the results, being sure that the group agrees that the vote prioritized ideas in a way that everyone is comfortable with;
- Eliminate ideas that clearly have no support; and
- Repeat to highlight the ideas that clearly have the most support.

I find that multi-voting works best when combined with a high degree of discussion. Talk about ideas before they are eliminated to give their supporters a chance to argue their merits. Discuss the rankings as they emerge, to make sure that good design alternatives are not being ranked poorly for the wrong reasons. Ideas can be eliminated because they are so "way out" that people are afraid to show their support. They can be eliminated because their supporters are not as articulate as other members. Ideas can be supported because members of a technical clique want to stick together. It's the facilitator's job to ensure that the outcome of this process is a true consensus on the most appropriate ideas for the client's situation.

The *decision matrix* is a tool for evaluating solutions against weighted criteria. This is a basic charting technique that can be used either by a group or an individual. It consists of a list of criteria, usually weighted by importance such as must-have or desirable options. These are listed down the left side of the matrix. The potential solutions are then listed across the top, and a matrix created, as illustrated in Figure 7.3.

This process is a method for identifying the priority of design criteria and then for ensuring that solutions under review meet those criteria. Whether done in a group or by an individual consultant, it enforces a specific and detailed review of each element of the objectives, ensures that the solutions will be able to meet those objectives, creates an opportunity to reject alternatives that are clearly inappropriate, and is useful for clarifying when iteration or going "back to the drawing board" is required.

To Create a Decision Matrix

- List the criteria that the system under review must have, then list the desirable options and assign a weight to each criteria, for instance a scale of 1 to 10, with the higher number indicating highest importance;

- Draw a decision matrix as illustrated in Figure 7.3;

- Rate each alternative as to its conformance with the must-have criteria and eliminate alternatives that are clearly inappropriate;

- Determine the extent to which each alternative meets the desirable criteria, by assigning each a score from 1 to 5; then, for each alternative, multiply the importance weighting number by the score (see Figure 7.3); and

- Determine the total score for each alternative and record it.

Obviously, this is not a mechanical process. Just because an alternative scores well does not automatically make it the best choice. Other measures, such as intuition or enthusiasm for specific alternatives, must always be taken into account. The decision matrix is simply a method of rationally evaluating alternatives. It

Figure 7.3. Sample Decision Matrix

Car Buying Decision	Honda	Chevy	Ford	Jeep	Isuzu
MUST HAVE					
V-6 Engine	✓	✓	✓	✓	
4-Wheel Drive	✓			✓	✓
Ability to Seat 6	✓	✓	✓	✓	✓
Air Bags	✓	✓	✓	✓	✓
CD Player		✓		✓	
NICE TO HAVE					
Leather Seats		✓		✓	
Split-Back Seat		✓	✓		
Anti-Theft Device		✓	✓		
Premium Sound	✓			✓	
LUXURY					
Sun Roof		✓		✓	✓
CD Changer	✓				
Electric Seat Warmer				✓	

should be used in combination with other techniques to devise the best options for presentation to the client.

Other Evaluation Techniques

Multi-voting and the decision matrix are just a couple of techniques out of many available to help consultants select the best solution options. Other methods such as T-charts, affinity diagrams, work flow diagrams, and Ishikawa (fishbone) diagrams can add real value to this process. See the bibliography for sources for using these techniques (Rees, 1998; Schwarz, 1994).

Remember that these methods are aids and not restraints. The best option can fall to the bottom of a multi-voted list because its supporters are not the most articulate or the most assertive. What one designer considers "nice to have," another can consider critical. The level of expertise of the supporters of various options must be taken into account as well. Use these design aids to assist in your decision process, not to dictate it.

A SOLUTION ARCHITECTURE

All of this creativity, input, interaction, and technical expertise is focused on producing one result: a quality solution that is complete and appropriate. We've reviewed the characteristics that make a design good. In the next phase of the engagement, when we present our solution options, the client will decide which of our options is the most appropriate. So let's briefly address completeness.

Every project is unique. The client's needs, budget, the organizational issues, the consultant's expertise and area of specialization, all will influence the complexity of the solution. In any IT consulting engagement, however, each element of the Enterprise IT Model that we've developed must be addressed. For an IT consulting engagement to deliver the "complete package," once the creative work of designing is done and the team (or individual consultant) believes that a solution is taking shape, that solution should be subjected to a review and documentation process. The purpose of this process is to ensure that, when we present our options for solution to the client, we can do so confidently, knowing that we have thought through the situation in depth. We want to be ready to answer any questions that come up, to educate the client, and to help to select the best option for the client's needs.

So, whether we are proposing to write a Java program to allow website visitors to sign an electronic guest book, or we are proposing to implement a worldwide network to allow commodities brokers to enter trading information and have it routed to the appropriate exchange in milliseconds, the architectural components we need to consider remain the same:

Infrastructure

- Document the computer platforms, operating systems, communications, and network requirements, storage, backup, input and output, and desktop software options.

- Document any special configurations required on these components.

- Prepare a graphical representation of infrastructure elements. Illustrations help make the conception clearer to the design team and the client.

- Describe how the implementation of the proposed architecture will affect existing infrastructure. Prepare the client for the impact of your proposed solution!

Data

- Document the data elements, such as information about people, places, things, numbers, or events, that the system will record. For instance, in a guest book application, document the data elements, such as name, address, and telephone number, that will be captured.

- Document the function of this data. Will the guest book data be the basis of a report or will it be available for queries on the web? Will the number of guest book entries be counted to obtain website visit metrics?

- Prepare a graphic presentation of data elements, for instance a mockup of an entry screen or a report.

- Describe how the new data will interact with existing data elements.

Applications

- Create a brief description of each application describing its purpose, its capabilities and functions, and its business benefits.

- Describe the interaction between proposed and existing applications.

Processes

- Describe the processes and procedures that will be required in order to obtain the benefit of your design.
- Describe how existing processes might change, based on the proposed system.

Business

- Put all of the elements listed above into a business context. Describe the business results your design will achieve, not the system you will implement.

We are not, at this stage, trying to create a design document that is detailed enough to actually implement. At this stage, we want to be sure that we understand our own design well enough to prepare a professional presentation that clearly and fairly outlines the options and their ramifications.

Consistent with the concept of step-wise refinement, we've now gone from a general conceptual approach to a very specific design. Typically, however, we have focused on the technical aspects of our solution. In order to complete the picture for the client, we now need to center our attention on the delivery aspects, namely the cost, schedule, and project management details that will assure the client that we can deliver the chosen solution successfully. We need to persuade the client, not only that we've designed the right solution, but that we have planned for its successful implementation.

PREPARING YOUR DELIVERY PLAN

This brings us to the project management aspects of our solution. We must be prepared to explain not only what we are proposing, but how we plan to deliver it. This means planning the tasks, resources, schedule, and costs associated with our options. One form of project planning is to simply state: "We'll start next Tuesday and be done by six weeks from Friday." Unless you have a long track record of success with the client, however, it's unlikely that this plan will give much assurance that you will deliver as promised. Neither does this plan help much in the daily management of the delivery effort. Although management is obviously critical to successful delivery, convincing the client that you have a methodology for tracking and reporting on project progress should be a major focus of your presentation. I've seen too many consultants focus their entire presentation on the technical details, but never discuss the tasks, technical resources, or costs associated with the solution. Knowledgeable clients will not be impressed by presentations that solely address technology issues. Conversely, those consultants who have taken the time to present a clear plan, timeline, and estimate convince the client that they are in the hands of a competent, thorough advisor.

Task planning is yet another example of the divide-and-conquer, step-wise refinement approach. Remember, the purpose of project plan preparation at this time is to give the client an overview of your delivery process, not to create a working project plan. A better name for your planning at this phase is *activity planning*, rather than task planning. Activities are broader, and each activity contains a number of lower-level tasks. For instance, performing a network audit is an activity, while setting up the network analyzer, running the tests, gathering the results, and analyzing them are tasks within that activity. There is some finesse and experience involved in determining how much detail is enough. At the presentation stage, we probably don't want to spend the time required to write a task-level project plan, because we don't yet know what choices the client will make. If we keep in mind the purpose, to give the client the information needed to make a decision, we'll design an activity plan at the right level of detail. See Exhibit 7.1 for an example of an activity plan used for a solutions presentation.

Use the Enterprise IT Model to do your project planning. Think through the tasks required to implement the infrastructure, data, application, and process aspects of your design. Include the business-related tasks like training, communication, support, maintenance, contingency planning, and documentation. Because we've used this model in the assessment and design phases, using it to plan the tasks required for delivery brings consistency to our thought process and better prepares us to present our approach. Also include management tasks such as progress meetings and status reports, to assure the client that you will keep him or her informed and involved throughout the delivery process.

Here are some tips on project planning in the solutions design phase:

- *Project Planning Is a Team Activity.* Unless you are a solo consultant and will be performing all the tasks yourself, involve the delivery team in the planning activity. No matter how well you believe you know the technology, involving the team in this process will result in a more realistic plan. Nothing alienates a

Exhibit 7.1. Sample Activity Plan

Activity Sheet as of Mon 8/16/99

Work Station Standardization Project

Superior Systems

ID	Task Name	Duration	Start	Finish	Resource Names
1	**Work Station Standardization Project**	**33 days**	**Mon 3/20/95**	**Wed 5/3/95**	
2	**Project Preparatory Activities**	**33 days**	**Mon 3/20/95**	**Wed 5/3/95**	
3	**Inventory**	**28 days**	**Mon 3/20/95**	**Wed 4/26/95**	
4	Hardware inventory and assessment	21 days	Mon 3/20/95	Mon 4/17/95	Desktop Tech
5	Application inventory and assessment	21 days	Mon 3/20/95	Mon 4/17/95	Desktop Tech
6	Evaluate inventory	4 days	Tues 4/18/95	Fri 4/21/95	Desktop Tech
7	Identify devices for upgrade	3 days	Mon 4/24/95	Wed 4/26/95	Desktop Manager
8	Meet w/Business Unit Managers	1 wk	Thu 4/27/95	Wed 4/26/95	Desktop Manager
9	Test new proposed technical standard	2 wks	Mon 3/20/95	Fri 3/31/95	
11	**Work Station Rollout**	**100 days**	**Thu 5/4/95**	**Wed 9/20/95**	
12	Prepare procurement list for upgrade project	5 days	Thu 5/4/95	Wed 5/10/95	Desktop Manager
13	Prepare project budget	5 days	Thu 5/11/95	Wed 5/17/95	Desktop Manager
14	Prepare project schedule	3 days	Thu 5/18/95	Mon 5.22/95	Desktop Manager
15	Review network bandwidth requirements	1 day	Tue 5/23/95	Tue 5/23/95	Desktop Manager
16	Procure devices	15 days	Wed 5/14/95	Tue 6/13/95	Purchasing
17	Set up testing, staging environment	7 days	Tue 5/23/95	Wed 5/31/95	Desktop Contractor
18	**Work Station Preparation**	**80 days**	**Thu 6/1/95**	**Wed 9/20/95**	**Desktop Contractor**
19	**Configure work stations**	**16 wks**	**Thu 6/1/95**	**Wed 9/20/95**	**Desktop Contractor**
20	Perform any required upgrades	16 weeks	Thu 6/1/95	Wed 9/20/95	Desktop Contractor
21	Configure for network connectivity	16 wks	Thu 6/1/95	Wed 9/20/95	Desktop Contractor
22	Test network, host connectivity	16 wks	Thu 6/1/95	Wed 9/20/95	Desktop Contractor
23	Perform data migration where needed	16 wks	Thu 6/1/95	Wed 9/20/95	Desktop Contractor
24	Test for application functionality	16 wks	Thu 6/1/95	Wed 9/20/95	Desktop Contractor
25	**Work Station Rollout**	**80 days**	**Thu 6/1/95**	**Wed 9/20/95**	**Desktop Tech**
26	Schedule with users	16 wks	Thu 6/1/95	Wed 9/20/95	Desktop Contractor
27	Perform desktop installation	16 wks	Thu 6/1/95	Wed 9/20/95	Desktop Contractor
28	Perform user acceptance test	16 wks	Thu 6/1/95	Wed 9/20/95	Desktop Contractor
29	Perform user training	16 wks	Thu 6/1/95	Wed 9/20/95	Desktop Contractor

technical team more than being presented with a plan that was created without their participation.

- *Project Planning Is an Iterative Exercise.* Once an outline of tasks is created, appropriate technical resources can be assigned, schedules can be estimated, and a rough budget can be defined. As we discussed in the design phase, once you get into the details of the delivery plan, you'll discover scheduling conflicts, product constraints, technical skills issues, and other forces that will require you to revisit your plan.

- *You Must Build in Time to Deal with Risks and Contingencies.* One of the cardinal sins of project planning by technicians is that we assume the best. We estimate time based on the most skilled individual doing the work and on everything going as expected. Inevitably, of course, the most skilled person is unavailable and everything that can go wrong, does. Yet we never seem to learn this lesson. Please BUILD IN TIME!

- *The Presentation Is a Marketing Process.* Always keep in mind the marketing nature of the presentation phase. Prepare your delivery plan so it is persuasive and convincing, so that it demonstrates that you can do the work on schedule and within the budget.

Using a project management tool, such as Microsoft Project, for this step is helpful both for organizing your ideas and for illustrating them to the client. Clients find it very persuasive that you've taken the time to rough out a project plan for each of the options you present. Having a project plan clearly delineated for each solution option gives you a tremendous advantage when you are in a negotiating session. With the plan in front of you, you are in a stronger negotiating position when the client says, "I still need to cut 20 percent from the project budget," because you can then reply, "Which of these tasks do you recommend we cut out of the plan?" or "Which of these tasks can your team take on in order to save consulting fees?"

The output of your delivery plan should include the following elements:

- An activity plan, like the one illustrated above, that shows the high-level tasks required to deliver each of your optional solutions;

- A schedule for each option;

- A roles and responsibilities document that describes the technical and project-management skills required to perform the activities; and

- An estimated budget for consulting services to deliver each option.

By thinking of design as a structured process, with specific inputs, outputs, and methods, we can apply a discipline to that mysterious human talent, creativity. Striking the correct balance between freedom and methodology, between inspiration and perspiration, enables us to create solution designs that work, fit, and last.

In the case study segment at the end of Chapter Six, we watched the Superior Systems team design a discovery process. The reason we perform discovery is that in every engagement there are issues and requirements that are not obvious, that need to ferreted out and brought to the design table. In the case study sample for this chapter, we'll watch as the Superior team struggles with one of those issues—their discovery that there is a government filing underway for Cap-State that cannot be interrupted by the move process. Let's see how they apply some of the techniques we've discussed in this chapter to devise a solution to this unforeseen event.

References

Buxton, J.N., & Randell, B. (Eds.). (1970, April). *Software engineering techniques.* Brussels, Belguim: NATO Scientific Affairs Division.

Naur, P., & Randell, B. (Eds.). (1969, January). *Software engineering.* Brussels, Belguim: NATO Scientific Affairs Division.

Osborne, A. (1993). *Applied imagination.* Buffalo, NY: Creative Education Foundation.

Yourdon, E. (1975). *Techniques of program structure and design.* Englewood Cliffs, NJ: Prentice Hall.

1972, October. The maintenence iceberg. *EDP Analyzer.*

"This is a disaster," Sara complained to Nick. "At this late date, we now have a department manager telling us that there's no way he can even think about moving his servers in the middle of this FDA filing. How could they not have known about this?"

"I agree this is an issue, but this is why we go through this due diligence process. There are always situations like this in big projects." Nick tried to turn this situation into a coaching session for Sara. "This issue is not going to go away, so we need to come up with a creative way to address it. What do you suggest?"

"I don't know what to suggest!" Sara exclaimed. "If we let them stay in their current site, we blow the whole move schedule, plus we have to figure out a way to connect them to the new building so they have access to corporate e-mail and other network services. If we try to move them, then we have a political nightmare on our hands, because they claim that the slightest interruption in their filing schedule could cause them to miss a filing cycle, and that could set them back years! I'm stumped!"

"The first step is to get the rest of the team involved," Nick advised. "You and I are not going to solve this ourselves. There may be some creative technical answer we're not even considering."

"There had better be!"

Sara scheduled a meeting with all the consultants, as she did not want to limit the creative ideas to just the CapState project team. She described the situation for everyone: "In our discovery process, we agreed that it would be important to meet with the document management team to review their special requirements and be sure we were addressing them. As part of that discussion, we discovered that they're in the middle of an FDA filing on a drug that CapState is developing with one of its clients, and that the document management team refuses to be moved on the original schedule. They claim that moving their servers puts their filing status at risk, and that the potential loss if they miss a filing date could be a billion dollars in revenue! We need to work together to come up with some creative solution to this problem, or we're at risk of missing our schedule and severely complicating the move."

"Let's frame this problem a bit differently," Nick added. "Is this a real technical problem, or a perception issue? What's the real risk if we go up the chain and try to get the steering committee to rule that they must move on schedule?"

"Well," Sandy joined in, "servers do go down after moves. I think that, with modern backup technology, redundant hardware, swappable hard disks, and such, we could devise a fail-safe scenario that would be reasonably secure. But do you want to take the chance? There's never a guarantee, no matter what you design."

"Let's brainstorm on this a bit," Nick suggested. "Let's go around the room and talk about some of the ways we could deal with this. Let's focus first on the issues we'd need to deal with if we do move them on time. Remember that any idea has potential merit in this exercise, so just let it flow. We'll evaluate the ideas later."

Nick used the "round-robin" approach to brainstorming, in which he gave everyone a chance to contribute an idea in turn. As ideas came up, he recorded them on the whiteboard. Some of the suggestions he recorded were as follows:

- Create a totally parallel network;
- Move their application onto the main server for redundancy;
- Migrate their servers to high availability servers before the move;
- Hire an offsite redundant processing location;
- Make multiple backups of the data before the move and test restoring them;
- Can CapState's partner in the filing take over some of the processing?
- Can they finish the FDA filing before the move?

"Okay, now let's talk about what we can do to leave them in place. What issues does this raise and how can we solve them?" Nick recorded the responses:

- How do we connect them to the new site?
- High-speed connections will cost a fortune!
- Maybe the cost is negligible compared to the risk of missing a filing.
- Can we connect them via the Internet?

- If they stay, how do we move them later, when all the crews and the movers are gone?

- If we contract with the movers now for a late move, maybe we can build that into the contract?

- What about leases and rent payments? Is the space even available?

- Are we going to have problems with reports, faxes, or mail that will need to be couriered back and forth?

- What about support services? If all the network support teams are in the new site, what will happen if they have a network outage? Remember that they're thirty minutes away from the headquarters building!

"Okay," Nick said, "this is good. Now let's evaluate some of the ideas. First, let's vote on the overall concepts. How many think that convincing them to move makes the most sense?"

A couple of consultants raised their hands. "How many think that we should let them stay?" Again, only a couple of votes. "That was pretty inconclusive. We clearly need to dig down into this a bit deeper. Let's examine some of these ideas in depth."

Nick led the team through a discussion of the pros and cons of each idea and of the cost and schedule ramifications of each and probed for any hidden bombs that could surface with any solution. He lead the team to develop some thumbnail estimates of the costs of developing a parallel network, of migrating to redundant hardware, and of migrating the document management application to the main servers. Then he explored the suggestions in the other column, of building high-speed connections between the sites or of creating an Internet-based connection. He helped the team think through the risks in each strategy, asking the questions over and over: "What can go wrong if we move the applications?" "What are the risks of an Internet connectivity strategy?" "Can we schedule a crew to go out after the moves and move just this department?" As the team weighed the options, Nick helped them develop a consensus about which options to present to the client. He knew that this would ultimately be the client's call, but he wanted to have a coherent series of options to present, in order to allow the client to make an informed decision.

After the session, Nick sat with Sara and reviewed the outcome. "How do you feel about this now?" he asked her.

"I'm still a bit uncomfortable, but I agree that this is CapState's call. I feel like we came up with some reasonable alternatives, and I'm confident I can present this to the steering committee and help them understand the options."

"That's our role," Nick reminded her. "The risk is theirs, so the decision must be theirs. But we played our part by uncovering this in our discovery sessions and by framing some alternatives to help them make a decision."

"I'll put a presentation together this weekend," Sara promised. "Let's review what I put together next week."

COLLABORATE TO SELECT SOLUTIONS

- Presentation of Options Is a Critical Deliverable
- We Advise, Client Decides
- Decision Process Can't Be Outsourced
- Present Delivery Plans for Each Option
- Document Selected Solution
- Create a Working Project Plan

Collaborate to Select Solutions

The difficulty in life is the choice.

George Moore

SUCCESSFUL COLLABORATION

The process of organizing our design into coherent alternatives, deciding how to present those options, and preparing for questions, objections, and negotiation is a sobering experience. Most consultants discover, when we prepare to present our solutions to our clients, how well or how badly we understand our own design. We see our solution through the eyes of the client and realize how much education, explanation, and justification we'll need to do to prepare the client to make the right decision.

The consequences of mismanaging this phase are dire. All of the work we have done in the assessment and design phases will have been wasted if our presentation is unclear, unpersuasive, or unprofessional. This presentation is a pivotal point of the consulting relationship. Apart from the actual system implementation, the solution presentation is the central deliverable of most engagements. If handled well, we can guide our clients to a successful implementation of IT that will have a significant impact on their business.

Our success at collaborating with clients is even more crucial. Our ability to create partnerships with clients, to help clients select the solution that they are most ready and able to implement successfully, and to negotiate an implementation plan that ensures results will define our success as action-oriented advisors.

WE ADVISE, THEY DECIDE

Back in Chapter One, one of our five principles for consulting success was: "You advise, they decide." One of the most significant lessons that all consultants must learn is the importance of the client's ownership of the solution. Client refusal or inability to commit to the solution is one of the biggest risks of the advisory relationship. This may happen because the client does not understand the technology, does not want to take responsibility if the system or the project fails, or simply wants a "blame agent" in case things don't work out as expected. I consistently refer to the designs we present during this phase as the "solution options" or the "solution alternatives." Presenting options, and insisting that the customer make choices, is a critical strategy in the consulting process. The decision process cannot be outsourced. It must be made by those who will live with the results.

Presenting our design in the form of a set of options and helping the client make choices to construct a solution ensures that we are not subject to the "consultant's system" syndrome. Many of the remedial projects I've taken on have begun with a statement by the client such as: "The consultant came in here and dropped this system on us—never bothered to inform us or get our approval." In some cases, inexperienced or incompetent consultants will implement a system that is inappropriate for the client's needs. Many times, however, a bit of digging has shown that the client purposely remained aloof from the decision process, delegated the decision to the consultant or a junior team member, made no effort to ensure the success of the project, remained insulated from the results, and then, when things went south, had a convenient scapegoat in the consultant. In order to protect yourself, the client, and the project, you must have a collaborative relationship, in which, based on the options you present, consultant and client negotiate a design you both support.

Maturity as an IT consultant also means *leaving our technical biases out of the mix.* I've worked with immature consultants who have seen every consulting job as an opportunity to convince the client that UNIX (or NetWare or Oracle) is the solution to every IT problem. By emphasizing in our IT Consulting Framework the importance of presenting options, we stress that consultants must get out of their technical rut and investigate technologies that may not be their specialty or preference, but might be the most appropriate for the client.

SOLUTION OPTIONS

When preparing a solutions presentation, I think of my options as "bicycle, car, or limousine" alternatives. This is just a personal method of simplifying my own thought process that allows me to organize my presentation. I've heard other consultants call their options the "hamburger, chicken, and steak" options and refer to the alternatives as the "menu." Whatever makes sense to you is fine.

The *bicycle solution* is low-budget, easily implemented, minimally disruptive to daily operations, uses off-the-shelf technology, and relies on existing technical skill sets within the client's organization. It addresses only the highest-priority objectives. Based on our principles of good design, it is robust and flexible and can be built upon incrementally to satisfy secondary objectives. Beside the obvious advantages of speed and economy, it can be sold on its merits as an unobtrusive system that is unlikely to raise political or technical objections, will be easily integrated into existing systems, and can serve as a pilot system to prove the business concept, demonstrate real business benefits, and act as a foundation for further enhancements. When consultants and clients have no track record of achievement together, selecting small, rapid, and attainable projects that demonstrate your capability to execute can go a long way toward laying the foundation for greater success later. By avoiding an "all-or-nothing" approach, the consultant demonstrates a focus on the client's interests and not billable hours. By counseling the client to select small, high-impact options, we can often obtain better results from existing systems, minimize risk and resistance, and give the organization a taste of what is possible.

The *car solution* is more ambitious, satisfies more of the objectives, is more expensive, and requires more intensive efforts to implement and integrate. This system should address all but the most aggressive of the client's goals and should take the client as far as possible without using nonstandard technologies or requiring extensive customization. This is typically a multi-phase effort that includes a pilot and a rollout phase, as well as significant training and documentation efforts.

Finally, the *limousine solution* should address all of the most ambitious objectives, including contingency planning, training, and documentation, as well as special customized technologies and applications. It may include "make versus buy" decisions for specialized software. Your presentation should inform the client of all of the integration requirements of a major system effort, including interfaces with existing systems and modifications to current business processes and procedures.

PREPARING FOR THE SOLUTION PRESENTATION

As discussed in Chapter Two, "thinking backward" from the desired outcome is a powerful means of organizing our communications. By focusing on the result we hope to achieve, we design our presentation from the beginning to further our purpose. This does not mean that we manipulate the content in order to persuade the client to choose our preferred solution. The result we desire is collaboration—and the selection of the client's best alternative. If we plan our presentation around those goals, our presentation will not be a dry recitation of technical choices; we will build education, interaction, and consensus-building elements into our presentation.

A good solution presentation must do a lot of things. It must restate the basic problem or opportunity we've been asked to address—not only to show we understand why we're here, but because we don't know who the client will invite to the presentation or what that audience will know about the engagement or about us. It's obviously critical to show that we've designed a quality solution and to present it in language that's meaningful to the audience. We must demonstrate that we've taken the client's wallet seriously, designing a solution that delivers the best "bang for the buck" and that gives the client budgetary options. And, of course, the presentation must be professional and polished, as would be expected from a strategic business partner.

It is critically important to have the right audience for your presentation. If geography and work loads allow, schedule the managers, department heads, and representatives of the technical teams and user groups to attend a single meeting for this presentation. Reaching consensus and commitment is the objective of this meeting, not just reporting on possible solutions. Assuming that you have followed the guidelines detailed above, have prepared your options in some sort of menu of alternatives, and are prepared to discuss not just the technology but also the delivery methodology, I recommend presenting to the client team in the following manner:

- Introduce all team members, and allow the client team to introduce themselves and describe their role in the project;

- Quickly recap your role in this engagement;

- Restate the limitations, problem, or opportunity being addressed;

- Present the vision statement you devised together, and expand on it to describe, in a manner that will be meaningful to all the attendees, the business objectives;

- Present a brief overview of the "as-is" model as you discovered it during your assessment activities;

- Walk through each proposed solution option;

- Describe the way each system option would look and feel for its users;

- Concisely state the business benefits of each option;

- Describe the impact on current systems and operations of each option;

- Present the activity plan, schedule, and estimated budget for each option; and

- Describe the sacrifices and risks of each option, for instance, for the "bicycle" option, explain which "nice-to-have" features would not be implemented and the implications of that for the vision and objectives.

Tips on Presenting

Remember when presenting:

- *Remember That This Is a Meeting.* It's not an opportunity to make a speech. Design interactivity into the meeting by stopping frequently and asking for questions or offering to clarify. To implement our strategy of making the client "own" the solution, it's crucial to involve the audience and give them a chance to raise objections or ask questions.

- *Avoid Technical Jargon.* Strive for complete clarity of the options and implications you present, so there are no misunderstandings or misgivings when the client team makes its decision.

- *Avoid Making Recommendations.* It is your job to objectively, clearly, and fairly describe the pros and cons of each solution and the possible outcomes of the client's decision. By making explicit recommendations, you risk bringing your own biases into the decision process, and you allow the client to make it your decision and, ultimately, your system.

- *Work with Your Client.* Approach this meeting as a facilitated work session and as a negotiation. Your role as the consultant is not to drive the client to a particular, or even to any, decision. You best serve your clients by helping them work through the issues that your presentation raises and by advising them regarding possible permutations and combinations of the options you have detailed. In many cases, some hybrid solution, combining elements of each alternative, is the best solution for your client's situation. Be a valuable advisor by helping your client find the best option.

- *Don't Push the Process.* Some clients may want to reach consensus in the room and walk out with a decision; others may want to digest the material, meet without you, and think through their options over days or weeks. Allow clients to reach consensus and decision on their own schedule and within their own corporate culture.

- *Be Ready to Make Changes.* Be prepared to redesign, rewrite, and re-present. As with all other activities in the consulting cycle, presenting solutions can be an iterative process, in which the client comes back with new ideas, new objectives, and new constraints based on your presentation.

Finally, when all of the options are on the table, all of the negotiating, synthesizing, and consensus building is complete, and you believe you have guided your client to the best decision, test the client's commitment and understanding of the decision. I recommend that this be done in a formal written report that states the solutions that were presented, the negotiations and modifications that took place, and the final result. This should be in the form of a proposal to proceed to the implementation phase and should include a final project plan, a schedule, a roles and responsibilities document, and an estimated budget. This document should be signed by the client in acknowledgement of the solution and delivery plan you've agreed to move forward with together. This is just another step in saying that this is not your system and that the client has made informed choices based on your discovery and design efforts.

We've almost reached the end of our case study. In this short vignette, we continue the issue we reviewed in the case study segment following Chapter Seven, in which Sara, during discovery, has found a special situation that she needs to bring to the client for a decision. In this scenario, Nick, our managing consultant, and Sara, the project manager, prepare for an options presentation with the client's project steering committee. Notice how they apply the techniques I've outlined in this chapter.

Nick and Sara met to prepare for the Steering Committee meeting. Sara had held a private meeting with Ron Gimble of CapState and had informed him of the issues with the document management department, and he decided to convene the Steering Committee to hear the options and make a decision. She was glad for Nick's guidance in preparing her presentation, as she had not had a lot of experience presenting before senior executives and was a bit nervous.

"One way I've found to get over the nerves is to remember that you have no agenda. You're not trying to convince them to decide one way or the other, so you really don't have anything personal on the line. You're there as an advisor; the decision is theirs. That takes a lot of the tension out of it for me," Nick advised her.

"I'm okay," Sara said. "I just want to be sure that I'm ready to help them make the right choice. After our team meeting, I feel that we can deal with whatever action they decide to take."

Nick walked her through the documents they had prepared: "So let's think through the options again. It's pretty basic, actually. They can allow the document management team to stay in place until the FDA filing is complete. That means paying extra rent and providing services in the existing building through April, or about four months. If they want to understand the details of that, refer them to the budget document we put together that outlines the cost of rent, courier services, and the two T1 lines that Sandy thought would be required for network connectivity. Remind them of the implications regarding keeping the phone switch running in the old building and interconnecting the two phone systems. Also, don't forget to inform them of the impact to the schedule, and that they'll have to engage another crew to come in later and disconnect them for their move."

"And I need to remember that we didn't factor in the cost of the phone interconnect, because that's not our area of expertise," Sara reminded herself as she rehearsed the meeting in her mind.

"That's right; Sandy didn't feel comfortable touching that because we never did a voice traffic analysis or really looked at the voice systems in detail," Nick replied.

"And if they do decide to move with everyone else," Sara said, "I'll walk them through the plan we put together for backing up all the data multiple times, for migrating a complete set of the data and applications to the main server farm, and for building some redundant servers just in case of a hardware failure."

"Please," Nick emphasized, "whatever you do, don't gloss over the cost of the redundant systems you'll need to build in order to assure the safety of the move. Also, remember what the lawyer said. You've got to mention that we can't take responsibility for consequential damages if they do move them and something goes wrong."

"That's the piece I'm most uncomfortable with," Sara replied. "I'm no lawyer; I don't even know what consequential damage is. I just hope they don't want to have that conversation with me."

"Don't worry," Nick reassured her. "They know you, they understand your role; they're not going to expect you to have a conversation about legal liabilities. Just remember, introduce yourself and remind them what you're there to review with them, explain the problem with the document management group, lay out the options clearly, walk through the documents with them, and wrap up with the schedule and budget implications. It's all laid out in the slide show and the handout."

Sara gathered up the material and prepared to leave for her meeting.

Nick saw Sara again that afternoon when she returned. "So, how'd it go?" he asked.

"It went great!" Sara replied. "Ron really helped me out. He sat down for a few minutes with me before the meeting and really coached me on how to present. Then, in the meeting, he set me up really well, introduced me as the project manager and told the committee that I was doing a great job. He made me feel really confident. I walked them through just as we rehearsed. They decided to let them stay. They asked us if we would manage the whole thing as a subproject, hire a phone subcontractor, put together a crew to prep them for their move, everything. That's good, right?"

"That's great," Nick told her. "We'll give it to Tim. I think he's ready for his own project. Great work!"

DELIVER BUSINESS RESULTS

- Deliver a Complete Solution
- Document What You Deliver
- Deliver Secure Systems
- Deliver Maintainable Systems
- Train Users on Your Solutions
- Test Client Satisfaction
- Measure Results Against Project Vision
- Document Client Acceptance

Deliver Business Results

*Man may work great changes, and accomplish great affairs
among mankind, if he forms a good plan and makes the execution
of that plan his sole study and business.*

Benjamin Franklin

HOW IS CONSULTING SUCCESS MEASURED?

In a June 1999 cover story, *Fortune* magazine asked the question "Why Do CEOs Fail?: The One Weakness That Brought Them Down" (Charan & Colvin, 1999). The authors reviewed the ascent and demise of high-profile CEOs such as Gil Amelio, the man tasked with saving Apple Computer after John Scully's departure, and Eckhard Pfeiffer, the Compaq CEO who was abruptly fired in April 1999, after Compaq surprised Wall Street with lower than expected earnings. Compaq's chairman, Ben Rosen, was quoted as stating that the change in Compaq's approach after Pfeiffer's departure would not be strategic. "The change will not be in our fundamental strategy," Rosen told *Fortune,* "but in execution." Charan and Colvin concluded that the single failing that unsuccessful CEOs shared was the inability to execute on the strategy and vision they'd articulated. "Bad execution: not getting things done, not delivering on commitments," they stated, was the one weakness that precipitated the downfall of the unfortunate CEOs profiled.

Although it is clearly the role of the CEO to ensure that the strategic vision is implemented, there is some controversy in the consulting world as to whether executing the vision is the consultant's responsibility or the client's. Many consulting organizations specifically state in their methodologies that "implementation is the client's responsibility!" I disagree. In my career over just the last year, I've encountered some situations that have helped develop my opinion on this question.

> A multi-national clinical research company hired a team of technology consultants to assist in the selection of a laboratory management information system. The consultants performed a review of the work flows and information needs within the organization, sat in on strategy sessions with department managers, and interviewed key decision makers. They evaluated many competitive software products, found the one they believed was the best fit for the client's needs, and prepared a complete findings document that outlined the key selection criteria and made a strong case for the software they recommended. They delivered their findings in a management presentation, and the managers who had hired them were very pleased with the completeness and persuasiveness of their work. Unfortunately, the software they selected ran on a different operating system than the one the organization was currently running, and the technical team, concerned over their own jobs and their ability to adapt to the new system, set up so many roadblocks that the consultant's recommendations were never implemented.

Unfortunately, solutions that are technically correct but not achievable are not found only in the world of IT consulting. Let me provide another example, based on my real-world experience as a practicing consultant.

> A small electronics wholesaler engaged a strategic planning consultant to help the company move from a product-based to a services-based business, with the goal of growing from $25 million to $200 million in annual revenues within three years. After many nights of SWOT analyses, competitive positioning exercises, and mission statement development, the planner and her client created a list of action items that included tasks such as:
>
> - Define a company-wide mission,
> - Create an employee development program,

- Organize to optimize the strengths of our teams; put "the right people in the right jobs," and

- Become a resource to our customers by engaging consultatively rather then "selling."

Following delivery of this "strategic plan," the consultant sent a bill and was off to the next client. After struggling with these goals for a few months, the company called in a consultant with a specialty in distribution services, who quickly reviewed their operations and identified five process improvements that could be implemented immediately, including a project management system, a client feedback loop, and a job-scheduling system. These improvements were structured as discrete, measurable projects with specific improvement goals and implementation timetables, and were credited with a 70 percent increase in customer satisfaction and with 30 percent revenue growth in the nine months after implementation.

Although the strategic planner helped the client identify meaningful goals, that's all they were: goals to strive for, not measurable results. They pointed to a destination, but provided no map to get there. Unfortunately, I could fill many pages with examples of creative IT solutions that were never implemented—and so provided no business benefits to the clients who paid for them. Were these engagements successful? The answer is clear: *Consulting engagements that provide no measurable results for clients are failures.*

Throughout this book, I've emphasized the contrast between the technical and the advisory aspects of consulting. The failures I've described above are attributable to an overriding focus on the technical goals of an engagement and a neglect of the advisory relationship. Technically focused consultants have a tendency to gauge their success based on the technical correctness of their findings. Advisors, on the other hand, work in partnership with their clients to ensure that the advice they give results in meaningful change—and in measurable benefit for their partners. Like the doctor who considers the patient's lifestyle, history, and temperament before prescribing, superior IT advisors consider the client's culture, readiness to change, ability to manage projects, willingness to take risks in order to achieve benefits, and many other "lifestyle" elements, before making recommendations. In short, IT consultants must *share* with their clients the responsibility for achieving results. Like the CEOs profiled in *Fortune,* consultants should ultimately be judged not only by their ability to develop a vision and a strategy, but by their ability to deliver on that vision.

BUILD IN SUCCESS FROM THE BEGINNING

Consultants can structure projects for implementation success from the start. By considering the client organization's culture, its readiness for change and tolerance for risk, its ability to communicate a project vision and to win stakeholder consensus, we can build our projects so they are realistic in terms of the client's ability to turn our advice into business results. To ensure that we deliver business impact, and not just "findings," I recommend concentrating on some basic principles from the beginning. I call these principles the "Three C's": *collaboration, communication,* and *culture.*

Collaboration

- When accepting engagements, concentrate on personality and cultural "fit" before you focus on your technical qualifications for the job;
- Avoid "thrown over the wall" types of relationships, in which the client wants to throw you problems and expects you to throw back solutions;
- Clearly establish, from the approach through the negotiation, and reinforce throughout the engagement, that this is a collaborative partnership with shared responsibility for results;
- Identify roles and responsibilities for the client as well as the consultant in all contracts and project plans;
- Run meetings as facilitated work sessions, not as presentations of conclusions; and
- Present solutions as options, not recommendations. Options support client ownership, while recommendations imply consultant ownership.

Communication

- Communicate throughout the project that your deliverable is not technology, but a business result;

- Clearly define the meaning of success; define the solution you and the client select based on specific, measurable results and outcomes to be delivered, not on vague objectives;
- Build communication planning into every engagement, to ensure that those to be affected by our solutions understand:

    What the benefits of the new system will be;

    How it will affect their job and daily activities;

    How it will be implemented, and how they'll be prepared and trained; and

    How their work with the new system will be supported in operation.

Culture

- Clearly identify from the start all risks, constraints, and assumptions that could impact your ability to deliver results, including cultural, organizational, and procedural as well as purely technical risks.

- Include implementation success factors in your planning from the start. Elements that will be important after the consultant is gone, such as documentation, operational support, policies and procedures, training, maintenance, and contingency planning, should be part of your solution.

- Help clients select solutions that are achievable. Many clients want the "big fix," even though their organizations are so risk-averse or resistant to change that only incremental change is possible. Many consultants are biased toward the total solution, to validate their image as strategic partners, and to maximize billings. Smaller, incremental projects can fit better with a client's ability to implement change and can create a momentum toward change by proving a concept and delivering immediate results.

PROJECT MANAGEMENT FOR CONSISTENT RESULTS

Although the principles outlined above can create a foundation of ideals with which to approach your advisory relationship, a code of ideals is not a plan. Every IT consultant needs a core of project management skills in order to deliver results in a consistent, manageable, and measurable way. For results-oriented consultants, project management skills are a deciding factor: You either have them, and can deliver, or you do not and you cannot. There may be some consultants with the innate ability to scope, plan, estimate, manage, and control ongoing projects without a formal project management methodology. I haven't met them. For the rest of us I recommend developing our project skills.

Many of the doctrines of good project management have a lot in common with the IT Consulting Framework developed in this book, but the framework is not a formal project management methodology. As mentioned before, the framework is designed to guide IT consultants through their advisory relationships with their clients. Formal project management is designed to provide tools and techniques for planning, managing, and controlling the details of task, schedule, and budget required to deliver a result. The different objectives of the IT Consulting Framework and formal project management complement one another, and I think of them as layers in the architecture of the client's solution. When it comes to guaranteeing the ability to deliver measurable results as a consultant, however, the skills and techniques of project management are tools that work. I know of successful IT consultants who make a deal with the client at the beginning of their relationship: If you agree to follow my project management methodology in this engagement, I guarantee that we'll achieve the objectives, or you don't pay. These consultants have proven to themselves over the course of their careers that, if they can convince their clients to participate in a rigorous project management process, they will achieve the desired results.

Project management as a discipline has progressed significantly since the development of the PERT technique during the nuclear submarine programs of the 1950s. The standards body for professional project managers, The Project Management Institute (PMI), has established a foundation Project Management Body of Knowledge (the PMBOK) that defines the required competencies for project managers. In addition to the four standard and obvious areas of competency, (1) scope management, (2) time management, (3) cost management, and (4) human resource management, the PMI also identifies (5) risk management, (6) quality management, (7) contract/procurement management, and (8) communication management as core areas of competency. The latter four areas underscore PMI's commitment to the delivery of quality results and its recognition of the importance of building consensus and cooperation for each project effort. Project management as a discipline is now concerned with more than just the conception, planning, execution, and closeout of projects, as the phases were defined in the traditional model. As Frame (1994) stated: "The project team members must be made to realize that their job is not simply to build something but also to assure that it works in a satisfactory way after it is delivered."

Another benefit of project management is that it can be used to formalize the roles and responsibilities of both client and consultant team members. It's one thing to tell the client that you'll be expecting the company's technicians to get involved in the setup of network servers, for example, and quite another thing when the technicians actually see their names and tasks on a project plan. This is the moment when, in many cases, the client suddenly discovers that the resources are not available. Clients will often volunteer their team members to perform implementation tasks as a way to shave costs during the planning phase, and then when it comes time for these resources to deliver, they're tied up in their regular jobs and support activities and aren't available for project work. Of course this may be seen as an opportunity to generate additional billable hours, but if the consultant lacks the technical skills or resources, this can be a serious setback for the project. Formal project management techniques concentrate the client's mind by turning vague conversations about shared responsibility into concrete planning documents with specific individuals assigned to specific tasks.

It's outside the scope of this book to include a detailed tutorial about project management. Some excellent sources are listed in the bibliography. Remember that the technical aspects of the IT consulting job are just a small portion of the repertoire we must bring to the engagement, and that the structured skills outlined in the PMI's Project Management Body of Knowledge are another example of essential tools we must be prepared to use.

AN APPROACH TO IMPLEMENTATION

The "Deliver Business Results" phase of the IT Consulting Framework can be made clearer by breaking it down into a "mini-framework" that outlines the steps that a successful implementation should take. This framework for the project delivery phase includes the following steps:

1. Implementation planning,

2. Communication,

3. Training,

4. Technical implementation,

5. Transition to operations,

6. Implementation review, and

7. Client acceptance.

This sequence of steps provides a method for implementing new technology, while ensuring that we keep our focus on the management and human issues that ultimately govern the success or failure of our solution. Let's review the activities within each phase.

Implementation Planning

When we were designing the solution options and working with the client to select the most appropriate solution, we created some preliminary project plans so that we could help the client understand the probable costs and schedule associated with each option. Because we did not know at that time what choices the client would make, it didn't make sense for us to build project plans in fine detail. Now that we've helped the client construct a viable solution, we need to dig into the details of the activities, tasks, and responsibilities required to make our solution a reality.

This is a good moment to reevaluate the vision of the project that was created in the early stages of engagement. If the vision reflects the "steak" approach, but the choices made in constructing the ultimate solution lean closer to the "hamburger" options, we need to recognize that now and be sure that we are managing expectations carefully. The next stage of implementation is communication, and it's critical to communicate clearly what the ultimate users of this system can expect. Also at this point, it's important to move beyond our vision statement and to develop detailed written criteria that will be used to evaluate the success of our system delivery. If the customer has specific productivity, financial, head count, or other quantifiable goals associated with this project, now is the time to state those and to negotiate any disagreements regarding your ability to deliver to those expectations. If the client wants to reduce head count in the accounting department by six in the first three months after implementation, and you believe it will take twelve months and probably only reduce the head count by one, you must ensure your ability to deliver successfully by negotiating reasonable expectations.

This is obviously the time to create itemized plans for the technical implementation, including materials lists, integration requirements, and any technical testing that will be necessary. Because, in most cases, the solution is constructed from a mix-and-match variety of the options you presented to the client, it's critical to refine the various elements into a final architecture that everyone understands and agrees on. Also critical at this time is the creation of detailed plans for the operational elements, such as training and documentation, technical support, policies and procedures, and system maintenance. Delivering results means delivering a total solution. It's important to remember that technology is not a deliverable; only a functioning system that delivers a sustainable result is.

Now that we know what the solution will look like, we need to recruit the implementation team. Will the implementation of our selected technology require network designers, software programmers, data analysts, database or application experts, desktop techs, or data communications experts? Will we need senior or junior staff in these positions, or a combination? What role will the client's team play? Is there a need for subcontractors, such as cabling or training experts? In larger projects, some project managers will actually create job descriptions to ensure that the roles and responsibilities of each position on the team are clearly documented. Although this may be overkill on many projects, it is important to communicate what each team player's role will be, what work standards will be applied to evaluate contributions, and how each person's work will contribute to the whole effort. This is also the time to review task assignments to ensure that resources are available as needed and that other project or daily operational duties do not interfere with any team member's ability to contribute as needed.

The key output of this step is the project plan. This plan, typically constructed in Microsoft Project or another project management tool, contains the activities and their tasks, the team member responsible for their delivery, the timeline, the materials required and when they're needed, all in a sequenced blueprint that is designed to help track and manage the daily progress of the delivery effort. Milestones, indicating successful completion of specific phases of the implementation, must be included, and should be associated with reporting events such as status reports and progress meetings. The project plan is a powerful communication tool. It should be written in language that the client and team can understand because they'll be using it as a guideline to assure themselves that you're delivering as promised. I recommend posting it on a website or printing an enlarged copy and posting it in a common work area, so the project team, the client, and the ultimate end users of your system can track progress toward the goal. See Appendix D for an example of a detailed project plan.

Communication

It is an axiom in the world of IT that many systems go uninstalled, unused, or under-utilized. Every client I've worked for, and every corporation I've been engaged with, has had a story of a development effort that was designed, installed, and made operational, but never used as intended by the targeted users. In my experience, lack of communication regarding the system, its benefits, and its impact is the culprit in the majority of these cases.

I look at the communication planning I do with my clients during the implementation phase as an extension of the initial marketing done during the "Visualizing Success" phase. During that phase, we developed a short tag line that broadly described the key benefits of the new technology we were planning. It was necessarily lean on specifics, because we had not done our discovery, design, or selection process yet. The information we imparted at that time was designed as a marketing effort and was focused on the general conception of the system we envisioned. Now we have a much more specific design in mind, and it's important to communicate the details of features and benefits to the entire organizational community. It's also critical to discuss the implementation process, such as which departments or teams will be affected by the changes, what the schedule for implementation will be, and how the users of the system will be trained and supported after it's operational. The success of the engagement is dependent on your ability to guide the client to communicate and market the new system effectively.

Every group communicates differently. Communication mediums vary from company to company, based on the company's size, organization, culture, or geography. The standard media, such as the memorandum from the president's desk, has been augmented by the website and by e-mail, as well as the video kiosk that is a common feature in some large organizations. When I work with clients to develop a communication plan, I focus as much on the medium as on the message. An interactive departmental meeting that allows the ultimate users of the system to comment and question sends a different underlying message than the memo from the president, regardless of the content.

Some basic principles to guide your advisory efforts in the communication process during implementation are described in the following paragraphs.

Multiple Media Are Better Than One, and Repetition Reinforces the Message.
Some clients will spend lots of time debating whether a memo from the president,

a website, or an auditorium presentation is better for communicating, to which I answer "Yes!" Advise your clients to *use all media at their disposal to over-communicate* the expectations for the new technology. Each medium has its own distinct type of impact, and some folks respond better to one or the other. Presidential memos display executive involvement and commitment, newsletters can present in depth the details of your technology strategy, websites allow the staff to review schedules and project plans at their own pace, while auditorium presentations with question-and-answer periods demonstrate willingness to discuss and debate the system and its implementation. Each of these mediums conveys a message, separate from the content, about your approach to the project and the client community.

Interactive Is Better Than Passive Communication. Presenting the systems benefits and features to a work team in a facilitated session is a powerful method of communicating. Not only does it allow you to customize the message so that it's meaningful to this particular group, but it states clearly that you encourage feedback and discussion. Don't discount the probable outcome of interactive communication; the client's teams are going to teach you how to implement the system effectively. They will tell you what type of training they expect, for instance, and they'll remind you (and their managers) that the tax department's system migration cannot be implemented during the first week of April.

You'll Need a Training and Operational Plan. System users are not interested only in the features and benefits of the new system. They also want to know how they are going to be prepared to make use of those features and glean those benefits. In short, they're concerned about how they will adapt. A major part of the message must be made up of assurances that they will be trained in the use of the new technology, that there will be an effective maintenance and support effort to keep them up and running, and that their comments and suggestions on improvement and revision of the system will be considered. The preparation of a training and support plan before communication efforts begin, so that it can be presented in detail, can go a long way toward reassuring the teams affected that the new technology will not be dumped on them with no preparation.

A Feedback Mechanism Should Be Included Up-Front. Voice-mail and e-mail mailboxes specifically dedicated to comments and suggestions regarding the new technology and a process for reviewing and evaluating that feedback are of great reassurance value to the teams affected. They also lead to better results for the client, because front-line work teams typically have the best insight into what works, what needs improvement, and what kind of support and training they need to be most effective.

Communication Is Critical Throughout the Implementation Process. *Communication is a process, not an event.* I've had many clients say, after the fifth newsletter or the third iteration of the website, "We've told them this stuff already!" My advice is not to underestimate the fear, resistance, and inertia of the human beings affected by new technology and changing jobs. Tell the customers of your new system where they're going, tell them the progress you're making as you make the journey, tell them when you near the destination, tell them when you get there, and remind them at every opportunity along the way of why this trip is necessary.

There's no such thing as too much communication, especially when it affects livelihood, prestige, and self-worth.

Training

Most clients will understand the importance of training to the success of their projects. Going from acknowledgment of its importance to the development of an effective program, however, is complex. In addition to training users on the daily operation of the system, including minute details of data entry and system administration, you must also train them about changes in work flow, process, and job function. Reports, forms, and other inputs and outputs may change and may need to be interpreted differently. Not only must the users of the new technology be trained, but the teams that support them must learn how to maintain and support the system. To further complicate the training process, there are many alternative methods of training available, from teachers in classrooms, to user manuals, to interactive computer-based training (CBT). The three major questions we must help our clients answer are:

- *Who Are Our Audiences for Training?* In addition to training for the workers or teams that will actually sit in front of terminals and enter or view data, we need to design training for the support staff that will maintain the technology and for the managers who will either manage the work teams or use the information produced.

- *What Is the Content of Our Training?* Each of the audiences will need to learn different skills. Each will require a different mix of technical details, business context, and work flow training.

- *What Methods and Materials Will We Use?* In many cases, a mixture of training methods delivers lasting results. For instance, most system users prefer classroom training with a detailed manual to refer to later and with an option for personal deskside tutoring if needed. Managers may be more interested in a flow chart of the new work process. Technical teams may want CBT so they can learn at their own pace.

Obviously, the size and scope of our project will dictate the depth and complexity of the training effort. The implementation of a new multi-site wide area network will have different training implications than the design of an accounting system. In all but the simplest IT implementations, designing programs targeted to the right audiences, with the right combination of training methods and materials, and with the appropriate level of technical and operational detail is an intricate task. It is also a task that is beyond the experience of many IT consultants.

In those lucky cases in which a client is large enough to have a training staff, we can collaborate with them from the beginning of the project to design an appropriate program. Internal trainers can contribute an intimate understanding of the organization, its culture and norms, and its history of training efforts, whereas the IT consultant can add the technology-specific content. In organizations without the luxury of internal trainers, IT consultants can partner with training consultants to prepare a program. Finally, of course, IT consultants can go it alone, working with their client one-on-one to create a training approach. However programs are developed, they must include some common tasks:

1. *Select the Trainees.* Not only must we select the audiences in general, but we must designate the specific individuals so we can do the necessary scheduling and notification.

2. *Develop Detailed Content.* This includes not only the creation of "slide shows" or classroom material, but also any takeaways such as manuals, flow charts, or report samples. The logic and sequence of your presentation must be mapped out. Many inexperienced trainers will attempt to train from a slide show and find themselves struggling to present the fine details not explicit in the outline.

A detailed lesson plan helps trainers present with confidence and gives a basis for specific improvements based on trainee reaction.

3. *Help the Client Market the Training.* Training is another opportunity to generate some enthusiasm for the project benefits. By promoting training, your client highlights a commitment to making the necessary investment so that work teams can be successful.

4. *Customize the Training.* Every client, organization, and individual learns differently. By using a combination of training methods, we ensure that individuals are treated individually, so that the worker who needs reinforcement of skills has the option to pursue one-on-one tutoring, for instance, or to review a manual.

5. *Evaluate and Revise Training.* Good training programs include a feedback loop that allows trainees to comment on the methods, materials, instructors, and content of training so that the learning experience can be continuously improved.

One unexpected benefit of developing a training program is that it often results in refinement of the system. By preparing to teach the details of operating the technology, we often uncover awkward, nonintuitive elements that should be revised to be more usable. Screens and reports that do not make sense or flow well are often flushed out when we try to articulate their features. Even after training is underway, we can learn a lot about the elegance of our design by observing the ease or difficulty of explaining it to others. Trainers themselves can become part of our evaluation process, as users will sometimes express to trainers fears and concerns about their ability to adapt that they would never express to managers.

Technical Implementation

When I teach consulting skills and project management to IT professionals, I see a common error in designing technical implementations. Many consultants, in their project plans, will include one or two lines that say something like:

Task 23: Install hardware

Task 24: Install software

Even consultants who are experienced enough to design extensive training, communication, and support processes into their plans will often assume that, as technologists, their ability to perform the actual installation of the technical components is a given.

Yet even the simplest technical implementation project, such as moving a network server from one side of the data center to the other, needs to be planned, and risks need to be considered. In my career as a network consultant, I've shut down many servers that had been running for years without being turned off and that would not come back up after being moved. This has happened so many times that I made a rule for my consulting teams that all servers must be shut off and restarted before being moved, so we could avoid liability for servers that would not reboot. Yet this common scenario, and many like it, are not addressed in the one-line "Install Server" task above. These experiences have convinced me that every technical activity in a technology implementation needs to be planned and that at every step we need to ask, "What can go wrong?" so that we can mitigate these risks.

Because we rarely install a system into a "green field" environment, in which no technology infrastructure exists, our planning for technical implementation must include integration and must address contingencies based on interactions between systems. Many times, new systems will work when tested in isolation, but produce unexpected results when integrated with existing technology. Disruption of current systems while implementing new technology is a serious blunder. To prevent this, we must analyze all the interactions of our proposed system with current systems. We have to review every "touch point" between our infrastructure, application, and data systems and existing ones, and we must think through the possible unexpected effects we could have. Then we must plan our response.

I see this basic risk planning neglected consistently in the consulting teams I advise. Yet its faithful application will protect against, I estimate, 85 percent of technical glitches. By thinking about all the software and tools that would be needed if a server died, for instance, a consultant could put together a software tool kit that would allow a quick response. By understanding the client's technical infrastructure, we can guide decisions about "hot spares" during implementation. By prioritizing systems by business importance, we can make judgments about which systems need backup capability in case of integration problems. By understanding the client's business, we can schedule "go/no-go" decisions that protect the client's ability to continue working. In brief, by protecting the client from foreseeable risk, we perform our professional obligation as consultants.

Quality Management

Although analyzing the risks is essential, it's not sufficient. We must also manage the quality of our deliverables. In today's competitive environment, speed to deployment can determine the ultimate business benefit of a technology solution. Some project managers will mistakenly try to save time by reducing the focus on quality management activities such as walkthroughs, team reviews, or testing. The reverse approach has been proven to be effective in shortening IT project delivery times. Studies of software development projects, as an example, have found that organizations that skimp on the quality management activities suffer from schedule overruns, project cancellations, and low user satisfaction (Kitson & Masters, 1993).

As part of the quality management process, I advocate that all IT practitioners take a page from the software developer's book and adopt the practice of the "structured walkthrough." The *walkthrough* is a team review process in which teams review technical designs to ensure that they are of high quality. Although I present this approach in the implementation phase of the framework, in reality it can be applied throughout the engagement to ensure that specifications, designs, and results are technically correct and meet the standards of quality we have developed. This process typically requires that the specific element under review, whether a module of code or a network design, be documented and distributed to the team and that the designers walk the team through the design concepts and their planned execution and allow the team to dissect, to criticize, and to recommend improvements. Apart from the quality management aspects of this approach, I find that a significant secondary benefit is that it helps build team ownership of the solution and reinforces the standards of the organization. In practical terms, structured walkthroughs should be scheduled as the first "gate" in the testing process for major technical elements that are about to be implemented.

The most obvious element in the management of technical quality is the execution test, in which we actually run the program or install the hardware and ensure that our design works as expected in this operating environment. Whether we're testing a software module or a network design, there are two main types of test we will use:

- *The System or Unit Test.* For this test, the individual element, whether it's a Java applet or a server installation, is tested, and
- *The Integration Test.* Here, the verified element is integrated into its operating environment and the whole system is tested.

These basic quality control measures protect the client from system elements that are not ready for release. As with any fair test, a passing grade must be established up-front. If, for instance, we are testing a network connection, an acceptable level of throughput should be agreed on. Collaborating with the client to develop tests that reflect the real usage of the system is key. In many cases the finer technical details of your system design will not have been seen by the client before. Designing measurements is an integral part of the design process and an important opportunity to reset expectations with the client. As well as testing the system, this is a chance to test the client's understanding of your technical deliverables. Systems can be fine-tuned, not only based on the purely technical results of testing but also based on your test of customer expectations.

Some of the results we're looking for when testing are as follows:

- *Logic Errors.* Especially in the testing of software modules, the most basic "bug" we are trying to eliminate is the logic error. Are there errors in the logic that causes a program to execute, branch, or calculate a result?

- *Capacity Errors.* Is the system designed to handle the capacity required? If it's a database, is there enough space in the data repository? If it's a network segment, can it handle the throughput required? If it's a website, can it handle the number of hits expected?

- *Recovery Errors.* As discussed in our design section, does the program, hardware, or communication device measure up to our standards of robustness? Does it gracefully handle unexpected usages or inputs? Are files corrupted if the system interrupts unexpectedly? Are the recovery processes documented and feasible?

- *Standards Errors.* Is the system element being tested consistent with our standards, or is it an example of a "quick-and-dirty" solution?

These criteria apply whether we are performing system testing or integration testing. In system testing we are asking whether the isolated module or device meets certain standards. In integration testing we have the additional complexity of ensuring that the unit, when integrated with the existing elements in place, does not violate any of these criteria or cause the newly created system to fail.

Pilot Testing

As we do throughout our consulting process, we must keep business results in mind as we test our implementations. Testing individual elements is important from a technical point of view, but only pilot testing can uncover business issues.

The technology may work exactly as expected, but workers may be unable to learn how to use it productively. It may conflict with unofficial work flows. It may clash with job descriptions or organizational boundaries. By carving out a representative community of users or a technical niche, we can run a simulation of a business environment for our system. This is the basis of pilot testing. The creation of a pilot test program before full rollout has become an accepted part of most design methodologies.

The basic rules for developing a pilot test are:

- *To Create a Formal Pilot Test Plan.* Define resources, schedule, and testing tasks in advance and in collaboration with the client. Make the client the owner and evaluator of the pilot test, with you as advisor. Define precise tasks that the users should perform as part of the test, such as opening every module, entering data into every field, printing and desk-checking every report, printing to every printer, or whatever other tasks will verify that the system will perform as expected.

- *To Predefine Measurements.* Part of the formal pilot test plan should be the criteria for deeming the test a success or failure.

- *To Select a Representative Sample.* The work team or department selected for the pilot test should be as representative of the general organization as possible, not a special department such as legal or manufacturing. Their schedules, work flows, and data traffic should be consistent with company norms. This can be quite difficult in many companies and can have political implications as well, as every team believes their environment is unique.

- *To Give the Pilot Group Special Handling.* They must be motivated to participate. They must be trained so they're prepared to give the system a fair workout. Their feedback and reaction to the pilot process must be considered, and they must be involved in validating changes to the system based on their input. In many technologically advanced companies, being on a pilot test team is considered an honor, an opportunity to influence the future technological direction of the organization.

- *To Plan to Incorporate the Results.* If the schedule leaves no time to respond to concerns that arise in the pilot phase, then it's merely a formality and does not improve the quality of your deliverables. Project plans must plan not only for the pilot test itself, but for the time and resources to incorporate changes and test them.

The evaluation of pilot results is best performed in a facilitated work session with the client, some members of the pilot group, and the system designers. In many cases, only by having members of the pilot user group present will you be able to interpret the results. The users can shed light on informal work flows, turf issues, work habits, and other factors that can show up in the pilot. Designers can use them as surrogates of the user community, to float possible fixes or enhancements, and to gauge the reaction.

Pilot tests uncover cultural issues, team training issues, and organizational issues that cannot be flushed out by system testing. Information technology consultants who plan well for pilot testing, and who build in time to refine their designs based on pilot results, give themselves a priceless margin of freedom to again set expectations and to ensure the delivery of business results.

A final comment about testing: *Document your tests and use them as baselines for future performance.* By performing system tests, integration tests, and a representative pilot project, we can set expectations for the performance of our system. We can then refer to these baselines in the future when we need to plan for enhancements or troubleshoot problems. When asked to do a network audit because users are complaining of poor response time, for example, it's helpful to have a documented baseline of the performance that was deemed acceptable during implementation. With no baseline, "acceptable performance" becomes extremely subjective and sets the stage for disagreement and customer dissatisfaction.

Knowledge Transfer

One other implementation strategy I want to explore is the transfer of knowledge to the client and the client's staff. I've heard consultants jokingly (and not so jokingly) state that they want to keep the client in the dark about the technology they install, so they can keep a steady stream of revenue from providing support services. Apart from the obvious ethical problems with this approach, it's bad business. Keeping the customer reliant on you for support does not pay economic dividends because the customer will typically call with minor support issues, like adding users or restoring data, and you'll often end up giving that support away as a courtesy. Support calls inevitably come at a time when you can least afford to break away from your current engagement. The nature of technologists is that we would rather be working on the next exciting project than supporting our last implementation, so we give short shrift to the support needs of our clients. Most importantly, clients have become sophisticated in the use of consultants and understand the importance of maintaining the technology that runs their businesses. They want to be self-sufficient.

In the discussion of training above, we mentioned that training must be developed for IT support teams as well as for user teams. I have found that the simple mention of knowledge transfer during project planning gets a positive response from clients, as it demonstrates my commitment to delivering a total solution and to putting the client's interests first. Information technology consultants should work with their clients to understand what the operational support program for their new system will be and to plan for a comprehensive training program for the IT team. This program can include vendor certifications, application training, customer service training, problem management techniques, or other components, depending on the requirements.

When clients use the term "knowledge transfer," they typically refer to the participation of their IT team with the consultants in the technical implementation of the system. Clients will often request, while I'm planning the technical deliverables of a project, that I build in time to allow their team to work with my team as we install and implement the hardware and software so they can watch over our shoulders, see us deal with the inevitable problems and glitches that arise, and obtain an overall understanding of the technology. If the client does not ask for this, I encourage it. The client's team may not be able to assist in implementation, especially in cases of unfamiliar technology; also, in most cases of knowledge transfer, it actually takes longer when the client's team is watching. Still, building in knowledge transfer as part of the technical implementation is perceived by savvy clients as adding significant value to your services.

Vendor Involvement

Finally, one observation about technical implementation: Consultants often wait too long to involve the vendor of the selected technology. Technical consultants want to work through problems themselves, to meet the challenge and overcome it. It's true that we learn some of our most valuable lessons by doing the detective work necessary to troubleshoot and solve technical implementation problems. Some of the most satisfying moments of my consulting career have come when I conquered mysterious technical snafus through sheer willpower and determination.

There comes a moment, however, when the client's best interest would be better served by reaching out to the vendor of the hardware or software and utilizing the experience and specialized expertise that only they can bring. Vendors, especially vendors of successful, widely installed technology, have seen permutations and combinations that even the most specialized consultants would not see in a lifetime. They have access to the development teams that wrote the software or designed the hardware. They have installations around the world where the very problem you are banging your head against may have been solved and documented.

Working through technical problems is a large part of our value to the customer. It serves clients well because it broadens our understanding of the solution we've implemented. Deciding when we've gone as far as we can go in solving a problem is a judgment call. By keeping our eye on the client's best interests, on the client's schedule and budget, we can make the right call on seeking vendor or outside assistance.

Transition to Operations

The focus throughout this book has been on the delivery of a total solution, one that not only brings new technology to bear to solve a client's problem, but also includes the training and support elements necessary to obtain sustained results. Our advisory role does not end when the system passes its integration test or when it moves from pilot testing to full implementation. Based on our understanding of our client and the solution we've implemented and our experience with a broad range of customer situations, we can advise the client in the creation of a support structure to enable our solution to deliver benefits for years to come.

Beside the fact that it's in the customer's interest for us to help design a support and maintenance process, it's also good business. The growth of outsourcing demonstrates that clients want help with the design and delivery of these operational functions. As hardware vendors have learned, support and maintenance contracts can be a source of significant revenue and can keep relationships alive long after the initial sale or project is done. Savvy consultants can bolster their earning potential by performing a range of operational duties, from selling a block of hours for ongoing support, to offering an onsite support individual for a few hours a week, all the way through building an entire help desk, hardware maintenance, network operations, or software support team and outsourcing that to the client. Whatever the size and scope of the support services you want to provide, it's your professional responsibility to advise the client on these matters so the transition to operation is successful.

When advising clients on the creation of a support function, key points to consider are these:

- *Develop a Separate Transition Plan.* Like the too brief implementation plans I mentioned before, many project plans include a line like "Go Live" or "Put into Production." Every IT project should have a transition plan that addresses in detail the elements discussed below.

- *Include the User Community.* Individual users and groups have unique needs. Each department or location will have specific support requirements. The only way to address these needs adequately is to give those users the opportunity to participate in the design of their support. Again, apart from the functional benefits of designing support to fit the requirements, this is a marketing opportunity to show the users that we're considering their needs at every step and not imposing a "one-size-fits-all" solution.

- *Arrange for Resources.* Help by advising your client to be realistic and reasonable in estimating required resources for support. Support teams that are already overwhelmed with existing systems cannot be reasonably expected to take on more responsibility. Technicians without the expertise or experience in a specific technology will require training and ramp-up time to become effective. Also help clients arrange for the equipment that will be required, such as network management workstations or network "sniffer" devices.

- *Arrange for Special "Day-After" Support.* Studies by the Gartner Group (Raphaelian, 1995) estimate that 70 percent of user support calls occur within the first month after implementation of a new technology. By building a special support process, such as roving support teams or a special hot-line number, you begin the user's experience with the new system on a positive note.

- *Develop a Support Process.* Advise the client to utilize a structured support process that tracks requests and resolutions so that the support function can be evaluated and managed. Some applications can cope with informal "hall-call," "ask your neighbor" support systems, but business-critical systems require formal, manageable processes that can be monitored and improved so they meet the users' needs.

- *Include Vendor Support.* As part of your support package, don't neglect to include hardware and software maintenance options from the vendors of your selected technology. Most vendors offer packaged support solutions, such as Cisco Systems' "SmartNet" product that give the client direct access to the vendor's expertise.

- *Do Some Contingency Planning.* Contingency planning is a required element of operational support. It's your responsibility to guide your client toward a backup and recovery plan for both data and systems. At the least, a data backup and recovery program should be established. Business-critical systems require you to dig deeper and consider business-continuity issues such as hot spares of critical components, redundant data links, and possible off-site processing in case of an emergency.

By designing support and maintenance as integrated parts of our IT systems, we ensure that our clients can become self-sufficient, can maintain a positive relationship with their internal customers, and can keep accruing the business benefits of the systems we design.

Implementation Review

As mentioned before, one of the critical questions every consultant must ask is: "When this engagement is concluded, what will you have?" The concluding phase of implementation, the review and evaluation phase, is our opportunity to discover whether or not we have been successful in guiding the client to the achievement we visualized. We've been preparing for this evaluation from the start, by visualizing success and developing completion criteria all through the project. Now that we are nearing the completion of our engagement, we can begin to match our performance against the metrics we've devised. Most project management methodologies include the post-project review as a discrete step of the process. These evaluations are done on a formal basis, with specific steps for monitoring adherence to the budget, schedule, and performance criteria committed to at the beginning. I recommend scheduling post-project reviews in the project plan, just as milestones and status reports are integrated into the project activities. These reviews should be run as facilitated sessions, and they should be conducted in an atmosphere of continuous improvement and not blame or reward.

I'll often hold a separate review session with my consulting team only, and then hold one with the client. My experience is that there are issues that the team will feel comfortable exploring together that would not be raised with the client in the room. The knowledge that project success will be formally evaluated is an assurance factor for clients, and is a motivator to keep project participants, whether employees or subcontractors, committed and focused.

Client Acceptance

If we've worked through all of the training, communication, and implementation details and delivered an IT solution to the client that fulfills the vision we defined, it should be easy to have the client sign an acceptance document. Unfortunately, there are some ambiguities that can complicate the essential process of having the customer acknowledge that we've delivered as promised.

How do we know when the project is done? One of the shortcomings of many IT consulting engagements is that projects just peter out, as the last pieces of software are installed and the last technical glitches are worked out. Systems will often go into production mode in one department or branch office, while technical problems are unresolved or implementation activities are incomplete in another. Phased rollouts often occur, and in many cases the responsibility for implementation slowly migrates from consultants to internal teams, as the client's IT folks become more familiar with the new system and want to take more ownership of the technology. In these and many other cases, it's difficult to point to a discrete completion date when the consultant's job is done.

Some projects will have a clear cutoff date, when the consultant can say, "I'm done." Others will need a more iterative acceptance process. Whatever the case, for reasons of client satisfaction and relationship, as well as for legal reasons, it's critical to obtain a formal acceptance from the client documenting the fact that we've delivered as contracted. Some rules about gaining client acceptance follow:

- *Define Acceptance Criteria Up-Front.* I've reiterated this multiple times, but it bears repeating. Without the usual quotes from the Cheshire Cat or Yogi Berra, it's nevertheless important to remember that clear destinations make for more purposeful journeys.

- *Negotiate an End Point for Your Involvement.* In situations like those mentioned above, in which implementation duties will migrate to client IT teams, it's critical to agree on when your involvement ends and the responsibility for the deliverables moves to internal staff.

- *Acceptance Can Be Phased.* In large, multi-site or multi-department rollouts or other complex rollouts with shifting responsibilities, phased acceptance can take some of the confusion out of knowing when the project is complete. By building in acceptance along with milestone and status reporting, we can document that we've delivered as contracted in part as well as in whole and can help the customer move on from phase to phase on the road to project completion.

- *Document What You Have Delivered.* Your acceptance document should describe the objectives of the project, the deliverables you've transferred to the client, and any ongoing responsibilities such as support or maintenance. It should clearly express what the customer has received and that the customer is satisfied with the result.

Some IT project methodologies are constructed as a circle, with an "end or extend" decision point, at which point the consultant and client decide whether they want to move forward together to implement additional objectives. My experience is that this complicates the client acceptance process, as it makes project completion even more ambiguous than it already is. Any project can be extended simply by agreeing to re-engage. As long as that re-engagement follows the techniques set forth in this book, clients can be assured of a quality delivery of the objectives and goals they set with the consultant.

Smart IT consultants look at the successful conclusion of an engagement as a chance to accomplish a couple of goals: (1) to build a portfolio of reference accounts, and (2) to build a relationship with the client that survives the completion of this project. I always ask my clients whether they would be willing to act as a reference account, so that I can leverage my success with their project into a selling point with other clients. If we have delivered with quality, clients will be glad to perform this service for us. I also make it a point to get in touch with every client I've worked with periodically, to ensure that the solution I delivered still fits their needs. These two final "project closeout" activities probably account for about a quarter of all my billable work.

A few years ago there was a particularly vivid advertisement for a brand of project management software that made the distinction between the planning process and the execution process. In one panel was a crew of rowboaters taking a leisurely float down the river, with the caption: "This is project planning." In the next panel was a raft going down the rapids with the team holding on for dear life, with the caption: "This is project management." In the final installment of our case study scenario, we'll listen in as Sara and her teams experience and deal with the myriad issues that can arise in the heat of the project management battle.

References

Charan, R, & Colvin, G. (1999, June 21). Why CEOs fail. *Fortune.*

Frame, J.D. (1994). *The new project management.* San Francisco, CA: Jossey-Bass.

Kitson, E., & Masters, S. (1993). An analysis of SEI software process assessment results 1987–1991. *Proceedings of the Fifteenth International Conference on Software Engineering,* pg. 68–77. Washington, DC: IEEE Computer Society Press.

Raphaelian, G. (1995, October 23) Client/server organization and training challenges. Stamford, CT: *Gartner Analytics* (Subscription service).

Nick had recommended that Sara set up a command center in the new building, and she was glad she had taken his advice. The CapState telecom folks had given her a few phones, and they were ringing off the hook from the moment the move started. She had four separate crews working in different locations on the first night of the move, disconnecting PCs and helping the CapState Distributed Computing team prepare the servers to move. The first call she received was from Jeff, her crew leader with the Distributed Computing Group.

"Well, we took your advice and shut down the servers before we moved them," Jeff told Sara, "and now one of them won't come back up. The CapState crew chief is being a real knucklehead about it; I can tell he's trying to figure out a way to make this our fault."

"We talked about this," Sara reminded him. "Don't even engage in that conversation. We delivered a contingency plan to his boss in which we predicted that there would be some servers that wouldn't make the move, and we built some spares on this side. Just document which server it is and move on."

"He doesn't want to move on," Jeff told her. "He wants to futz around with this server and see if we can get it up. Meanwhile the clock is ticking and the movers are coming in two hours."

"Remember who the customer is," she coached him. "Our commitment is to Ron and his team, and the plan we made was to document failures and move on. If he wants to play around with the server, that's his call. You need to remain on plan and keep on moving through the servers. If the movers come and we're not ready, then that will be our fault, and that will be a bigger problem than a server that's down."

"Okay, we'll move on. Just wanted to let you know."

"Great," Sara replied. "That's just what I want—to be in the loop. Just let me know."

The second she put that phone down, another one started ringing. She pressed the speaker button so she could keep working while she talked.

"Sara, this is Eric. Problem. The tags that the moving company gave us to tag the PCs are falling off. We've had to go back and retag about half of the ones we've disconnected. If the tags are falling off sitting here on the desks, imagine what's going to happen when the movers get their hands on them. If we can't get these tags to stay on we're going to have chaos on the other side."

"Why are they falling off? Are they old tags that have lost their adhesiveness? Or what?" Sara asked. Nick walked in and sat down next to Sara. As the conversation continued, he rolled his eyes and laughed.

"CapState wanted tags that wouldn't mar the surface of the PCs," Eric reminded her, "so we used these light-adhesive peel-off tags, but they're just not sticking."

"Can you just tape a piece of paper to the PC or something?" she asked.

"I guess we could, but that's going to take time. Remember, we had the tags pre-printed with the to and from locations. We'd have to copy that off to a sheet of paper for each one. We're on a minute-by-minute schedule here."

"Well, what do you recommend?" she asked.

"I could send one of the guys out to the all-night copy store and see if they have some heavier labels, but that's going to mar the surfaces of the PCs. Or we could just write the destination in pencil on the back of the PC and erase it when we get to the other side. Or, like you said, we could just tape on a little note."

"How about if I send you an administrator to stick the labels onto sheets of paper, so you can keep moving?" she asked him. "I've got an admin here I can give up for a couple of hours."

"That would be great; then whatever we decide to do I can get the admin to help us and we can keep on going forward."

"This is the kind of stuff that comes up when you're in the thick of it," Nick told her after she hung up. "It's never the technical stuff that you spent all day worrying about; it's whether the little stickers stay on the computers."

After a couple of hours, the first wave of PCs started to show up on the moving trucks. Sara's crew of installers began to place some of them on the high-priority desktops. Less then twenty minutes after they began, Bobby, the crew chief, came running in to the command center: "Sara, Nick! We've got a major political problem here. Some of the PCs are coming in with no memory. It looks like somewhere between the old and new site, the boxes are being opened and the memory is being lifted. I've got one of the department managers standing over my shoulder, and he's acting like it's our guys who are doing it. I heard him say to one of the other CapState guys that the movers wouldn't know how to take the memory out, and then he looked at me like it was obviously us."

"This is a hot one," Nick responded. "I don't want to make a call on this. Let's bring Ron and Zane, from the moving company, in here right now."

"Jerry, please page Ron and Zane 911 to this number," Sara requested.

When Ron and Zane arrived, Sara walked them through the issue. Ron asked Bobby who on the CapState side had made remarks about blaming someone for this, and Zane asked a couple of technical questions about how long it would take to open a PC, get the memory out, and close it.

"So, Nick, what do you suggest?" Ron asked.

"First thing is that we need to figure out our recovery plan. This is one of those things that we couldn't foresee, so we don't have spare memory on hand. I'll get one of our sales reps on the phone with our distributors and get some replacement memory in here. Bobby, get a list of the types of PCs affected and how much memory we need."

"Zane," said Ron, "let's huddle about this. Sara's teams are disconnecting these PCs out in the open, and they have department managers and staff all around them packing their desks and such. I can't believe they'd be able to open PCs, even if they wanted to."

Nick and Sara spent the rest of the evening working through issues like these. They received a call from one of the crew chiefs to say that the users were milling around and getting in their way as they attempted to break down PCs. Another call came from the moving company to tell them that one of their guys dropped a server on the way to the truck. They worked through all the issues, and the evening flew by. It was one in the morning before Sara realized she hadn't eaten anything since breakfast.

The following couple of days, as they reconnected and tested all the relocated equipment, they experienced more of the same. Moving truck drivers left the old site and disappeared for hours, only to radio in from the other side of town that they were lost. Printers that were supposed to be set up by the CapState team for testing were hours late. Again Sara and Nick and their teams worked through every issue as it arose.

On the fourth day, pilot teams of users showed up to test their network connectivity and access to applications. Ron had requested that all technical teams meet him in the new auditorium after the pilot test for a review of the results.

"Well," Ron told the crowd, "I have good news and bad news. The bad news is that we had some unexpected issues, including some theft and vandalism, as well as some old hardware that just didn't make it through the move. We have some disgruntled users and department managers, and we're going to have to deal with that when we go live on Tuesday. The good news is that the steering committee met today, and we agree that you all did a great job of working through every issue that came up. I especially want to commend the Superior Systems team, who worked through the night to get our servers up and running and to implement the fallback policies we had implemented for the dead hardware. Thanks also to. . . ."

As Ron went through the list of CapState employees and contractors who had assisted in the move, Sara and Nick sighed in exhaustion. They'd made it through.

part three

Developing Superior Consulting Skills

The artist is nothing without the gift, but the gift is nothing without work.

Emile Zola

In Chapter Seven I discussed in depth the structured programming techniques that were developed in the 1970s by pioneers such as Niklaus Wirth and Larry Constantine. This period was a time of great creativity and experimentation in the realm of computer science, as researchers struggled to develop theories that would help tame this undisciplined art and turn it into a science. One of the seminal research projects of this period was the famous "superprogrammer project" (Aron, 1971). This project applied academic research techniques to the conventional wisdom that there existed some extraordinarily gifted programmers who could do the work of five or ten ordinary coders. The results of this study confirmed the existence of these "super-programmers," individuals who, through a lucky combination of skills, training, character, and desire, could become the central specialists in teams of system designers, and who could lead those teams and ultimately the organization to new heights of achievement. These findings became the basis of a type of software development unit called the "chief programmer team," an organization focused on providing the superprogrammer with the support and services required to achieve Herculean feats. This team construct is still in wide use.

This illustrates a concept I want to convey here: the idea that great variation exists in the ability of individuals to contribute to a project effort. And, as I mentioned, this ability to contribute—this high level of competence—is rooted in skills, training, character, and desire. Obviously, some of these elements are more subject to our control than others. For those of us who have the desire to be superachievers, there are techniques for advancing our skills, both interpersonal and technical, and these techniques are the subject of the following chapters. High competence enables us to become high achievers, to deliver superior results in our engagements, and to distinguish ourselves from the competition in this increasingly competitive world.

Reference

Aron, J.D. (1971). The superprogrammer project. *Software Engineering Techniques, NATO Scientific Affairs Division,* pp. 50–52.

Delivering the Full Value

*All beautiful things are made by those who strive
to make something useful.*

Oscar Wilde

LIFELONG RELATIONSHIPS

There's an expression used in the Midwest, which I heard for the first time when I moved to Kansas City a few years ago: "Stepping over dollars to pick up dimes." I think of that phrase every time I work with IT consulting teams that deliver simple technology systems to their clients when they could be delivering strategic solutions. Information technology consultants have the opportunity to build a comprehensive package of services around many of the projects we take on, yet many of us instead go for the "quick hit," offering a hardware and software based solution to our clients and neglecting the elements that can turn that technology into a complete, sustainable system. Worse then leaving money on the table, however, is walking away from potential lifelong client relationships. By learning how to deliver the value-adding ingredients of a total solution, we can create the ultimate win-win scenario: We give the client a better result, create a delighted customer who has received superior value for the money, and differentiate ourselves from the run-of-the-mill technical contractor, plus we get to bill more hours in the bargain.

I consistently see consultants struggling to meet new prospects, writing lengthy proposals for new engagements, and spending dozens of sales hours trying to get in the door at new accounts, instead of focusing on gaining depth and breadth within the accounts they already have. Every sales book ever written emphasizes the high relative cost of gaining a new client versus retaining an existing one. This is especially pertinent in our business, where every hour spent marketing or selling is an hour not spent billing. Many savvy consultants have realized that it is scope within each client, rather than the number of clients on your roster, that builds consulting practices. Being seen as a strategic partner to your clients, so that you are the one they call when they are considering any IT investment, is the ultimate compliment and the consultant's ultimate business strategy.

What are these strategic ingredients I'm referring to? They are the add-ons that allow us to turn technology, such as a local area network, into a sustainable, running business asset that is maintainable, manageable, and secure. Specifically, every IT consultant should be prepared to advise clients on the following:

- Operational policies and procedures,
- Support and maintenance services,
- Documentation,
- Asset management,
- IT human resource planning,
- IT product procurement, and
- Security.

Each of these elements is large, and many IT consultants build their careers specializing in one or another of them. I'm certainly not going to attempt to train consultants on these practices here, as each of them is worthy of a book this size. My goal here is to present a brief outline of each, in order to convince you that developing your depth of knowledge in these areas will pay returns in additional billings and, more importantly, in your feeling of accomplishment at having engaged with your clients on a strategic level and delivered a complete solution.

OPERATIONAL POLICIES AND PROCEDURES

The defining element of a complete solution is its ability to deliver business results reliably over time. Sophisticated clients have experienced "technology-driven" systems and are now smart enough to expect "process-driven" solutions. When they ask for a turnkey system, they don't just mean hardware bundled with software. They're looking for an operating environment that includes integrated network management, problem resolution procedures, software upgrade services, and hardware maintenance services, just to name a few examples. Less sophisticated clients need our advice in these areas even more.

Information technology consultants, whether they are installing a software module or a mainframe data center, should visualize what the client will need after the project is complete and they have gone. During implementation, we're around to fix the software bug or reboot the router. When we obtain the client's sign-off and leave, the client often feels panicked and abandoned. Client and consultant may have reviewed the procedure for creating a backup tape or for adding users to a group, but clients doubt their ability to remember all the details. By developing standard operating procedures for the daily tasks of running the system, we help clients become self-sufficient. We help them create a disciplined, standardized environment, as befits a critical business process.

Procedure writing is an art and is one of the most challenging tasks for any technical writer. It requires an understanding of the system itself, of the reader's technical competency, the business processes, and the organization's culture. Some IT consultants, such as those who specialize in business process reengineering or enterprise resource planning implementation, may be skilled enough to write operating procedures themselves as a billable service. Even those consultants who are not business process experts, however, can help their clients design standard procedures for tasks like the following:

- *Problem Resolution.* Give the client a path to follow when diagnosing a problem with the systems you've designed. A simple flow chart that instructs the IT staff to first check the system log, then the network management station, then restart the application, and then reboot the system can build confidence and self-sufficiency for the client. A vendor escalation list, with a roster of all the hardware and software suppliers and their technical support contact numbers, is an obvious and essential document that many consultants fail to provide.

- *Software Upgrade Services.* Clients need help defining procedures for installing hardware and software patches and upgrades. Many consultants will sell periodic software maintenance visits as part of their solutions and consider it a great annuity source of revenue as well as a chance to keep the client relationship warm. For consultants who don't want to provide these services themselves, most software vendors now offer Internet-based update subscriptions.

- *Hardware Maintenance Services.* Some consulting firms also have "break-fix" capabilities and will sell warranty upgrades or on-site maintenance services as part of their solutions. Solo practitioners can help their clients contract for these services, either from the product vendor or from independent service providers such as Decision One or IBM Global Services. Consultants should also help clients design policies for deploying spare hardware, rules and, "time windows" for performing maintenance.

- *Backup and Restoration Procedures.* All systems fail. Robust systems are recoverable. Information technology consultants must build backup and restoration capabilities into their solutions. "Capabilities" doesn't refer only to technology. Client IT teams must have a standard discipline for backing up, storing, and recovering corporate data.

- *Security.* Policies for adding and deleting users, for modifying user access rights, and for protecting data and systems must be documented. Consultants need to consider seriously their responsibility to build systems that are secure and that can be administered by the client. Website designers, for instance, have been taken to court by clients whose sites were "hacked."

In most IT shops, documented procedures for standard daily tasks are typically nonexistent or buried in an operations manual and then never referred to again. By helping our clients develop a foundation of standard processes, we give them a deeper sense of ownership and confidence in the systems they depend on.

SUPPORT AND MAINTENANCE SERVICES

The outsourcing of IT support services is one of the most influential trends in modern business. The giant IT consulting firms, such as Andersen Consulting, EDS, Computer Sciences, and many others, now derive a substantial portion of their income from relationships in which they contract to take over IT services that were formerly provided by internal staff. Some buy their clients' entire data center, including the IBM mainframes, the peripherals, and applications, and may even take on the existing IT staff, and then sell it all back to their customer in the form of a guaranteed service level. Others focus on the network, providing offsite network monitoring combined with onsite help desk and hardware repair services. Whatever the permutation, the trend toward supplying clients with packaged support services is profound for all IT consultants. Whether or not outsourcing is a part of your consulting business model, this trend demonstrates that clients understand the importance of a successful support system and that they believe IT specialists can provide these services better than they can internally.

Whether you are a member of a large-firm consulting team or an independent working out of your basement, you can help clients support and maintain the systems you implement. The large-firm consultant can migrate clients into an outsourced model, taking over some of these support services, thereby developing the project-oriented relationship into an operational partnership. Independents not prepared to deliver outsourced services can sell ongoing support in the form of a prepaid retainer. Other consulting services could include advising the client in the design of support and maintenance procedures and helping to evaluate service providers.

Support services that some clients might need to consider are:

- *Help Desk.* Most clients with more than about 250 users will want a central facility for answering system questions, reporting outages, and tracking adds and changes. Many organizations use complex, industry-specific applications and must provide access to expert advice for their users.

- *Laptop Depot.* Clients with mobile work forces, such as sales organizations or insurance adjusters, use laptops as an integral part of their business. They cannot be without these devices and so require a depot where users can drop off a problem device for repair and borrow one that's working.

- *Moves, Adds, and Changes.* Workers and teams move around; employees leave and are replaced; companies upsize, downsize, and rightsize. Devices need to be moved. For large companies, IMACs (installs, moves, adds, changes) can be a resource-intensive and demanding activity. Consultants can help clients develop optimized processes for the deployment of systems.

By cultivating our foresight into the future needs of our clients we can learn to help them become self-reliant.

DOCUMENTATION

I'm going to make a strong statement here: I've *never* seen an IT operation that was properly documented. From the major New York banks and brokerages where I spent my early career, to the manufacturers, hospitals, and retail chains I've had as clients, every single IT shop neglects documentation. There are lots of reasons for this: Technicians don't like to document and typically aren't good at it, systems change so fast that by the time something is recorded the documentation is obsolete, there are no standards or models for IT teams to use when writing documentation, and so on. Yet it's clear that lack of documentation hurts maintenance and upgrade activities tremendously. With no map of the existing network, how does an IT team know where to place the new router in order to enhance throughput? With no operating manual, where does the nontechnical user turn for detailed information on performing a complex transaction? With no record of the interaction between applications, how does a software developer predict the effect a new module will have on the overall system?

We've discussed, as an integral part of our IT Consulting Framework, the documentation that should accompany any system we deliver. But project-specific documentation is only one part of an IT organization's needs. You can fulfill your role as a strategic partner by helping clients to develop a complete process to document their IT architecture and to maintain that documentation so that it remains relevant.

It's usually during a project effort that clients realize how inadequate and outdated their current documentation is. Although, as noted in Chapter Six, I always ask to review the existing diagrams, maps, flow charts, and manuals, I've learned from experience that I'm more likely to get a sheepish look than I am to find any meaningful documents. When documents are forthcoming, they usually come with the disclaimer that they're out-of-date, incomplete, and inaccurate.

Skilled advisors can use this opportunity to the benefit of the client. By diplomatically illustrating the importance of valid documentation during our project efforts, we can prepare clients to make the necessary investment in time and talent to produce it. I'm not suggesting that we necessarily contract to write this documentation ourselves; for many of us that would be a poor use of our skills. My proposal is that, as strategic advisors, we counsel our clients on the importance of a good documentation program, we help them identify information that needs to be recorded, and we assist them in finding, either internally or externally, the resources to keep their documents current and complete.

Some of the types of documentation we should advise clients to consider are listed below:

Project Records. As discussed previously, every project should have a record that includes the following elements:

- The original request that initiated the project,
- Any RFPs or proposals,
- The project vision statement or project description,
- Project plans, budgets, and schedules,
- Project work papers, milestones and status reports, and presentations,
- Any agreements with consultants or other contractors,
- Records of any testing or validation,
- Implementation records, and
- Close-out documents.

Systems Documents. When projects become operational systems, those systems need to be documented for future maintenance and support. System documentation should include:

- A system concept statement,
- System specifications,
- System work flows or flow charts,
- Technology infrastructure components,
- Application components and version levels,
- Source code,
- Data layouts and schemas,
- Inputs, such as data-entry screens,
- Outputs, such as reports,
- Operations manuals for users, and
- Maintenance manuals for IT teams.

Information Technology Architecture Diagrams. Diagrams of the technology infrastructure include:

- Network topology map;
- Network components map: servers, routers, hubs, and switches;
- Interconnection map: data links, such as T1 lines, dial-in lines, wiring closets;
- Network addressing schemes: TCP/IP addresses and MAC addresses, for instance; and
- Protocol maps: map of protocols supported on various network segments.

Operational Procedures: The procedures required to keep the organization's data-processing plant running, including:

- An overall IT plant description, including data centers in operation, their locations, hours of operations, and special purposes;
- Detailed listing of all hardware and software components, operating systems, revision levels, and patches;
- Start-up, shutdown, and reboot procedures;
- Backup and recovery procedures;
- Disaster plans;
- Setup instructions for any special jobs;
- User maintenance procedures, such as password resets and user addition/deletion;
- A contact list of all key personnel in case of emergency; and
- Security, user rights and allowances, and any accounting or charge-back procedures.

This is just a representative listing. Other types of documentation that are commonly maintained are workstation standards, approved application lists, system performance baselines and audits, and IT job descriptions. To fully add value in advising on documentation, we should assist the client in designing an ongoing documentation maintenance program. For clients with deep budgets, this can mean the creation of a permanent staff whose only responsibility is to keep records up-to-date. For most clients, however, documentation maintenance will take the form of documentation standards that apply to every new project undertaken, and perhaps to a periodic "spring cleaning" type of review, during which documentation is examined on a periodic schedule and updated as appropriate.

Some consultants take a unique approach to documentation: They write the operating manual first, then use it as the design specification for the system. By working with the client to develop a manual that reflects the functionality the customer wants, these consultants create a detailed design document that can be followed closely by the development team, with the added bonus that when the system is delivered, the documentation is nearly complete. This approach can be taken not only with software design, but with IT architecture design as well. By documenting the "to-be" design up-front, we can come to a clear understanding of the client's requirements, build to those specifications, and deliver a documented system. The downside to this is the possibility that we become married to a specific design too early in the process. With this caveat in mind, however, the design of system documentation early in the process can set a powerful precedent that can be followed throughout the engagement and ensure that the client receives a fully documented solution.

Documentation projects are not trivial. A project focused solely on diagramming a wide area network or documenting an existing bank lending application clearly could be lengthy and complex. It requires you to delve deeply into the client's business, which is part of the point. Documentation, like these other value-added services, crosses the line that separates projects from operations. It allows you to develop your client relationships by migrating to more customer-intimate activities. These services give you the chance to "touch" the organization at a strategic level and profoundly influence the way they conduct business.

ASSET MANAGEMENT

Fifteen years ago, the assets of most IT departments consisted of mainframes, cluster controllers, and huge disk drives, along with assorted card readers and CRTs. Since the PC and distributed computing took over, however, the assets of the IT group are dispersed throughout the organization. Many are mobile, such as laptops and at-home PC's. In many organizations, purchasing and control of these devices is decentralized. Many users go to CompUSA and buy software and then install it on their office PC's. Obviously, keeping track of the ownership, whereabouts, and configuration of PC's and networks is difficult.

Yet it is crucial. Every project manager planning a network migration needs a record of the hardware and software that make up the server infrastructure in order to design the right migration, continuity, and contingency plans. Every consultant managing a desktop upgrade project needs an accurate inventory of the applications in use for compatibility and testing purposes. Any attempt to measure the total cost of ownership or return on investment of IT technology will require asset inventory numbers for calculations. Any major project planning effort requires, as part of the "as-is" analysis, a catalogue of existing devices.

Consultants can assist clients in managing their assets by helping them select from these approaches:

- *Outsourcing of Asset Management.* There are many companies that will take full responsibility for a client's asset management operation, performing an initial inventory, entering it into an asset management database, and maintaining it.

- *Consulting on Asset Management System Implementation.* Many consulting shops will help clients build their own asset management systems by reviewing their purchasing and deployment trends and procedures and helping them decide where in the process asset data should be captured, where it should be stored and manipulated, the types of reporting required, and the process for maintaining the data. This could be a service you decide to provide, or you can assist clients in selecting specialists.

- *Building Asset Management In-House.* Many organizations decide that asset management is a core competency, and that there is strategic value to developing the in-house expertise to plan, design, and manage an asset management capability. For organizations that are reliant on cutting-edge technology, and so refresh their technology frequently, it may be more cost-effective to own this task rather than pay an outside agency to administer it. For some companies there may be security or competitive reasons to keep information about their use of technology secret. Some companies have a robust asset management system in place for control of non-computer assets, and adding technology to that system is simply more cost-effective than building a whole new system.

Whatever approach the client decides to take in sourcing asset management, a good asset management program should address the following:

- *Current Inventory.* What is the state of any current inventories? Are there any practices in place?

- *Acquisition Process and Rules.* How are hardware and software assets acquired? Is this strictly controlled or can users go to Best Buy and install any software they want on company PC's?

- *Software License Tracking.* Is a process in place?

- *Current Level of Compliance.* Based on any existing inventory data, is the company in compliance with software laws or does a "crash program" need to be implemented?

- *Level of Inventory Detail.* Is there value to the organization in recording inventory data to a very granular level? For instance, some companies will upgrade PC's rather than replace them. These clients may need to record information on add-in cards and peripherals.

- *Asset Management Database.* How will the inventory data be recorded and manipulated?

- *Asset Tagging.* Will assets be tagged, for instance with a bar-code system?

- *Periodic Audit Process.* How will compliance with asset management policies be enforced?

I was involved in a consulting engagement this year in which a major regional cable television provider was raided by the Software Publisher's Association, who police software piracy, and threatened with public exposure and legal action unless proof of ownership of all software was provided. This company had no asset management policy, and their purchasing records were inaccessible or incomplete. An emergency asset management system had to be implemented, which was intrusive, disruptive, and expensive. Every single PC in this 20,000-person company had to be individually inventoried. This effort took four consultants, including a database administrator and a project manager, and six inventory technicians, lasted six months, and was considered 75 percent accurate at its completion due to ongoing changes. The effort cost almost $1 million, which was expensive but nowhere near the $20 million the SPA estimated their lawsuits could cost the company.

Once this forced effort was completed, however, this cable company found the information so valuable to their ongoing development and maintenance efforts that it has become a critical part of their IT strategy. Their asset management system has since been enhanced to reside on the corporate intranet with a web interface, so departmental managers can track the software compliance of their teams, and so project managers can review system hardware and software configurations online before planning a migration or upgrade.

IT HUMAN RESOURCE PLANNING

In my engagements I often run into a scenario like this:

> The client calls me into an office and shuts the door. He then consults the staff roster and asks me: "What do you think of Ronnie? How would you rate Ronnie's technical skills? What about project management skills? How would you rate his maturity? What about Nancy?"

These conversations can be sticky, because you need to be an honest advisor, yet you must be sensitive to team dynamics as well as people's livelihoods. Rather than engaging in a personality dialogue, however, I recommend offering to help the client develop an IT staffing plan. Advise the client that you will help catalog not only the technology skills you believe the team needs, but the project, business, and relationship skills as well.

Few IT consultants are professionally prepared to go too deeply into their clients' HR functions. Where we can help, however, is in developing the philosophies behind recruiting and retaining an IT team. We can help our clients in the following ways:

- *Prepare Recruitment Profiles.* These would include the technical, project, and consulting skills mentioned above.

- *Prepare Team-Development Programs.* We can advise our clients on certifications and vendor training programs that would be beneficial.

- *Develop Career Paths.* We can work with the client to create job descriptions that define the roles and responsibilities of positions within the team.

- *Develop Evaluation Programs.* We can help clients define performance criteria for IT staff.

When the client asks your advice about an IT team, that is a measure of superior trust and confidence. I've been asked by many clients to interview candidates for their teams, to reassure them that the recruits had the right stuff. I recommend extreme caution when directly influencing hiring decisions; as with technology decisions, the client must own the decision, and you must be an advisor only.

IT PRODUCT PROCUREMENT

Unlike the custom-coded systems of the mainframe days, many of the solutions we design today are composed of packaged software and off-the-shelf hardware. Some of our clients will have relationships with computer resellers or direct hardware vendors. For other customers, our ability to assist in the procurement of hardware and software, our advice on the relative merits of one brand of server over another, for instance, and our influence with vendors in negotiating better pricing and warranty terms can be valuable.

Many large IT consulting firms of today have their roots in the PC reseller channel. As the margins have eroded in the hardware business, these firms have realized that in order to survive they need to migrate to a services-based business model. For these companies and for their consulting teams, the inclusion of hardware and software in an integrated package is a natural fit, building on expertise and business relationships that already exist. For many solo practitioners, and for consultants who work for services-only firms, bringing products into the solution mix can be a bit more difficult. Yet most of the systems we design today are based on an architecture of industry standard products, such as Cisco routers, Dell servers, Novell NetWare network software, and Microsoft Office applications, for example. Clients, especially smaller ones who lack internal purchasing agents and pre-negotiated volume discounts, can benefit from our advice and assistance in the product procurement process.

Some of the ways we can assist clients in this process follow:

- *Keep Up with Developments.* Whether it's *Data Communications* or *Network Computing* magazine for the network infrastructure components, or *PC Magazine* or *InfoWorld* for desktop applications, there are many sources that consultants can use to keep abreast of the latest developments in the industry.

Reviews, product "shootouts," and evaluations in these trade publications can help consultants make informed suggestions to clients, and the columns and case studies can help you avoid known bugs and advise your clients of "work arounds" for solving specific problems.

- *Develop Vendor Relationships.* Most vendors have programs specifically designed to help consultants offer their products to clients. From Microsoft's Solution Provider program to Gateway's Reseller Partner program, vendors want to make it easy for you to recommend their products, to support them after the sale, and to receive expert advice so you can configure and maintain solutions based on their products. Microsoft's *TechNet* CD, published monthly, and Novell's *Support Connection* CD set are specifically designed to provide consultants with the latest information on product lines, new products, known bugs, and innovative uses of the technology. Visit the websites of vendors whose products fall into your area of specialization and join reseller partnering programs to gain the advantage of direct support from your vendors of choice.

- *Develop Local Relationships.* Many local hardware and software resellers will welcome the chance to partner with a consultant in order to sell products to your client accounts. This can be a classic win-win scenario: Product-focused vendors have the opportunity to sell more products, often into accounts for which they have no relationships, and you can broaden your scope of services to include product procurement—and perhaps support and maintenance services, if your reseller provides those.

- *Help Your Client Negotiate.* If your client will purchase system components, help find the best deal by keeping in touch with the latest products and prices and by advising your client to build the appropriate warranty and support provisions into contracts or purchasing arrangements.

- *Help the Client Develop Vendor Relationships.* If you have a relationship with your local Microsoft or Compaq representative, for instance, and those products are part of your solution, bring the rep to your client's site. Show the vendor that you are using their products to deliver solutions, and show the client that you have good relationships with the vendors that the client will be relying on for their business systems. This raises your standing in the eyes of the vendor, who sees you advocating and integrating products into customer solutions, and it is another reassurance factor for the client, allowing the client to develop a direct relationship with the vendor.

In the quest for a total solution, our ability to add value to the product procurement process is another way we can broaden the scope of services we bring to the table.

SECURITY

In these Internet-focused times, mention of security often brings to mind the latest hacker penetration of a high-profile website or the latest virus scare. Security, however, is a much broader topic and covers everything from the physical security of the servers or data center to the assignment of user access rights, to the policies regarding e-mail message content and the disposition of reports produced by data systems. As mentioned earlier, apart from our professional responsibility to deliver a complete solution, consultants now need to consider legal liabilities as well. We must be prepared to advise clients on data security, system access security, physical data center security, and virus protection, as well as contingency plans and backup-and-restoration policies, all of which fall under the umbrella of security.

Obviously, the size, scope, and nature of your engagement will determine how stringently you need to review security options. The e-commerce developer, creating a website that will accept customer credit card data, needs to evaluate security concerns at a deeper level then the C programmer designing a reporting module. As an example, in my work as a member of the Security Cross-Functional Committee for a major New York bank, we developed detailed policies regarding the shredding of reports, including instructions as to whether single-shreddings or multiple shreddings were required for certain bank loan reports. This is obviously overkill in most situations. When we broaden our definition of security to include such things as virus protection and contingency planning, however, it should be clear that IT consultants must apply some consideration to security in almost every engagement.

Security is an area in which, if your application calls for it and it is not your specialty, I strongly recommend that you engage (or advise the client to engage) a specialist. Whether you are developing security plans yourself or working with a specialist, here are some of the issues you should consider.

Access Security

- How are users added and deleted from systems? On whose authority?
- How are the access rights of those users determined?
- How are hirings and firings communicated, so that access rights can be controlled?
- How are passwords administered? Are there password protection and periodic change policies?
- Are unauthorized access attempts tracked?
- Are Internet-connected networks secured by firewalls or proxy servers?
- Are administrators and others with specialized access rights monitored?

Data Center Security

- Are data centers or servers locked or access-controlled?
- Are there key-card readers or other tracking devices?
- Are data centers properly protected against fire, excess heat, power outages, and construction hazards?

Contingency Planning

- Are there disaster recovery plans in place? Are they current?
- Is data stored in an offsite location?
- Are backup and restoration plans in place?
- Is there a backup processing site in case of flood, earthquake, or other natural disaster?
- Are contingency duties assigned?
- Are there periodic run-throughs of contingency plans?

Virus Protection

- Is virus protection software in place on all servers and desktops?
- Is there a virus "SWAT team" ready to deploy?
- Is there a policy about, and communication to users about, the use of downloaded or borrowed software?

This list is meant to be a representative sample and is necessarily an incomplete examination of this complex subject. Data encryption, e-mail policies, report retention standards, and firewall and proxy server use, as well as many other topics, must be explored, and policies determined, with your clients.

CONCLUSION

This chapter, I hope, makes a couple of clear points:

- The deployment of technology-only solutions, without these value-added elements, does a disservice to our clients, and
- By developing our capabilities in these areas, and by including them in every system we design, we deliver superior solutions and elevate our strategic value to our clients.

chapter eleven

Troubleshooting the Consulting Relationship

*Advice is seldom welcome; and those who want it the most
always like it the least.*

The Earl of Chesterfield

INERTIA AND MOMENTUM

Engineers, whether designing cars or spaceships, need to deal with physical forces like inertia and momentum. Consultants must also develop strategies for dealing with outside forces. In engineering, these forces are based on the immutable laws of physics and are ignored at the engineer's peril. In consulting, inertia and momentum, as we discussed in Chapter Five, are based on laws of human emotion and are ignored at the peril of the engagements we undertake.

Yet many consultants discount these forces. They attempt to convince themselves that if they focus solely on delivering technical excellence to their clients, they can bypass the complex and uncomfortable world of politics, compromise, conflict, and influence. Yet, as we've seen throughout this book, technical solutions never exist in a vacuum. The human aspects of the advisory relationship, which we've emphasized throughout, are designed to help us anticipate and prevent some of the more common and obvious problems of the consulting relationship. No measure of anticipation, however, can inoculate consultants from the need to exercise political skills, to influence others to achieve project goals, to overcome resistance and fear, and to negotiate and compromise in order to consummate our commitments to our clients.

It's also critical to acknowledge that consultants are uniquely vulnerable to political pressures. As outside contractors, we typically have no positional or formal authority to compel anyone to take our advice or follow our direction. For that reason, any decisions that are made or actions that are taken on our projects are based solely on our ability to persuade and influence. We typically cannot wield the usual tactics of corporate power, such as employee evaluations or performance reviews. As much as we may scorn and condemn organizational politics, every experienced consultant will agree that adept use of power, influence, negotiation, and compromise are as central to our success as knowledge of our technical disciplines.

POLITICS

All projects, in fact all human activities, involve compromise and conflict. Decisions must be made regarding the allocation of scarce resources. Features and benefits must be weighed against cost, disruption, and schedule. The desires of one department or stakeholder must be balanced against those of another. Whether it's the married couple deciding which movie to see on Saturday night or the IT department managers arguing over who controls the network, conflict and compromise are the basis of human interaction. In some cases, these decisions are made purely on the basis of merit. Only the most naïve of consultants, however, would propose that power and influence hold no sway in the outcome of these decisions.

Wherever there are conflicting desires, opposing forces, and different levels of power and authority, there are politics. It may be unfortunate, but it is nonetheless true, that many projects that would clearly be of benefit to the organization are derailed due to the inability to satisfy conflicting constituencies. Politics can kill projects. Successful consultants, however, take a positive viewpoint on the subject of politics. They understand that politics are inevitable, and the greater the scope and impact of the project, the greater the need to exercise political skill.

As mentioned above, consultants typically have no formal authority. We are *influencers,* not bosses. This lack of formal authority does not, however, imply that we have no power. Authority and influence can be developed by the adept consultant, even though we have no purse strings, titles, or promotions to brandish.

The most obvious type of authority for the consultant is *transferred authority*. The fact that we are involved in a project with the president or department head can often bestow on us some borrowed authority, so that our requests are perceived as requests of the leader. This is complicated by the fact that, as an outsider, it's difficult for us to gauge how meaningful this conferred power really is. We all know of leaders with little authority to lead and of informal lines of authority that are much more powerful than the lines on an organization chart.

As technical specialists, we can often gain the respect of technicians purely as a result of our expertise. The converse is also true: We can dilute our influence if we are perceived as "not technical enough." This is one of the reasons to keep current with developments in technology. Not only is it critical to our ability to design the best solutions, but it's also a key tool we need in our arsenal of influence.

In Chapter Ten, I noted that breadth and depth in a client's organization is a successful strategy for building a consulting business. It's also a great strategy for enhancing your authority on the projects you undertake. By developing a network of contacts in the client's company, learning the bureaucratic ins and outs of the system, and building a "favor bank" of IOUs, you can accumulate political power without resorting to the negative aspects of politics.

Because political skills are not taught in technical certification classes and because many consultants have not had political skill-building experience as inside players in large organizations, how can we develop these skills? Here are some suggestions:

- *Overcome Negativity.* Although most managers or consultants will sneer at politics and consider political activities counterproductive and inelegant, we must acknowledge that as long as there are different individuals with different desires, politics will be part of our environment. By developing a personal code of conduct that defines acceptable and unacceptable political behavior and by regarding politics as the necessary lubricant of human affairs, we can exercise political skills without become politicians.

- *Develop Your Natural Authority.* Whether you are comfortable wielding authority as a technical expert, a quiet influencer, a trader of favors and IOUs, a name dropper (as in, "I was chatting with the chairman yesterday, and he asked me to see if you would . . ."), or some combination of these, recognize the importance of working from a base of authority and develop an effective style that you can live with.

- *Understand the Political Environment.* Although there are no formal measurements for the degree of politics in an organization, everyone knows what we mean when we say: "XYZ is the most political company I've ever worked for" or "QBC is amazingly free of politics for such a large company." Just as important as it is to understand the technical "as-is" state, it is crucial to gauge the political state as well. Who has power, and who doesn't? Where are the formal lines of influence at odds with the org chart? Who wields power for the good of the organization, and who plays politics for the sheer ego gratification of it? In short, where in the organization are politics healthy, and where are they unhealthy?

- *Remain Pure.* Becoming embroiled in organizational politics has been the death knell for many consultants. The more you are perceived as a center of influence, the more folks will try to recruit you for their own ends. In almost every large project I've ever undertaken, some faction or other has tried to enlist me as a referee or an advocate. The consultant's main value, apart from technical expertise, is the ability to remain objective and without prejudice. It cannot be emphasized enough that you can easily dilute or destroy your credibility, and with it your ability to successfully advise your client, if you are viewed as siding with a faction or pursuing an agenda.

- *Learn Negotiation and Compromise.* As we discussed in Chapter Four, no consultant can be successful without a foundation of skill in negotiation and compromise. Bring facilitation skills, objectivity, and a results orientation to your project negotiations and you will be perceived as a value-adding strategic partner.

Everything we do as consultants, from the moment we approach our client to the final signoff on our deliverables, is a process of negotiation and interaction—in other words, politics. Politics themselves, despite the negative connotations, are neutral. Only the motivations and strategies behind them can be categorized as good or evil.

RESISTANCE

Many of the techniques in this book are specifically designed to preclude resistance. By building a project vision, communicating a compelling reason for change, including affected users in the decision process, and building sponsorship and momentum, we've attempted to forestall resistance proactively rather then react to it.

Despite our best efforts, however, change will generate opposition. Whether their motivation is fear of failure, the protection of power, inertia, or simply disagreement with the ends or means of your effort, "snipers" and resisters can and will sink your project.

Dealing with resistance is an intricate exercise. Its motivations, such as fear, are based on desires for prestige and self-preservation. Resistance manifests itself in mysterious and indirect ways: interviews that keep being canceled, surveys that are never returned, teams that sit mute during project meetings. Consultants must learn to look beneath the exterior, to use experience, compassion, and empathy to identify resistance and address it. I say "address it" rather than "overcome it," because I don't believe it's our duty to roll over resisters, to sell them, or to convince them. Resistance is a positive tool for the client and the consultant. It indicates places where we have done an inadequate job of communicating, justifying, reassuring, or involving our customers. Our job is not to persuade every single individual in the organization to "drink the Kool-aid," but to do the necessary preparation to deliver the business results. Judgment calls must be made regarding the depth of consensus required to move forward. As results-oriented consultants, we want to avoid "analysis paralysis," a disease of endless consensus building that's fatal to projects. Yet we obviously must build a foundation of agreement before proceeding.

I'm reluctant to call these tips for dealing with resistance a "strategy," because that wording makes it seem like a scheme rather than a human interaction. Whether we're working with a group that has doubts about the compelling need to migrate from the old system, or with an individual who is spreading negative rumors about the project, I recommend a simple set of ideals:

- *Assume Resistance Is Your Fault.* Look at yourself and the way you've conducted this engagement and assume that resistance is due to your errors in communication, specification, or politics. Review your own behavior and consulting skills before you analyze the client.

- *Do Not Assume Bad Intent.* In many cases, people resist your ideas because they're bad ideas, not because people are stupid, stubborn, or cowardly. Your ideas may be technically correct, but totally inappropriate for the organization, the department, or simply for that individual. Again, look to your solution and its suitability first.

- *Approach Resistance with Compassion.* Look for the underlying human motivations that are driving the resistance, then work together with the client to devise a counterstrategy.

- *Take Your Ego and Emotion Out of It.* Don't interpret resistance to the project as resistance to you or to your expertise. Only by bringing maturity and lack of ego to the challenge of resistance can we overcome it.

- *Help the Client Take the Emotion Out.* Try to help the client separate the emotional content from the technical and business content. By listening actively, rephrasing and clarifying, and remaining impartial and nonjudgmental, we can help identify the real issues.

- *Be Prepared to "Agree to Disagree."* Dealing with resistance is not a contest you must win. Some resisters will continue to resist. Do your best to build consensus, then move on.

Although it may not be encouraging to the novice consultant, experience is a great teacher in these areas. Seasoned consultants learn when an unreturned phone call means a busy client and when it means a political problem that must be addressed. As we work with many clients in diverse circumstances, we learn how to use political skill to the client's advantage and how to diagnose relationship issues before they become problems. I hope I've been able to convince IT consultants that this most high-tech of professions requires the deepest of human relationship skills.

A Blueprint for Development

*On the mountains of truth you can never climb in vain: either you
will reach a point higher up today, or you will be training your powers
so that you will be able to climb higher tomorrow.*

Friedrich Nietzsche

ENHANCING COMPETENCE

The information technology that is the IT consultant's stock-in-trade has completely changed the competitive business landscape. Internet access to detailed information on price, performance, and competitive offerings has leveled the playing field for consumers of everything from stocks and bonds to automobiles and computer software. No matter what products or services our clients are selling, their potential customers can now choose from a global marketplace, with choices that are unrestricted by location and local availability. Electronic commerce and worldwide overnight delivery are making the textbook fantasy of "perfect competition" a reality.

These developments create a competitive environment in which organizations must become as productive and cost-efficient as possible. The explosion in the use of consultants and other outsourced resources is one effect of these changes. Consultants, project managers, and outsourced service providers, however, add nothing to the competitiveness of their clients unless they bring enhanced competence to the engagement. In this climate, where organizations depend on information technology as a baseline condition of entry into the global market, the competence that we as IT consultants contribute can be a make-or-break element for our clients.

Obviously, these competitive pressures affect us and our marketplace as well. Clients are more sophisticated technically and can no longer be dazzled by technobabble or "speeds and feeds." Many are also experienced in the effective use of consultants and can look beyond the merely technical to gauge our competence as team players, communicators, and strategic business advisors. As the use of consultants expands, the pool of experienced clients grows as well, challenging each of us to develop our repertoire so we can distinguish ourselves from the crowd.

Staying current with developments in technology is clearly not enough. To elevate your game as a consultant, you need to develop business skills, project skills, communication skills, and a multitude of additional proficiencies. In this final chapter, we'll cover an approach to skill development that will help us keep broadening our horizons and increasing our value to the clients we serve. Whether we work for ourselves as independent contractors or are employees of professional services firms, our career development as IT consultants is largely our own responsibility. By applying a disciplined planning process to that development, we can ensure that we continue to derive the pleasure and payoff of remaining at the top of our game.

A CAREER DEVELOPMENT PROCESS

Throughout this book, we've taken complex problems and applied structured processes to their solution. Career development is another difficult and complicated activity that lends itself to a process-driven solution. In fact, the simple steps of the consulting method that we identified in the beginning chapters of this book, in which we assess the as-is state, visualize the desired to-be condition, and perform a gap analysis, can form the basis of a personal development process. The consulting and analysis process, used by organizations and their advisors to design strategies and development plans for their enterprises, can help the individual practitioner create a personal road map to lifelong professional development. In fact, I suggest that consultants look at career development planning much as companies look at strategic planning, as an ongoing exercise that uses the discipline of periodically reviewing and assessing their current state of competitiveness and then creating a plan of action to enhance their positions.

PROFILING OUR SKILLS

Assessing the as-is state of our competencies is known in the training and development industry as *profiling*. Because career development for consultants is largely an individual responsibility, profiling is a self-discovery process that requires maturity, honesty, and self-awareness. Each of us who chooses to engage in a personal development regimen must first look inward and determine where our strengths lie in the disciplines of consulting; and then we must decide on which skills we need to concentrate our development efforts. Because self-assessment can be difficult, professional career coaches have developed tools and techniques to stimulate and guide this activity. The first, and most obvious, is a series of questions that can help us appraise and categorize our own skills and competencies, as follows:

- What do you do in your work as a consultant that often gets good results?
- What do you often struggle with in your consulting work?
- Which skills and talents do you believe your clients value highly?
- Which parts of the IT consulting profession appeal to you the most? Which appeal to you the least?
- Which personal values do you believe you bring to your consulting work that make you effective?

Notice that these questions are focused on results and on past success or difficulty. When self-assessment questions are framed in this way, most consultants find it easy to state that they, for instance, love the detective work of troubleshooting a system problem and dislike the tasks of paperwork and billing, or that they believe clients prize highly communication skills but that they personally abhor presenting to an executive committee meeting. By focusing on capabilities in the context of the work we need to accomplish, we can target areas for improvement, based not on a negative assessment of our individual talents, but on building competence in the skills we need for the task at hand.

Other tools that development coaches recommend for self-assessment include the use of the following:

- *Success Stories.* By focusing on real-world situations in which we have successfully applied our skills to the solution of a client problem or the delivery of a superior solution, we can highlight our strengths to obtain a clearer picture of our current competencies. Conversely, failure stories, while perhaps not as pleasant, can, if honestly applied, help us determine our target areas for development.

- *Typical Day.* This exercise is similar to the visualization techniques we discussed earlier; by imagining the tasks that we would encounter in a typical day as an IT consultant, we can ask ourselves which skills help us succeed at those tasks and which we could develop further to allow us to be more effective.

- *Work History.* By walking through our personal work history, we can ask ourselves which skills we developed and improved on to allow us to progress from, for instance, desktop technician to network designer. We can then extrapolate those developments to ask what skills we need to move to the next level in our career growth.

The result of this self-review should be a skills inventory, whether formal or informal. By documenting our findings, we have a baseline by which to target our efforts and measure our progress. Keeping in mind some broad categories, such as technical, advisory, business, and project skills, and outlining our specific comfort and competence in these areas, we can create an informal scorecard to guide the targeting and execution activities to come.

TARGETING OUR DEVELOPMENTAL NEEDS

In professional career development, the prioritization of developmental goals is often driven by the strategic needs of the organization. Projections of human resource requirements, prospective job openings, and new strategic directions or areas of business development will all influence the objectives of a corporate development program. Similarly, the IT consultants must perform an analysis of their business direction to determine where development efforts should be concentrated. Although it's clear that competence in technology, communication, and business skills are required, how to translate that into a specific plan of action may not be obvious. Our technology concentration will be different if our practice is moving toward a specialization in Internet development than it would be if we were focusing on implementing ERP solutions. Our communications skills-development program will differ sharply if our daily engagements bring us in contact with the owners of automobile service stations versus Fortune 500 executives. If we are specializing in selling accounting packages to CPAs, our business context skills should develop differently than if we are targeting law firms with document management software.

Additionally, current circumstances may drive us to develop a particular skill at a particular time. The fact that we have a remote-access project coming up in the next few months will obviously give us an incentive to brush up on those technical skills. In the same way, an impending presentation to a senior management committee will inspire us to prepare, practice, and rehearse in order to refresh our presentation skills. Doing our homework about the issues affecting the specific industry for a prospective client is also a form of circumstance-driven personal development.

By using the analytical skills we have developed as consultants and by reviewing our profile, skills inventory, business projections, and circumstances, we can create a prioritized developmental target that will be our focus through our career-long learning effort.

EXECUTING THE DEVELOPMENTAL PROGRAM

Now that a career development program is a key component of your success as a consultant, this does not automatically translate into action. One of the difficulties of executing a program like this is the simple mathematics of business. Every hour spent in development is an hour not spent on billable activity. Every personal hour spent in development is an hour not spent rejuvenating from the pressures and stresses of the consulting lifestyle. For these reasons, the best laid plans of self-development often go unfulfilled.

Yet it's critical that we overcome these obstacles if we want to remain valuable to our clients and fulfilled in our work. Some of the techniques I have found to be useful in motivating me to execute my development plan are as follows:

- *Build Development Time into Your Billing Rate.* Many consultants build their rate structure by guesswork, or by working backward from their household budget, or by some other less-than-scientific method. I recommend performing a financial analysis that factors in sales, marketing, and personal development activities, estimates their proportion of time versus billable hours, and builds these activities into billing rates. Apart from the "reality check" that this exercise provides, it has the psychological benefit of allowing you to feel as though you are being paid for the marketing and development efforts you put forth. It also allows you to budget time for these activities without feeling that you're stealing from your earning potential.

- *Make Development a Social Activity.* By joining user groups or consulting associations or by partnering and networking with other IT consultants, you can mix skill development with social activity. This is the concept behind successful organizations such as Toastmasters, and it can make development an enjoyable activity that you look forward to, rather than a necessary evil.

- *Build in Financial Rewards.* If you believe that your new-found skills permit you to charge your client a higher billing rate (and competitive pressures allow that), then reward yourself by giving yourself a raise. Some consultants will develop a personal "pay for certifications" program, for instance, by targeting a specific technical certification and then raising their rate by $10 an hour when they achieve it.

These techniques can help us to motivate ourselves and to continue on the path to continuous improvement of our skills.

Developing Technology Skills

One of the central premises of this book is that IT consulting is a profession on a par with engineering and architecture. One price of entry into those professions, and other professional callings such as law and medicine, is the requirement for continuing education. In an industry like ours, in which the specialized knowledge required changes as rapidly as in any of these other professions, keeping up with change is especially critical.

Technology skills become stale at an extraordinary rate. The explosion of Internet-based technology in the last five years has created entirely new areas of specialization. Who had ever heard of HTML, Java, or web-page design five years ago? Now specialists in these technologies constitute a large proportion of IT consultants. In the same way, gigabit ethernet, voice over IP, firewalls, proxy servers, Linux, and who knows what else between the time I write this and the time you read it. The body of technical knowledge that we need to keep up with grows and mutates at a geometric rate, and our clients expect us to have insight into these subjects and what they mean to their businesses.

Obviously, keeping on top of our technical discipline and expanding our range of technical understanding are central. I've reviewed many of the tools and techniques I recommend for achieving this, so I'll just mention them briefly in this chapter.

Trade Publications. There are over one hundred IT trade publications, ranging from the general, such as *PC Magazine* or *ComputerWorld,* to the very specific, such as *Embedded Systems Journal* or *Cabling Business.* For keeping up with the short-term gyrations and developments in technology, these publications are essential. I'm always amazed at the number of "consultants" who never read any of these; this is unacceptable on my consulting teams. It is our professional responsibility to remain informed on developments in our field.

Vendor Training. Most consultants, when thinking about vendor training, think of the formal training programs that award titles, such as Microsoft Certified Systems Engineer (MCSE) or Novell Certified NetWare Engineer (CNE). Yet vendors provide a multitude of additional training material. Both Novell and Microsoft have their own publishing companies that issue in-depth self-study material covering their entire product lines, as well as case studies, field guides, and other valuable material. Both of these vendors, and most other technology vendors, including Cisco, 3Com, Compaq, Hewlett-Packard, Nortel, and hundreds of others, publish both technical and marketing CDs periodically, designed to help sales and technical professionals keep current on their products. Develop relationships with local representatives of these companies; they are then glad to sponsor seminars, "lunch and learn" training sessions, and technical "chalk talks" for consultants and clients.

Technical Books. Of course, the bookstores are crammed with technical reference books on all things computer-related, from HTML to Java to Internetworking and all points between.

Classroom Training. There are both national chains and local independent operations focused on providing technical training to both users and technical providers.

User Groups. User groups, special interest groups, and vendor-supported forums provide an opportunity for consultants to meet and exchange information with other specialists in their discipline. Whether you are an SAP expert, a NetWare guru, or a Linux technician, there is likely a user group in your city where you can attend seminars and gatherings and gain exposure to diverse experience and knowledge in your discipline. For independent IT consultants, the Independent Computer Consultant's Association (ICCA) is a national professional organization that has local branches in most major cities. In addition to the knowledge-sharing features highlighted above, the ICCA offers consultants advice on contracts, professional standards and ethics, and practice development.

Internet. For many consultants, the first source of technical reference is the Internet. The vendor-supported sites, the communities of interest, and the user groups and discussion groups give us a forum to search for answers, to post difficult questions to a worldwide community, and to gather minute-by-minute updates on developments in both technology and business.

Team Reviews and Seminars. For those consultants who work in teams, one of the most powerful methods of development is cross-teaching. I encourage the teams I work with to teach each other the basics of each member's specialties, so that the entire team benefits from the knowledge of each member. A structured program of cross-training not only expands the team's technical depth, but gives consultants a chance to practice their presentation skills.

Technical Mentoring. I'll often team up a junior technician with a senior consultant on client projects, which allows the junior to watch and learn and to gain exposure to various clients, businesses, and technical situations.

One of the most uncomfortable situations a technical consultant can encounter is one in which the client is more in touch with an emerging technology than the consultant. Conversely, the most fulfilling of consulting situations is one in which, due to your technical expertise, you can help the client gain real business benefits from a new technology that fits all the requirements perfectly. Information technology consulting can be a lucrative and exciting business, but it requires a fundamental commitment from its practitioners to keeping their skills sharp.

Developing Business Skills

Today's hot sales approach is "customer intimacy," alternatively called "results-based selling" or "partnership selling." Rather than selling the features and benefits of your product, proponents of these techniques say, partner with your clients and help them obtain results with your product. Books like *Bottom-Line Selling* (Malcolm, 1999) or *Customer Intimacy* (Wiersema, 1996) exalt the sales professional who understands the customer's business, can review and interpret the client's financial statement, knows clients' competitive challenges, and can help clients turn the products or services sold into measurable results. In an nutshell, these books recommend that salespeople become consultants.

Yet many IT consultants cannot do these things. The number of IT consultants I've met who can read and interpret a client's financial statements could dance on the head of a pin. This is not because we're not bright enough; it's simply a matter of interest and mental bandwidth. Most of us are so busy keeping up with technical developments that we don't have a lot of time to become experts in financial analysis as well. Frankly, most of the IT consultants I've met are also not interested in doing so. For the rare IT consultant who does expend energy in these areas, however, the payoff is enormous. From the sales cycle through the design and delivery process, clients are more likely to develop partnerships, rather than mere transactional relationships, with consultants who understand their business and can add value at a strategic level.

Some of the resources consultants can explore to expand their business knowledge are listed again below:

- *Business Press. The Wall Street Journal, Fortune, Business Week,* and *Barron's.*

- *Business TV.* CNBC, PBS Nightly Business Report, CNN's Moneyline.

- *Business Books.* From books on selling to general treatises on management, through books on financial analysis, the use of a library or bookstore and the assistance of a reference librarian can add tremendously to any consultant's business background.

- *Industry Trade Publications.* For consultants specializing in a specific "vertical" industry, such as insurance or media, reading the trade publications for that industry give a valuable lesson in the language and concerns of that niche.

Every development effort we invest in for our personal growth as business experts makes our technology skills more pertinent to our customers' needs.

Developing Project Management Skills

Project management has gone, in the last twenty years, from an obscure and inconsistent specialty to a mature, systematized discipline. Much of the credit for this transformation must go to the Project Management Institute (PMI), a nonprofit professional association that has taken the lead in organizing the various areas of project management competency into a structured body of knowledge. In fact, the Project Management Body of Knowledge (PMBOK) and the Project Management Professional Certification program have made systematic study of, and certification in, project management accessible to all who are interested. As consultants, I believe we benefit from their efforts tremendously. I recommend that all IT consultants become members of the PMI, study the PMBOK, and consider taking the PMP certification program. Although the PMP test is not trivial (it's an all-day affair requiring months of study), it is a significant advantage in both the sales effort and in delivery.

Developing Communication Skills

Communication is our product. Every phase of the IT Consulting Framework is based on our ability to communicate effectively across the client's organization, with our peers and contractors, with vendors and suppliers, and with the ultimate users of our solutions. Exchanges of information about requirements, capabilities, goals and objectives, budgets, schedules—and all the other details of our complex work—must be clear and open, or we toil in vain. The inability to perform at the highest possible level of effectiveness in this area nullifies excellence in all other areas of IT consulting.

The migration from the "glass house" of the mainframe days to the desktop PC has changed the skill requirements for IT professionals. We now must communicate not only with managers, but with everyone from clerical staff to stockbrokers, all of whom depend on IT technology to do their jobs. The ability to train and support users one-on-one, to write usable documentation, to listen effectively, and to present our findings in a business-oriented, jargon-free manner has become as important to our effectiveness as our technical skill. Communication skills can be learned. The results of organizations like Toastmasters proves that folks who previously feared public speaking more than death can learn to be comfortable and confident presenters. Training programs in active listening, effective technical writing, and clear communications can help all consultants elevate their games and become better advisors.

Consultants should make development of communication skills a priority. By seeking out training, books, and videos and by embracing opportunities to give presentations to user groups, clients, prospects, and peers, even the most recalcitrant or awkward communicator can develop the skills necessary to become a confident advisor.

When we refer to communication, we are actually talking about a bundle of related skills. The abilities to speak, write, negotiate, facilitate, present, interview, persuade, and listen are equally critical to consulting success. *Advising is an interactive process.* It requires that the advisor create confidence and lead the discussion, whether a one-on-one interview or a group facilitated session, into fruitful areas of discourse. It demands of us that we clearly delineate options for the solution of technical problems, outline the pros, cons, and likely outcomes of client decisions, and persuade clients to act (for we have no authority other than our persuasiveness). We must impart both the technical and organizational aspects of an engagement to our teams and partners and must coach, mentor, and motivate our staffs or subcontractors to achieve quality in our delivery of service.

Developing Sales Skills

As mentioned before, sales professionals are using the tools of consulting to gauge their clients' business needs and to become intimate with their customers' challenges. The converse should also be true; consultants should learn some of the skills of diplomacy, persuasiveness, and marketing that sales professionals are proficient in.

Diplomacy can be in short supply for many IT consultants. I've been in countless situations in which an IT consultant either implied, or stated outright: "The person who designed the current system was a moron." Beside the obvious fact that that person was sometimes sitting at the same table, implications like this create resistance, resentment, and defiance, rather than the cooperation, trust, and enthusiasm a good advisor needs. This is not to say that we cannot be bearers of bad news. Sales professionals learn early in their careers how to inform the customer that their current situation is less than optimal without challenging the integrity or intelligence of the stakeholders.

Persuasiveness and marketing are skills of the sales pro that all consultants must acquire. Many sales training courses present a marketing methodology based on the following steps:

- *Know the Audience.* Understand who you are targeting your marketing message to, what they are likely to find persuasive, and what style and medium of presentation will be most effective for them.

- *Understand the Competition.* Other providers of products or services provide competition, but there are other competitive issues as well. For the consultant, the client's inclination to use internal staff rather than external consultants can be a competitive pressure. Technologies or solutions other than the one you are recommending can also be competitive.

- *Develop a Competitive Strategy.* Once you understand the audience and the competition, develop a competitive strategy. Decide how you propose to persuade this audience, with these competitors, that your service or solution is superior.

Some sales strategies delve much more deeply. Proprietary sales systems, such as the highly successful Target Account Selling® program developed by Target Marketing International, Inc., present a structured sales process that requires sales professionals to perform an in-depth opportunity assessment, to build a comprehensive competitive strategy, to identify the key players and to categorize them as friends, foes, mentors, or enemies, and then to plan and test various selling strategies based on the specific situation.

I've seen IT consultants who have participated in these sales programs become not just better at selling, but better advisors and consultants. The skills taught at these seminars are not new; they are all borrowed from the consulting skill set. Techniques that help us understand our clients as individuals, dig into their unique problems and opportunities, assess their cultures, identify traits of their key players, and then create custom strategies to guide them toward success are what consulting is all about.

It should be gratifying for all consultants to see that our specialty has progressed from the cliché that we "borrow your watch to tell you the time, then keep the watch," to the current realization that every facet of business, from sales through management, benefits from the consultative approach.

References
Malcolm, J. (1999). *Bottom-line selling.* Lincolnwood, IL: Contemporary Books.
Wiersema, F. (1996). *Customer intimacy.* Los Angeles: Knowledge Exchange.

Conclusion

*There's only one corner of the universe you can be certain of improving,
and that's your own self.*

Aldous Huxley

In my practice as a trainer of consultants, I often refer my classes to a diagram I call "the cornerstones of a successful consulting practice." It's a pretty simple diagram for such a portentous title, as you can see in Figure 13.1.

The figure illustrates the three factors that the manager of a consulting practice must keep an eye on. Obviously, *financial achievement* is essential. We, as business people, must be sure that our billable utilization and the rates we charge our clients remain at a level that compensates us for the work we do. I want to conclude, however, by focusing on the other two factors in my diagram, *customer satisfaction* and *consultant satisfaction*.

My ideas about consulting are not original; they have developed as a result of the talented consultants I've known and the books I've read. Two of the authors I especially admire, Elaine Biech and David Maister, have one thing in common: They both strongly advocate the customer satisfaction guarantee. When you review the sample proposal in Appendix B, you'll see that I include a guarantee when I propose on engagements. My aim with this book has been to prepare consultants, through the use of a structured delivery discipline, to help clients obtain the results

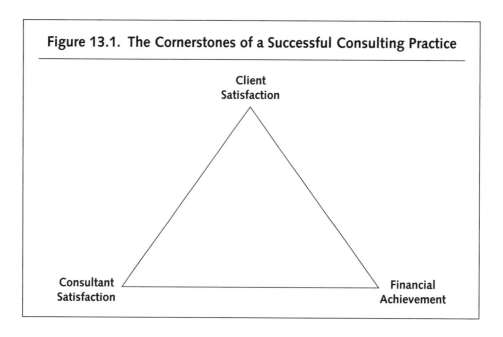

Figure 13.1. The Cornerstones of a Successful Consulting Practice

Client
Satisfaction

Consultant
Satisfaction

Financial
Achievement

they expect and so to have a better shot at generating the customer satisfaction that leads to referrals—and ultimately to a thriving practice. Although there is undoubtedly a bit of risk in guaranteeing work that is by its nature intangible and ambiguous, I can say from personal experience that nothing reassures the customer, and focuses the mind of a consulting team, more than the idea that you won't be paid if the client is not pleased. This strategy demonstrates to the client that you trust your ability to deliver, that you take your responsibility seriously, and that you are willing to share the risks of the advisory relationship. As one of the original mentors of consulting, Gerald Weinberg, states in his book *The Secrets of Consulting* (1985), "If they don't like your work, don't take their money." This simple declaration is central to the ethics of our business.

The average tenure of IT professionals is about eighteen months. In these times of extraordinary job mobility for talented folks in our industry, consultant satisfaction can be the make-or-break element for the manager of a consulting firm. A recent study by the employment consulting firm Kennedy Information of New Hampshire (Yamada, 1999) found that, although 1998 revenue for systems integration firms rose by 27 percent over the previous year, the factor limiting them from even greater growth was the difficulty of finding and retaining IT talent. Clearly, those of us building consulting practices need to figure out how to keep technical teams committed and motivated. I believe our achievements as consultants, our ability to point to a website, a network, or an application and say, "I built that," determine our job satisfaction. Again, my hope is that, by introducing a disciplined methodology that can lead consultants through the brambles of the client relationship, this book can help consultants build confidence and competence in the delivery of meaningful business results. Nothing in my experience has contributed to my personal satisfaction more than the feeling of accomplishment I've had when I've worked closely with a client to solve a thorny business problem and delivered a superior solution. By working to master our profession, to improve our competence, and to become adept advisors, we can turn the promise of technology into enriched lives for ourselves, our teammates, and our clients.

References

Weinberg, G. (1985). *The secrets of consulting.* New York: Dorset House.
Yamada, K. (1999, August). IT consulting market soars. *Solutions Integrator,* p. 13.

Appendices

Sample Request for Proposal: CapState Chemical Company Relocation Project

RFP, Capitol State Chemical Corporation Relocation Project, Distributed Systems

This document is a Request for Proposal for services required to plan, manage, and implement a distributed systems relocation project for Capitol State Chemical Corporation. This document will define in detail the objectives of this project and the levels of service we expect from the chosen service provider on this project.

Capitol State Chemical Corporation, the world's largest supplier of pharmaceutical chemicals, is consolidating its multiple offices into our new World Headquarters building. We are seeking a Technical Project Team to assist us with the move of our distributed computing environment, made up of servers, storage devices, desktop PC's, workstations, laptops, and network-connected printers and peripherals. This team will be composed of a Technical Project Manager and specific Subject-Matter Experts as required.

This Request for Proposal will document the business and technical requirements for our selection of a Technical Project Team to assist us with this move. It is organized as follows:

- Project Background
- Services We Seek to Acquire
- Selection Criteria and Process
- Bidders' Guidelines
- Schedule

Project Background

Capitol State Chemical designs and manufactures customized chemical compounds for the pharmaceutical industry. Our technologically advanced Research & Development department uses sophisticated molecular-imaging workstations to design effective and efficient chemical products for our clients. We rely on information technology to design, record, document, store, and protect our intellectual property. Currently our computing resources are scattered through multiple departments and locations. Consolidation of our computing assets is a primary goal of this move. Also key is ensuring that no disruption to availability of our computing resources is caused by this move.

Capitol State typically closes for the week from Christmas Eve to New Year's Day every year as a benefit for our associates. We will use that period this year to move. Our expectation is for all systems to be moved, installed, tested, and in production on Tuesday, January 2, when our associates return from their holiday break.

Capitol State has 19,000 employees who will be affected by this move. We have a complete asset-management database, which is current and includes user ID, serial number, installed software, and inventory information for every computing device. We have about sixty Novell servers, in a mix of 4.1 and 5.0 version levels. We have about six hundred networked printers, about twenty-five networked CD jukeboxes, and about fifteen networked scanners. We are standardized on IBM servers, desktops, and laptops.

We have two areas that have specialized needs: the R&D Department and the Production Department. Research and Development is composed of about fifty chemists who use graphic workstations and UNIX servers. Due to previous client commitments, there is no provision for downtime for moving the R&D servers, so a special plan must be created to move these servers and have them in production without interruption.

The Production area is a factory floor, requiring special planning for cabling, and perhaps special furniture or millwork for the PC's to protect them from the harsh environment.

Services We Seek to Acquire

We are seeking to hire a Technical Project Team, made up of a Technical Project Leader and Subject-Matter Experts with certain skills, including:

- Network infrastructure design skills,
- Novell NetWare expertise,
- IBM server and desktop hardware expertise,
- Project management skills, and
- Technical knowledge of the following:

  Video conferencing

  Imaging,

  Network address (IP) design,

  Data/voice communications, and

  Desktop applications.

We will also consider using a team of workers who would perform the actual disconnection and preparation of all desktop devices and the reconnection after the move, as our moving company will not perform this task.

Project Management. CapState will assign a full-time project manager to this project, with accountability for all CapState activities required to fulfill this project. This manager will be the single interface for project directions, status reporting, scheduling, and problem resolution. Our expectation is that bidders will also provide a project manager with the same central interface responsibilities related to bidder activities on this project. The selected contractor will work with CapState's project manager to prepare detailed project plans and bills of materials, to provide ongoing weekly status reporting to management, to direct and control the activities of contractor resources, and to resolve any open issues that arise during the provision of these services.

Follow-Up Support. Bidders should describe in detail their warranty policy for services and materials. We require that a documented problem resolution and escalation process be in place and agreed to before any bids are awarded on this project. Bidders should describe any ongoing onsite or telephone support they will provide for our users during and after relocation. We expect bidders to be prepared to provide "hot spare" systems for deployment in case of station problems and to provide spare parts in case of discovery of faulty parts or systems during this process to ensure that the project schedule is not impacted.

Selection Criteria and Process

We have held a series of pre-RFP interviews, at which we reviewed the qualifications of a group of potential bidders. This RFP is the next step in our selection process. We will review all proposals submitted in response to this bid fairly and completely—and will then select the three bids we believe are most responsive to our needs. We will allow those three vendors to present their recommendations to the Selection Committee, after which we will make a selection and begin negotiations. Capitol State Chemical is committed to fair bidding practices.

Bidders' Guidelines

All bidders for this engagement must follow these guidelines:

1. Present detailed corporate literature describing your organization, its areas of expertise, its structure and longevity, and financial information that describes the stability of your organization.

2. Present the resumes of the management and technical personnel that you propose to assign to this project.

3. Include three (3) detailed local references for projects your organization has undertaken that are similar in scope, technical expertise, and duration to this project.

4. Present a draft project plan that defines the tasks you believe are required to manage and implement this project. Include all estimated durations on a task-by-task basis.

5. Specify your estimate of the total cost to CapState of the services required to perform the relocation project outlined above. Our expectation is for a fixed bid to provide the entire range of services described. If you cannot provide a fixed bid, describe in detail your proposed pricing policies for this project.

6. Any and all costs to CapState for the bidder to perform these services must be included in the bid. This includes any permits, insurance, project management costs, travel or other expenses, or any other miscellaneous charges related to the bidder's services on this project.

7. Describe the process for handling any changes to the scope of the project after it is undertaken. Include the process for providing overtime, weekend, or other special work if required.

8. Describe your process for problem resolution if any issues arise during your services on this project.

Schedule

Our Selection Committee schedule for this process is as follows:

What	Date
Pre-RFP meetings	July 1–17
RFP mailed to bidders	July 21
RFP response due	Aug 5
Proposal review	Aug 6–12
Bidder presentations	Aug 15–17
Final selection	Aug 25
Negotiations begin	Aug 26

All bidders are advised that they must respond in detail to each element of this RFP in order to be considered for the award of this bid. Late bids will not be considered.

Any questions regarding this Request for Proposal should be submitted by FAX to:

> Ron Gimble, Fax: 999-999-0000.

All responses to this RFP must be made in soft-cover format, six complete copies, and submitted by close of business on August 5, to:

> Ron Gimble
> Director of Network Infrastructure
> Capitol State Chemical
> 111 CapState Road
> Commerce City, STATE 00001

Sample Proposal: Superior Systems Proposal for CapState Relocation Project

To CapState Chemicals

Proposal for Computer System Relocation Project

Presented by Superior Systems

Prepared by John Ryan, Superior Systems, August 5, 1999

BACKGROUND

CapState Chemicals, Inc., is a chemical company based in Commerce City, providing custom chemical compounds to the pharmaceutical industry. Based on a Request for Proposal issued on July 21, 1999, and on an informational meeting between Ron Gimble, CapState Chemicals, and John Ryan, Nick Campbell, and Sandy Root, Superior Systems, Superior Systems understands that CapState Chemicals intends to relocate its computer systems and networks from multiple locations in the metropolitan area to its new world headquarters, currently under construction. Based on the information presented in the RFP and subsequent meeting, we understand that CapState wishes to engage an IT consulting firm to provide the following services:

- Technical assistance in the planning and execution of the relocation project;

- Project management skills to create detailed project plans, schedules, and budgets and to ensure effective execution of those plans;

- Assistance with the disconnection, reconnection, and testing of all computing devices affected by this relocation project; and

- Follow-up support to provide CapState associates with uninterrupted use of their computer systems following the relocation.

This proposal describes Superior Systems' understanding of the goals CapState Chemicals has for this relocation project. It defines our proposed approach to achieving those goals, the deliverables to be generated, and our proposed budget of time and expense estimated to produce the described deliverables.

SUCCESS CRITERIA

Based on the information presented to Superior Systems, our consulting team has identified a series of success criteria for this project. In the interest of clear communication and mutual understanding, we have enumerated in this section the priorities and success criteria of this engagement as we understand them. As identified in the RFP, critical success criteria include the following:

- Avoidance of disruption of user access to IT services.

- Provision of special handling for CapState's Research and Development Division, including a plan for relocation of this division with no interruption in service. This includes the provision of technical subject-matter expertise in the UNIX systems and graphics workstations that are in use in the R&D group.

- The complete relocation and testing process must be performed over the holiday break between Christmas Eve and New Year's Day.

- Special provisions must be made for the relocation of the production department.

- The provision of "hot spare" systems and spare parts is an important component of this relocation.

- Other specialized technical skills, such as expertise in IP addressing, video conferencing, voice communications, and imaging may be required.

We have catalogued these success factors in order to ensure agreement regarding their priority, the budget and schedule associated with them, and the risks and assumptions inherent in each. Our experience with projects of this type indicates that clear and open understanding of these success factors leads to greater probability of project success.

APPROACH

Superior Systems approaches information technology projects with a unique perspective: We believe that the application of a structured project management discipline is the deciding factor in the success of IT projects. Every engagement we undertake follows our IT Consulting Framework, which enforces a strict project discipline to ensure that we deliver the expected results. Our discipline requires that we perform a detailed project assessment, which results in documented objectives, milestones, and deliverables for every project. In addition, our IT Consulting Framework also enforces the use of a detailed discovery procedure, in which we review the client's current business work flow, technology architecture, application usage, and data needs, in order to certify that we have a clear understanding of the current environment before we attempt to design a solution. Our experience with this methodology allows us to make the following assurance to our clients:

> If you agree to follow our project methodology, and you are not satisfied with the results of our engagement, you don't pay.

We are proud to say that, in our nine years of providing IT services, we have never had a client ask us to honor this pledge. In addition, we have never had a client who has not agreed to be a reference site for our project work. We have built this record because our methodology works, because we focus on client service, and because we honor our commitments. We appreciate the opportunity to present our proposed approach to CapState Chemical Company.

Superior Systems proposes to deliver the CapState System Relocation Project in the following manner:

Project Assessment Phase

Superior Systems will collaborate with the CapState Chemicals project sponsors to create a joint CapState-Superior Systems Relocation Project Team, with the responsibility of defining the objectives, priorities, and deliverables for this project. A Superior Systems project manager and a CapState Chemicals primary project sponsor will be designated. Superior Systems will then meet with the designated IT and departmental resources, and other CapState Chemicals associates, for the purposes of:

- Defining the requirements, time frames, and priorities of the relocation project;
- Developing consensus regarding the success criteria;
- Understanding the roles and responsibilities of the CapState team and the Superior Systems team;
- Assessing the requirements for post-move support;
- Assessing the requirements for hardware support, such as spare parts or "hot spare" systems;
- Performing site walk-throughs of all current sites to be relocated;
- Reviewing all blueprints and schematics for the new site; and
- Designing project status reporting formats.

The desired outcome of the assessment phase is an accurate profile of the objectives, success criteria, expectations, and skills required to deliver this project successfully.

The deliverables from this phase include the following:

- A Preliminary Project Objectives statement,

- A Project Success Criteria document,

- A Roles and Responsibilities document,

- A Project Status Reporting procedure, and

- An assigned project team from CapState and Superior Systems.

These documents will be presented for review to the CapState project sponsors. Upon acceptance, they will form the basis of the agreement between CapState and Superior Systems to collaborate on this project.

Current State Discovery Phase

In order to assure a complete understanding of the devices, systems, and applications affected by this relocation project, Superior Systems will perform a discovery process that will include the following activities:

- Review of the asset management database to increase our familiarity with the asset base to be relocated;

- Review of any existing system documentation, such as network diagrams, domain structures, addressing schemes, and cabling diagrams;

- Review of any network baselines or traffic statistics, such as those generated by a network audit or network management station;

- Review of any business process work flow documents, such as flow charts or operating procedures manuals;

- Observation of existing data centers;

- Review of any data warehouse or database schema documents;

- Review of backup and contingency plans;

- Creation of a user survey form, to collect data regarding CapState associates' use of technology and expectations for relocation;

- The scheduling of facilitated work sessions with IT staff and with user departments, to discover special needs and requirements for the relocation. (This will be especially important with the R&D and Production Departments, to ensure that all special requirements are documented and addressed.)

The purpose of this discovery phase is to prepare an accurate "as-is" model of the enterprise and to enable the project team to create a detailed project plan, budget, and schedule for the relocation project. By developing a complete understanding of the technology, application, and business needs of the R&D and Production Departments, as well as all functional areas affected by the move, we ensure that each CapState department receives the specific handling and attention required to assure uninterrupted system access.

The deliverables from the discovery phase include the following:

- A technology architecture document describing our findings regarding the current technical infrastructure. This may include any diagrams, network maps, or other material discovered or developed in the effort to document the current systems.
- A work flow diagram, documenting the interactions of major systems and procedures.
- A verified asset inventory, or, if asset verification is not possible, we will submit a plan for asset discovery.
- A data storage map, to ensure that all data that are required for uninterrupted processing are available after the move.
- These detailed "as-is" documents will form the basis for the project plans to follow.

Project Design Phase

Based on the information discovered in the assessment and discovery phases, the CapState-Superior Systems Relocation Project Team will collaborate to create a detailed project plan. This plan will define the specific tasks associated with this project, the resources assigned to those tasks, the sequence of events and schedule of deliverables, as well as any risks or open issues for further review. This plan will present to the CapState project sponsors the team's estimates of time and expenses required to deliver the relocation according to expectations set out in the previous phases.

The deliverables from the Project Design Phase would be as follows:

- A Scope of Work Document that would contain the final agreements regarding objectives, success criteria, priorities, and deliverables;

- A detailed project plan, including tasks, task sequence, assigned resources, estimated task durations, and a Gantt chart;

- A project schedule including estimated start and finish dates for each task;

- A materials list enumerating any hardware or software products, tools, or other materials required to deliver this project;

- A project estimate, including estimates for services, materials, and expenses;

- A risk management plan, including backup and contingency plans to ensure that all systems have data backups and that essential equipment has spare parts or hot spares;

- A change control mechanism for managing changes or impacts to the project;

- A special plan for the relocation of the R&D Department;

- A plan for special handling of the Production Department;

- A support plan for providing after-move support to CapState associates; and

- A communication plan to ensure appropriate participation among all the entities involved.

Project Implementation Phase

During the implementation phase, Superior Systems and CapState will work together to execute the plans designed during the previous phase. We will manage and control the resources to ensure that budget and schedule expectations set forth earlier were met and will deal with any open issues or scope changes that arise. We will apply quality control procedures to ensure that all deliverables and activities meet our expectations and standards.

Deliverables of the implementation phase include:

- Status reports based on the reporting process laid out earlier,

- Change control reports,

- Periodic budget and schedule updates, and

- Open issues reports.

Project Review and Maintenance Phase

At the completion of the relocation, we will perform a structured review process with CapState project sponsors to ensure that all open items were addressed, that the project delivered the results expected, and that CapState was properly prepared to resume system operations in the new facility. As is our standard process with all engagements, we will request that CapState project sponsors fill out a project review and acceptance form, to document acceptance of project completion and to record any issues or comments regarding our performance.

The maintenance activities include any after-move support that we have agreed on, as well as any warranty work or other additional activities that CapState requests us to undertake.

P R O F E S S I O N A L   F E E S

Superior Systems estimates that the consulting budget for the assessment and discovery phases of this effort, as described above, would be $ 22,500.00. This estimate is based on our rate of $150.00 per hour for System Consultants and Project Managers. Professional fees are billed monthly based upon actual hours expended in your behalf.

This estimate is presented for budgeting purposes only, and should not be construed as a fixed bid or "not-to-exceed" price. CapState Chemicals will be billed for actual effort expended at the professional rate defined above. This estimate of professional fees is based on the scope and assumptions identified herein. Changes in scope or variances in assumptions can impact engagements either negatively or positively. Should any changes or variances occur that may affect the outcome of this engagement, Superior Systems will notify the designated CapState Chemicals Project Sponsor within seventy-two hours.

Please note that the fees estimated in this section apply to the assessment and discovery phases only. They will result in the delivery of the documents as described under "Deliverables" for those phases. The planning, implementation, and review phases outlined in this document are not included in this estimate, and will be separately proposed, priced, and delivered.

ASSUMPTIONS

The following is a list of assumptions made during the development of this proposal and its related work plan.

Client Participation. CapState Chemicals will appoint a Project Sponsor to oversee the direction of the project. The appointed Project Sponsor will have decision-making authority over all aspects of the project.

The success of this project is dependent on the participation of CapState Chemical's employees. CapState will provide access to required personnel to perform assigned tasks, review documents, and approve deliverables in a timely manner in order to avoid negative impact on the project schedule.

CapState Chemicals will review interim and final deliverables and report acceptance or discrepancy within forty-eight hours of the submission of deliverables.

Other Agreements

Guaranteed Satisfaction. The guarantee of satisfaction alluded to in this document is subject to certain restrictions and guidelines. These restrictions are documented in a separate document entitled "The Superior Systems Customer Satisfaction Guarantee," which will be presented as an addendum in the event this proposal is accepted and our services are contracted for this project. Superior Systems will devote its best efforts to the engagement defined in this proposal. In no event shall Superior Systems be liable for indirect, special, or consequential damages arising from its service.

Expiration. The terms of this proposal expire in ninety days from the date of receipt and are subject to renegotiation at that time, unless a formal extension is provided by Superior Systems.

Quality Management. All engagements performed by Superior Systems are subject to quality assurance reviews to assure they are being performed to the highest standards. During the course of this engagement, Superior Systems' quality personnel will be calling on key CapState Chemicals personnel as part of this process.

Post-Engagement Review. The success of CapState Chemicals in this initiative is our prime interest. Therefore, as part of this process, Superior Systems will be conducting a Post-Engagement Review within ninety days after the completion of the engagement. By accepting this proposal the client agrees to participate in a project review session.

Proprietary Information. All materials, ideas, concepts, knowledge, and techniques presented to CapState Chemicals during the performance of this engagement by Superior Systems shall belong to Superior Systems. Deliverables produced remain the property of Superior Systems until all invoices for services provided are paid in full, at which time ownership of the deliverables produced will transfer to CapState Chemicals.

(*Note to readers:* References, financial data, and other information requested in the CapState RFP are not included in this sample proposal.)

Sample Communication Plan: Superior Systems Communication Plan for CapState Relocation Project

CapState Relocation Project Communications Plan

Presented by Superior Systems

Superior Systems' experience in our consulting engagements indicates that communication is one of the most critical variables in the overall success of any IT project. We propose in this plan to collaborate with CapState to prepare a communications program that will create positive anticipation regarding the relocation project and that will transmit in a regularly scheduled manner the essential status issues that senior managers need to know.

Benefits of a structured communications program include the following:

Expectation Management. When users learn that an IT project is underway, they begin to form expectations regarding its potential impact. They may wonder whether the program will meet their needs. They may look for service improvement in areas that are not directly related to the target areas of the engagement. Some associates may even question the security of their positions and begin to look for alternative employment. When these expectations are not managed, IT teams may find that even outstanding project results do not generate corresponding levels of customer satisfaction. Setting and managing expectations through the participation of affected departmental management and staff is a critical step in the creation of positive anticipation and ultimate satisfaction among affected associates.

Education. Changing the behavior of associates is a difficult and challenging task. Team members have invested significant time and energy in learning how to use current systems to their best advantage, often creating informal or "shadow" processes and organizations to work around system deficiencies. Associates affected by changing technology and work processes need to understand the strategic reasons for implementing change, and they must be brought up to speed on the new systems in order to achieve their maximum value. Simply implementing technology, no matter how well designed and suited, will not generate better business results. Additionally, the development and marketing of an associate training program sends a positive message of inclusion and commitment.

Business Unit Consensus. One characteristic of effective adopters of information technology is their commitment to gaining buy-in of the business units affected by change. We believe that the involvement of business units in designing the work flows, processes, procedures, and support systems that accompany new technology leads to better designs and more client satisfaction. The technology delivered must be perceived as relevant to the goals of each business unit. Skepticism and resistance to changing technology must be addressed.

Our IT Project Communication Program consists of the following activities:

1. Define constituencies,

2. Determine message content and media, and

3. Plan and execute communications strategy.

Define Constituencies

Different people within the organization have varying concerns and different needs for communication.

The *executive level* typically prefers brief, big picture updates on the status of the engagement and of open issues that must be addressed or arbitrated at their level. Executive level managers are focused on the alignment of technology with strategic objectives and on the overall effectiveness and business justification of technology initiatives.

Business unit managers must understand how new technology will affect their departments, its interaction with other functional units, and the output of the unit, whether that output consists of financial analysis or finished goods.

They want assurances that training and support issues are being planned and managed appropriately and that their ongoing operations will not be unduly disrupted by the implementation efforts.

Associates need to understand how to utilize the new technology to do their work. They want to be assured that their concerns and support needs will be addressed and that the new technology will be convenient to use and not threaten their job performance or security.

Information technology staff members are interested in their roles and responsibilities in the planning and implementation of the new technology. They want to understand the technical aspects of the new systems, and they want assurances that they will be prepared to be effective in supporting and maintaining that technology. They must trust that their job security is not at risk based on technical change.

An effective communications program must target each constituency with a message specific to its needs.

Determine Message Content and Media

Superior Systems will partner with CapState to create a communications project plan that will define the frequency, media, and content of the messages to be broadcast throughout the organization. Some of the communications activities we recommend are described in the following paragraphs.

Executive Briefings. Meetings should be scheduled on a regular basis between the relocation project managers and CapState executives, in order to brief executives on project status, open issues, questions or disputes requiring arbitration, and other issues affecting schedule, budget, quality, and risk management.

Associate Auditorium Presentations. Presentations by senior executives to assembled teams of associates, explaining the strategic reasons for relocating the organization to its own building and the benefits in productivity, cooperation, and teamwork, can alleviate resistance and build momentum. Specific presentations regarding particular aspects of the move, such as IT, security, or building amenities, could be presented in detail at these meetings. Question and answer sessions during these assemblies allow associates to express concerns and suggestions directly to corporate officers and project teams.

Newsletter. A periodic newsletter, intended as a general informational vehicle for the entire organization, would be distributed to all associates of CapState. The format would be entertaining and informative. This newsletter would include photos and drawings of the new site, information on topics of general interest such as parking, access, services such as cafeteria and company store, and move schedules. It would be structured to generate excitement and anticipation about the benefits of the new building. Special inserts, such as open letters from corporate management to the associates describing the objectives and benefits of the relocation, would be incorporated into the newsletter. Associate feedback and suggestions would be also be included to promote interactivity.

Lunch and Learn. The "lunch and learn" format, in which a trade show environment is set up in the cafeteria or other associate gathering place and representatives of various project teams present information to their associates, provides a valuable opportunity to communicate a positive message to the CapState community. Associates can interact directly with project teams and with their peers and learn the plans for implementing IT, security, telephone systems, parking, food service, and other areas of interest. The participation of the corporate training department in this exercise is crucial, as this is the perfect venue to begin assuring associates that their needs for education on new processes will be addressed. Superior Systems' representatives would work with CapState to prepare a comprehensive presentation regarding the IT aspects of the relocation project.

Posters and Brochures. Consistent, repetitive exposure to the project goals and benefits will help effectively overcome skepticism and build momentum for the project. Posters in strategic areas throughout the existing sites, explaining the features and benefits of the new building and the process of preparing for and implementing the relocation, will create an atmosphere of anticipation and mental preparedness for the move. Brochures that present more detail, including specific move dates of specific departments and methods of registering concerns or resolving issues, should be prepared and distributed.

Focus Groups. Allowing users and managers to participate in the design of the relocation project is an excellent way to build buy-in and assure that requirements are addressed. Superior Systems proposes the implementation of scheduled focus groups, including associates from all departments and locations. We recommend conducting one focus group session per month, in different existing sites, and then incorporating the comments and feedback into the move planning process. User "champions" will sometimes rise from these situations to become conduits of project information to their respective teams.

Customer Surveys. An ongoing series of customer surveys, gauging concerns and issues that are arising among the staff and that may not be visible at the planning team level, will create an atmosphere of participation and enthusiasm.

Electronic Suggestion Box. The creation of e-mail and voice-mail suggestion boxes that can be accessed by all associates to leave messages of concern, suggestions, and issues is a powerful communications tool. Issues raised can then be included in the newsletter, to demonstrate that the planning team is listening and incorporating user suggestions in the process.

Intranet Web Page. A project-focused web page that broadcasts status information, schedules, and project benefits can be a convenient and entertaining method of communicating. Both associates and executives can access the data at their convenience and can immediately feed back via e-mail links posted prominently on the page. Online documentation that describes the technology of the new site, any new or modified systems, or any reengineered processes will give users a chance to educate themselves at their own speed.

Other methods of communication, such as memorandums from executive management or departmental status briefings, should also be considered.

Plan and Execute Communications Strategy

Communication should be planned as a project, with specific goals, objectives, deliverables, roles and responsibilities, and schedules. We recommend that a communications team, consisting of associates involved in the planning of the relocation project as well as representatives of corporate training and communications departments, be created and tasked with the responsibility to design a plan that includes the elements outlined above. This plan should then be scheduled and budgeted as a discrete element of the overall relocation effort, and its activities should be integrated into the master relocation project plan. Superior Systems has significant experience in the design of IT project communication plans and would be pleased to participate in this effort.

We recommend, as an integral part of any effective communication program, the creation of a features and benefits statement. We often refer to this statement as the "project vision." This marketing message should be compelling, persuasive, and easy to understand and communicate. We recommend that a project vision session be convened that includes representatives of various organizational constituencies, and that a consensus vision statement be constructed that can then form the nucleus of the communication effort.

Superior Systems is committed to assisting CapState in the design and delivery of an effective communication program that will generate enthusiasm and anticipation for the CapState relocation project. We again thank you for the opportunity to participate in this critical project.

Sample Project Plan

CapState Relocation Project Plan

CapState Relocation Project Plan

CapState Relocation Project

Superior Systems Project Plan

Master Summary

ID	Task	Who	Start	Finish
1	Inventory/Audit	SupSys Project Manager	9/1	11/18
2	Data Network/Infrastructure Inventory	SupSys Network Engineer	11/1	11/28
7	WAN Connections Inventory	SupSys Network Engineer	12/7	12/7
10	Facilities	CapState Premises	1/6	1/6
14	Distributed Systems/Processors Inventory	CapState Distributed Computing	12/15	12/15
19	Desktop Inventory	SupSys Technician	12/27	1/18
35	Application & Services Inventory	SupSys Application SME	2/1	3/31
40	Voice Systems Inventory	CapState Telecom	2/13	2/13
42	Security Inventory	CapState Security	9/1	1/5
44	Videoconferencing Inventory	CapState Video	1/5	1/5
46	Contracts	CapState Project Manager	3/1	12/21
49	Human Resource Issues	CapState HR	3/29	5/30
55	New Site Requirements Definition & Design	CapState Project Manager	4/15	11/22
56	Data Network/Infrastructure Requirements & Design	CapState Network	12/26	1/6
63	WAN Requirements Definition & Design	CapState Network	12/22	12/22
79	Facilities Requirements & Design	CapState Premises	1/6	1/15
97	Distributed Systems/Processors	CapState Distributed Computing	12/22	12/22
101	Desktop Requirements & Design	CapState IS	1/13	11/22
106	Application/Services Requirements & Design	CapState IS	4/3	6/30
110	Voice Systems Requirements & Design	CapState Telecom	1/6	7/14

ID	Task Name	Responsible		
121	Security Requirements	CapState Security	1/27	2/1
124	Videoconferencing Requirements	CapState Video	4/15	1/27
134	Contracts Requirements	CapState Project Manager	8/16	11/19
135	HR Requirements	CapState HR	11/17	1/6
138	Implementation Plan	SupSys Project Manager	11/9	8/16
139	Data Network/Infrastructure Implementation Plan	SupSys Project Manager	3/1	10/2
145	WAN Implementation Plan	SupSys Project Manager	1/6	12/15
170	Facilities Implementation Plan	SupSys Project Manager	1/31	9/1
188	Distributed Systems/Processors Implementation Plan	SupSys Project Manager	11/9	8/16
295	Desktop Systems Implementation Plan	SupSys Project Manager	3/15	3/15
297	Applications & Services Implementation Plan	SupSys Project Manager	3/31	6/30
302	Voice Systems Implementation Plan	SupSys Project Manager	11/10	12/22
316	Security Implementation Plan	SupSys Project Manager	2/1	12/1
324	Videoconferencing Implementation Plan	SupSys Project Manager	12/15	1/1
336	Contracts Implementation Plan	SupSys Project Manager	3/15	3/15
337	HR Implementation Plan	SupSys Project Manager	3/15	3/15
339	Detailed Move Plan (item-by-item)	SupSys Project Manager	1/3	8/15
340	Data Network/Infrastructure Detailed Move Plan	SupSys Project Manager	8/15	8/15
341	WAN Detailed Move Plan	SupSys Project Manager	8/15	8/15
342	Facilities Detailed Move Plan	SupSys Project Manager	8/15	8/15
343	Distributed Systems/Processors Detailed Move Plan	SupSys Project Manager	8/15	8/15
344	Desktop Systems Detailed Move Plan	SupSys Project Manager	8/15	8/15
345	Applications & Services Detailed Move Plan	SupSys Project Manager	8/15	8/15
346	Voice Systems Detailed Move Plan	SupSys Project Manager	1/3	1/3
348	Security Detailed Move Plan	SupSys Project Manager	8/15	8/15
349	Video Conferencing Detailed Move Plan	SupSys Project Manager	8/15	8/15
350	Contracts Detailed Move Plan	SupSys Project Manager	8/15	8/15
351	HR Detailed Move Plan	SupSys Project Manager	8/15	8/15

BIBLIOGRAPHY

Consulting Business

Biech, E. (1999). *The business of consulting.* San Francisco, CA: Jossey-Bass/Pfeiffer.

Maister, D. (1993). *Managing the professional service firm.* New York: Free Press.

Consulting Skills

Arnoudse, D.M. (1993). *Consulting skills for information professionals.* New York: Dow-Jones Irwin.

Arredondo, L. (1994). *The McGraw-Hill 36-hour course: Business presentations.* New York: McGraw-Hill.

Block, P. (1999). *Flawless consulting* (2nd ed.). San Francisco, CA: Jossey-Bass/Pfeiffer.

Hanan, M. (1990). *Consultative selling.* New York: American Management Association.

Maister, D. (1997). *True professionalism.* New York: Free Press.

Rees, F. (1998). *The facilitator excellence handbook.* San Francisco, CA: Jossey-Bass/Pfeiffer.

Salacuse, J. (1994). *The art of advice.* New York: Times Books.

Schaeffer, R.H. (1997). *High-impact consulting.* San Francisco, CA: Jossey-Bass.

Schwartz, R. (1994). *The skilled facilitator.* San Francisco, CA: Jossey-Bass.

IT Design

Bouldin, B.M. (1989). *Agents of change: Managing the introduction of automated tools.* Englewood Cliffs, NJ: Prentice Hall.

Brooks, F. (1982). *The mythical man-month.* Reading, MA: Addison-Wesley.

Demarco, T., & Lister, T. (1987). *Peopleware: Productive projects and teams.* New York: Dorset House.

Demarco, T. (1979). *Structured analysis and systems specifications.* Englewood Cliffs, NJ: Prentice Hall.

Demarco, T. (1982). *Controlling software projects.* New York: Yourdon Press.

Gane, C., & Sarson, T. (1977). *Structured systems analysis: Tools and techniques.* St. Louis, MO: Improved System Technologies.

Gunton, T. (1989). *Infrastructure: Building a framework for corporate information handling.* Englewood Cliffs, NJ: Prentice Hall.

Horton, F.W. (1985). *Information resources management.* Englewood Cliffs, NJ: Prentice Hall.

Jenkins, G. (1997). *Information systems policies and procedures manual.* Englewood Cliffs, NJ: Prentice Hall.

Jones, C. (1986). *Programming productivity.* New York: McGraw-Hill.

Maguire, S. (1994). *Debugging the development process.* Redmond, WA: Microsoft Press.

Martin, J. (1982). *Strategic data planning methodologies.* Englewood Cliffs, NJ: Prentice Hall.

Martin, J. (1991). *Rapid application design.* Indianapolis, IN: Macmillan.

McConnell, V.C., & Koch, C.W. (1991). *Computerizing the corporation.* New York: Van Nostrand Reinhold.

McConnell, S. (1996). *Rapid development.* Redmond, WA: Microsoft Press.

Osborn, A.F. (1993). *Applied imagination.* Buffalo, NY: Creative Education Foundation.

Page-Jones, M. (1988). *The practical guide to structured systems design.* New York: Yourdon Press.

Spewak, S. H. (1993). *Enterprise architecture planning.* Wellesley, MA: QED Publishing.

Tom, P. (1987). *Managing information as a corporate resource,* New York: Scott Foresman.

Walford, R.B. (1990). *Network system architecture.* Reading, MA: Addison-Wesley.

Weinberg, G.M. (1971). *The psychology of computer programming.* New York: Van Nostrand Reinhold.

Weinberg, G.M. (1982). *Becoming a technical leader.* New York: Dorset House.

Yourdan, E. (1975). *Techniques of program structure and design.* Englewood Cliffs, NJ: Prentice Hall.

Project Management

Cleland, D.I. (1997). *Project management: Strategic design and implementation.* New York: McGraw-Hill.

Frame, J.D. (1994). *The new project management.* San Francisco, CA: Jossey-Bass.

Frame, J.D. (1987). *Managing projects in organizations.* San Francisco, CA: Jossey-Bass.

Hallows, J. (1998). *Information systems project management: How to deliver function and value in IT projects.* New York: AMACOM.

General Business and Management

Drucker, P. (1993). *Management: Tasks, responsibilities, practices.* New York: Harper Business.

Drucker, P. (1980). *Managing in turbulent times.* New York: HarperCollins.

Fisher, R., & Ury, W. (1981). *Getting to yes.* New York: Penguin Books.

Grove, A. (1983). *High-output management.* New York: Random House.

Hammer, M., & Champy, J. (1993). *Reengineering the corporation.* New York: Harper Business.

Humphrey, W.S. (1997). *Managing technical people.* Reading, MA: Addison-Wesley.

Lowe, J. (1998). *Jack Welch speaks: Wisdom from the world's greatest business leader.* New York: John Wiley.

Seitz, N. (1983). *Finance for non-financial managers.* Reston, VA: Reston Publishing.

INDEX

A

Abstract thinking, 122–123

Acceptance criteria, 176

Access security, 200

Acquisition process and rules, 195

Action items, from facilitated work session, 99

Active listening, 98

Activity plan, 136; development of, 134; sample, 135

Advising and advisory skills, 5–13, 17; focus on, before technical skills, 1–4, 5–6, 155–156; general principles of, 6–13; for handling resistance, 207–208; IT consultant deficiency in, 73; political, 203–206; professional approach to, 5–6; for total solutions, 185–201

Affinity diagrams, 131

Agenda setting, in facilitated work sessions, 99

Agreement, in "negotiate the relationship" stage: documentation of, 51; testing of, 53

Agreement on action items, 99

Alpha testing, 116

Ambiguous nature: of consulting, 47–50; of human emotion, 73

Amelio, G., 153

Andersen Consulting, 188

Apple Computer, 153

Apple mouse, 108

Applications (component of Enterprise IT Model), 82, 83, 84; design at level of, 123; review of existing documentation on, 86–87; solution architecture at level of, 132–133

Applications statement, 123

"Approach the client" stage, 30–44; assessment in, of potential for success, 32–37; business situation assessment in, 34–37; in case study, 38–44; client evaluation and counter-evaluation in, 32–34; client motivations and, 31–32; documentation of, 37; Engagement Profile Form for, 34–37; overview of, 28, 30. *See also* Initial meeting

Aron, J. D., 183–184

Arrogance, 114. *See also* Emotion and ego; Technology bias

As-is model, 80, 101–102. *See also* Current state analysis; Discovery process; "Understand the client's situation" stage

Asset management: advising clients on, 91, 193–196; approaches to, 194; audit of, 195; characteristics of good, 194–195; decentralization and difficulties of, 194; importance of, 194, 195–196; in-house, 194; outsourcing, 194; use of data of, for inventory project, 89, 90

Asset tagging, 195

Assumptions statement, 52
Assurance factors, building in, 56
Atmosphere assessment: in "negotiate the relationship" stage, 49–50; in "understand the client's situation" stage, 88–89
Atmosphere of facilitated work sessions, 99–100
Attitudes, observation of, 88
Authority, consultant's, 204–205

B

Backup and restore mechanisms, 112, 174–175, 188, 200
Bacon, F., 5
Barron's, 217
Baseline, 171
Bay, 110
Bedside manner, 16
Berra, Y., 87
Best practices, 25
Beta testing, 116
Bicycle solution, 145
Biech, E., 221
Billable hours, 15
Billing for development time, 213–214
Bloomberg News, 19
Books: business, 20, 217; technical, 18, 215
Bottom-Line Selling (Malcolm), 217
Boundaries: defining relationship, 48–49, 176; defining scope, 54; of IT consulting framework, 25–26
Boundary testing, 111
Boyle, D., 118
Brainstorming: for fostering creativity, 108; for ideation, 125–126; rules for, 125–126
Break-fix services, 188
Brown-paper session, 101
Budget: estimate, in solutions presentation, 137; preliminary, 52, 55–56; value focus in, 55
Budget and expenditure reviews, 56
Bugs, 113, 116, 166–167; pilot testing for, 169–171; testing for, 168–169

Burke, E., 47
Bush, G., 67
Business-centered approach, 16, 186–188
Business (component of Enterprise IT Model), 82, 83, 84; review of existing documentation on, 87; solution architecture at level of, 133
Business Periodicals Index, 20
Business process reengineering (BPR), 72–73, 187
Business processes: advising on, 186–188; analysis of, 72–73
Business projection, IT consultant, 212–213
Business publications, 19, 217
Business results stage. *See* "Deliver business results" stage
Business situation assessment, in "approach the client" stage, 34–37
Business skills, 18–21; for business process analysis, 72–73; deficiency in, 18–19; development of, methods and sources of, 19–20, 217
Business strategy: analysis of, 72–73; vision communication linked with, 70–71
Business Systems Planning, 81
Business Week, 19, 217
Buxton, J. N., 121, 137

C

C++, 110
C programming language, 122
Cabling Business, 215
Cannonball run, 108
Capacity errors, 169
"Capstate Chemical Company Relocation Project." *See* Case study
Car solution, 145
Career development, IT consultant, 209–220. *See also* Development
Career path definition, for client staff, 196
Cascade communications, 70–71
Case study (Superior Systems/Capstate Chemical Company Relocation Project): "approach the client" stage in, 38–44; "collaborate to select

ment approach in, 157–159; quality management in, 167–169; technical implementation in, 166–167; training in, 164–166; transition from, to operations, 173–175; vendor involvement in, 172–173. *See also* Implementation; Results orientation

Deliverables: of "approach the client" stage, 37; client acceptance of, 175–177; description of project, 52; importance of clarifying, 52; of "negotiate the relationship" stage, 51–52; of solutions presentation, 148; of "understand the client's situation" stage, 101–102. *See also* Documentation

Deliverables document, 52

Delivery plan, 133–137; development of, 133–136; output of, 136–137

Delivery process. *See* "Deliver business results" stage

Dell, 110

Design: characteristics of good, 109–118; communication and training component of, 114–115; creativity and, 107–109; diligent, 117–118; documentation of, 114; flexible, 115; maintainable, 112–114; robust, 111; secure, 112; sources of, 118–119; standards-based, proven, 113, 116–117, 118; stealing, 118–119; that fits client requirements, 110–111; that solves the problem, 110

Design process, 118–131; evaluating ideas in, 128–131; flow charting in, 126–127; graphical representation of, 120; ideation techniques for, 124–126; iterative, 121, 136; product engineering methodology applied to, 119–121; structured programming methodology applied to, 82, 111, 121–122; top-down, 122–125

"Design solution options" stage, 106–141; in case study, 137, 138–141; creativity and, 107–109; design process in, 118–131; design standards for, 109–118; overview of, 29, 106; project management in, 133–137; solution architecture development in, 131–133

Design work flow, 119–121

Desktop computing, IT consulting and, 22

Development, IT consultant: of business skills, 19–20, 217; of communication skills, 22–23, 208, 218–219; of creativity, 108–109; executing the plan for, 213–220; of facilitation skills, 96, 97–98; financial rewards for, 214; goal setting for, 212–213; importance of, 183–184, 209–210; plan for, 212–213; of political skills, 205–206; for product procurement services, 197–198; of project management skills, 157–159, 218; of sales skills, 219–220; self-assessment for, 211–212; as social activity, 214; strategic approach to, 210–211; of technical skills, 17–18, 214–216; time for, billing for, 213–214. *See also* Skills

Diagramming, 114

Digital Equipment, 66

Dijkstra, E., 122

Diplomacy, 219

Disagreements, in "negotiate the relationship" stage, 51. *See also* Conflict

Discovery process: approach of, 80–81; as-is model creation in, 101–102; budgeting and, 55; in case study, 102, 103–104; data collection methods for, 85–101; Enterprise IT Model as basis for, 81–85; enterprise inventory for, 89–91; facilitated work sessions for, 85, 95–100; findings report of, 101–102; goals of, 80–81; interviews for, 85, 100–101; observation for, 87–89; review of existing documentation for, 85, 86–87; sequencing of, 85; surveys for, 85, 91–94. *See also* Current state analysis; "Understand the client's situation" stage

Distributed computing, 193

"Divide and conquer" approach, 82, 97, 124, 134. *See also* Enterprise IT Model

Doctors: characteristics of highly utilized, 16; consulting process of, 2–3

Documentation: advising clients on, 190–192; of agreements in "negotiate the relationship" stage, 51; of decisions from facilitated work sessions, 99; of deliverables, delivered, 176–177; of deliverables, planned, 52; of design process and solutions, 113, 114; of information technology architecture, 192; of initial contact, 37; methods of, 114; of operational procedures, 187–188, 192; of pilot tests, 171; of project records, 191; review of existing, 85, 86–87, 190; of solution architecture, 132–133; of systems, 191; total solution approach to, 190–193. *See also* Deliverables; Recordkeeping

DOS, 66

Doyle, A. C., 79

Drucker, P. F., 20, 72

Due diligence: approach of, 81, 102; defined, 80. *See also* Discovery process; "Understand the client's situation" stage

Dun & Bradstreet directors, 20

E

Edison, T., 107, 125

EDP Analyzer, 112

EDS, 188

Education and wellness program, doctor's, 3

Ego. *See* Emotion and ego

Embedded Systems Journal, 215

Emerson, R. W., 65

Emotion and ego: accepting blame and, 207; advisory skills for dealing with, 73; in "negotiate the relationship" stage, 50; overcoming, 205, 208; politics and, 203–206

Engagement Profile Form, 34–37, 51; sample, 35

Enterprise Information Management, 81

Enterprise IT Model, 81–85; as-is model of, 80, 101–102; discovery methods and, 85–101; graphical representation of, 82; layers of, described, 84; layers of, listed, 82; project planning based on, 134; solution architecture based on, 131–133; top-down design based on, 122–125

Enterprise resource planning (ERP) implementation, 69; business analysis requirements of, 72–73

Environment: observation of, in "understand the client's situation" stage, 88; understanding political, 206

Euripides, 31, 32

Evaluation techniques, 128–131

Execution test, 168–169

Expectations: managing, in "deliver business results" stage, 160; role definition for clarifying, 10, 48–49; visualization of success for managing, 11

F

Facilitated work sessions, 85, 95–100; atmosphere and flow of, 99–100; for brainstorming, 125; goals of, 96; impartiality in, 98; inclusion in, 98; listening in, 98; participants in, 95; preparation for, 96–97; questioning technique in, 97–98; recording of, 98; summarizing technique in, 98; tasks in, 98–99; unproductive meetings versus, 95–96; use of, for discovery, 85, 95–100

Facilitation skills and tools, 95, 96, 97–98, 99, 206; for interviews, 100–101

Facilitator role, 99

Facts and theories, 79–80, 101

Fast, good, or cheap, prioritizing by, 56–57

Favor bank, 205

Fear, 207

Feedback and interactivity: building in, 71; in communication, 163–164

Feedback session, from facilitated work session, 99

Financial achievement, 221, 222

Findings report, 101–102

Fishbone (Ishikawa) diagrams, 131

Fixed-bid pricing, 56

Flexibility: of design, 115; in negotiation and renegotiation, 57

Flip charts, 98

Flow charting, 126–127, 187

Forbes, 19

Formal atmosphere, 88

Fortran, 121–122

Fortune, 19, 153, 156, 217

Frame, J. D., 158–159, 177

IT consulting framework: advising principles underlying, 7–13; "approach the client" stage of, 28, 30–44; boundaries of, 25–26; "collaborate to select solutions" stage of, 29, 142–150; "deliver business results" stage of, 29, 152–181; "design solution options" stage of, 29, 106–141; graphical representation of, 27; "negotiate the relationship" stage of, 28, 46–63; overview of, 25–29; project management and, 157; seven stages of, 27–29; "understand the client's situation" stage of, 28–29, 78–104; "visualize success" stage of, 28, 64–77

Franklin, B., 153

Frink, L., 91, 102

G

Gale's Encyclopedia of Associations, 20

Gane, 114

Gap analysis, 2–3. *See also* As-is model; Discovery process; "Understand the client's situation"

Gartner Group, 91, 174

Gateway's Reseller Partner program, 198

General Electric, 68

Glass room, 22, 218

Go/no-go decisions, 167

Goal setting: for facilitated work sessions, 97; for IT consultant development, 212–213

Good, fast, or cheap, prioritizing by, 56–57

Graham, R. M., 121, 124

Green field environment, 167

Guarantee to client, 221–222

H

Hackers, 112, 188, 199

Hammer, M., 72

Heisenberg, 88

Help desk, 189

Hewlett-Packard, 110, 215

HP OpenView, 114

Hoffman, T., 18, 23

Holmes, S., 79, 101

Honest communication, 71

Hosting of meetings, 97

Hot spares, 167

HTML, 214

Human resource planning, 196–197

Huxley, A., 221

Hypothesis, 79–80

I

IBM Global Services, 188

Ideas, filtering of, 128–131

Ideation, 119–121; techniques of, 124–126

IDEO Product Design Services, 108

IDEO University training program, 108–109, 118

Impartiality, in facilitated work sessions, 98

Implementation, 29; approach to, 159–177; building in, from the beginning, 156–157; in case study, 177, 178–181; communication during process of, 161, 162–164; in "deliver business results" stage, 152–181; failures of, 153–155; IT consultant's responsibility for, 154–155; knowledge transfer and, 171–172; pilot testing, 169–171; planning, 160–161; planning, in design stage, 133–137; project management for consistent, 157–159; quality management of, 167–169; review of, 175; technical, 166–167; testing, 168–169; training and, 164–166; transition from, to operations, 173–175; vendor involvement in, 172–173. *See also* Business-centered approach; "Deliver business results" stage

Implementation team, 161

Inclusion, in facilitated work sessions, 98

Independent Computer Consultant's Association (ICCA), 216

Industry-standard components, 113, 116

Industry trade magazines, 217

Inertia, 65–66, 67, 68; generating momentum versus, 66–71; politics and, 203–204

Influence, 203–204

Information Movement and Management, 81

Information technology architecture diagrams, 192

IT consultant(s): average tenure of, 18, 222; career development for, 209–220; characteristics of highly utilized, 15–17; client's initial assessment of, 32–34; cornerstones for successful, 221–223; deficiency of business skills in, 18–19; deficiency of communication skills in, 22, 73; political relationships of, 203–206; responsibility of, for implementation, 154–155; role definition of, 7, 10–11, 48, 50; role of, in solutions presentation meeting, 147–148; satisfaction of, 221, 222–223; shortage of, 18, 222–223; skills critical to, listed, 17; technology bias in, 12, 144–145; value-added services of, 185–201. *See also* Development; Novice IT consultants; Role definition; Skills; Solo IT consultants; Team-based IT consultants

IT consulting: advisory skills for, 5–13; ambiguity in, 47–50; client motivations for seeking, 31–32; cornerstones for successful, 221–223; desktop PC revolution and, 22, 193; IT contracting versus, 1–2; migration of resellers to, 2, 197; politics in, 203–206; total solutions approach to, 185–201

IT consulting firms, 188

IT consulting skill set. *See* Skills, IT consulting

IT human resource planning, 196–197

IT trade publications, 18, 118–119, 197, 215

InfoWorld, 197

Infrastructure (component of Enterprise IT Model), 82, 83, 84; design at level of, 124; discovery tools for, 86, 114; review of existing documentation on, 86; solution architecture at level of, 132

Infrastructure statement, 124

Initial meeting, 28, 30–44; assessment in, of potential for success, 32–37; in case study, 38–44; client evaluation and counter-evaluation in, 32–34; client motivations and, 31–32; Engagement Profile Form for, 34–37. *See also* "Approach the client" stage

Innovation: inertia and, 66; techniques for fostering, 108–109. *See also* Creativity

Installed base: advantages and disadvantages of working from, 65–66; design issues and, 110

Installs, moves, adds, changes (IMACs), 189

Integration team, 69

Integration test, 168–169

IBM, 110

Internet: for business information, 20; for technical skill development, 18, 216

Internet connectivity strategy development, 47–48

Internet explosion, 214–215

Interviews, for discovery, 85, 100–101; facilitation skills for, 100–101; participants in, 100; preparation for, 100; roster for, 100

Intranets, project communication on, 71

Introductions: in facilitated work sessions, 98; in solutions presentation meeting, 146

Inventory database programs, 90

Inventory, in discovery process, 85, 89–91; asset management data for, 89, 90; collection form or program for, 91; components of, 90–91; questions for, 90; reporting structure for, 91; strategy for, 91; update mechanism for, 91

Inventory management. *See* Asset management

Ishikawa (fishbone) diagrams, 131

Itemized plans, 160–161

J

Jargon, 147

Java, 110, 214

Jefferson, T., 15

of, 57; overview of, 28, 46; role definition in, 11, 47–50; scope definition in, 53–55; six rules of negotiation for, 50–51; support and commitment issues in, 53; testing your agreement in, 53. *See also* Role definition

Negotiation skills, 50–51, 206

Nerds or propeller heads, 18, 22, 116

NetViz, 114

Network Computing, 118, 197

Network mapping, 114

Network technology, 82, 110, 118, 166–167, 194

Networking, personal: in client organization, 205; with colleagues, 18, 119, 214

Neutrality, 12

New clients: cost of gaining, versus retaining existing, 186; role definition with, 10–11

Newton, I., 79

Nietzsche, F., 209

Nortel, 215

Not-to-exceed pricing, 56

Novell: NetWare, 110, 118; *Support Connection* CD, 198; training materials of, 215; website of, 118

Novell Certified NetWare Engineer (CNE), 215

Novice IT consultants, business inexperience of, 19

O

Observation: in discovery process, 85, 87–89; in initial meeting, 33

Obsolescence, avoiding, 115

Office of Technology Policy, U.S. Department of Commerce, 18, 23

Olsen, K., 66

Open Systems Interconnect (OSI) model, 82

OpenView, 114

Operating manual, 193. *See also* Documentation

Operational procedures: documentation of, 192; writing, 187–188

Operations, 28; advising clients on, 186–188; design and provision of, 187–188; managing the transition to, 173–175; staffing of, 196–197

Options: design of, 106–141; final report of, 148; levels of, 145–146; presentation of, 142–150. *See also* "Collaborate to select solutions" stage; Design; Design process; "Design solution options" stage; Solution architecture; Solutions

Oracle approach to consulting, 8

Oracle of Delphi, 8

Organizational change, 72–73

Osborne, A., 125, 137

Outsourcing: of asset management, 194; of IT support, 26, 173, 188–189

P

Partnering for results, 3. *See also* "Collaborate to select solutions" stage; "Deliver business results" stage

Partnership selling, 217

PBS news shows, 19, 217

PC Magazine, 197, 215

PC Week, 18

Performance criteria development, for client staff, 196

Perlis, A. J., 121

Personal computer (PC) revolution, 22, 66, 193

Personality assessment, 9

PERT technique, 157

Pfeiffer, E., 153

Phased acceptance, 176

Physical security, 112

Pilot test team, 170

Pilot testing, 116–117; as baseline, 171; documentation of, 171; evaluation of results of, 171; formal plan for, 170; rules for conduct of, 170

Politics, 203–206; skills of, 205–206

Porter, M., 72

Post-it Notes, 101

Preparation: of delivery plan, 133–137; for facilitated work sessions, 96–97; for interviews, 100; professionalism of, 96–97; of solution options presentation, 146

Presentation of solution options: audience for, 146; delivery of, 142–150; preparation for, 133–137, 146; results orientation in, 146; tips on presenting, 147–148

Presentation of training, 165–166

Pricing, 56, 214. *See also* Budget

Prioritizing: of ideas in "design solution options" stage, 128–131; in "negotiate the relationship" stage, 56–57

Problem diagnosis and resolution support, 187

Problem statement, 28. *See also* "Visualize success" stage

Procedure writing, 187–188, 192

Process (component of Enterprise IT Model), 82, 83, 84; design at level of, 123; review of existing documentation on, 87; solution architecture at level of, 133

Process-driven solutions, 186–188, 210–211

Process statement, 123

Procurement, assisting clients with, 197–199

Product engineering methodologies, 119–121

Product procurement, as value-added service, 197–199

Professional organizations, 119, 216

Professional standards and professionalism, 5–6; in assessment of potential success, 36–37; in design, 115, 117–118; discovery process and, 80, 85–86; due diligence and, 80, 102; personal code of conduct and, 205; preparation and, 96–97; in solutions presentation, 146; in technical implementation, 167

Profile of skills, 211–212

Programmer for hire, 47, 48

Programming history, 121–122

Project delivery phase. *See* "Deliver business results" stage

Project management and planning, 177; in case study, 177, 178–181; for consistent implementation, 157–159; in design stage, 133–137; developing skills in, 157–159, 218; IT consulting

framework and, 158; teachability of, 16; tools of, 136. *See also* Implementation

Project Management Body of Knowledge (PMBOK), 16, 158, 159, 218

Project Management Institute (PMI), 16, 158, 159, 218

Project management methodology, 29

Project Management Professional certification, 16, 158, 218

Project plan: as output of implementation planning, 161; sample (Superior Systems/Capstate case study), 249–251

Project sponsor, 49

Project sponsorship teams, 68–69; creating a vision communication plan with, 69–70

Project steering committee, 68–69; creating a vision communication plan with, 69–70

Project vision. *See* Vision statement; "Visualize success" stage

Project website, 71, 162–164

Proposal, sample (CapState Chemical Company Relocation Project), 52, 57, 233–242

Prototyping, 108

Purity, political, 206

Q

Quality management, 167–169

Questioning, in facilitated work sessions, 97–98

Questionnaires. *See* Surveys

Quick-and-dirty approach, 115, 117, 169, 185

R

Randell, B., 121, 137

Raphaelian, G., 174, 177

Rapid design contest, 108

Recordkeeping: in brainstorming sessions, 125; in facilitated work sessions, 98; of interviews, 101; of project, 191. *See also* Documentation

Recovery errors, 169

Recruitment profiles, 196

Rees, 131

Reference checking, vendor, 116, 117

critical coverage of, 17–18; development of, sources and methods of, 18, 197–198, 214–216; focus on advisory skills versus, 1–4, 5–6, 155–156; Internet-related, 214–215

Technological change, and need for continuous skill development, 17–18, 214–215

Technology bias, 12, 144–145

Technology for technology's sake, 72–73, 113

Technology infrastructure. *See* Infrastructure

Television business news, 19–20, 217

Testing, 113, 168–169; methods of, 168–169; pilot, 169–171; results to look for in, 169

Theories, facts and, 79–80, 101

Thomas Register, 20

Three C's (collaboration, communication, and culture), 156–157

3Com Palm V hand-held organizer, 108

3Com routers and switches, 110, 215

Time, building, in project plan, 136

Time contract, for facilitated work sessions, 97

Tivoli, 114

Toastmasters, 214, 218

Top-down design, 122–125

Total solutions, 185–201. *See also* Value-added service

Trade publications: industry, 217; IT, 18, 118–119, 197, 215

Training: audience identification for, 164, 165; built-in to design, 114–115; communication of plan for, 163; content for, 165–166; customizing, 166; to ensure maintainability, 113; evaluating and revising, 166; marketing of, 166; methods and materials for, 164, 165–166; planning and implementing, 164–166; staff for, 165; as value-added service, 115; vendor, 215. *See also* Development, IT consultant

Transfer of knowledge, 171–172

Transferred authority, 205

Transition to operations, 173–175

Triple constraint, 56–57

Troubleshooting the consulting relationship, 203–208

Trusting atmosphere, 89

Try-before-you-buy services, 51

Typical day visualization, 212

U

Uncertainty principle, 88

"Understand the client's situation" stage, 78–104; as-is model creation in, 80, 101–102; budgeting and, 55; in case study, 102, 103–104; data collection methods for, 85–101; deliverables of, 101–102; discovery process approach in, 80–81; discovery process methods in, 85–101; Enterprise IT Model for, 81–85; goals of, 80–81; importance of, 79–80; overview of, 28–29, 78. *See also* As-is model; Current state analysis; Discovery process

Uniform communication, 70–71

U.S. Department of Commerce, Office of Technology Policy, 18, 23

U.S. Manufacturers Directory, 20

Unproductive efficiency, 113

Upgrades, 89, 187–188, 190, 194

User-groups, 18, 216

Users: as clients, 9, 49; communication with, 13, 162–164; interviews with, 100; involving, in transition to operations, 174

Utilization rates of IT staff, 15

V

Value-added service: asset management as, 193–196; documentation as, 190–193; IT human resource planning as, 196–197; operational policies and procedures as, 186–188; product procurement as, 197–199; rationale for, 185–186; security as, 199–201; support and maintenance as, 188–189; total solutions for, 185–201; training as, 115; visioning as, 73

Vargo, M., 91, 102

Rick Freedman is the founder of Consulting Strategies, Inc., an IT training and consulting firm. He has sixteen years of experience as an IT consultant, both as an employee of Fortune 500 firms such as Citicorp and Dun & Bradstreet, and as a principal consultant for Cap Gemini America and ENTEX Information Services. Rick presents seminars on information technology and consulting skills to organizations nationwide.

Consulting Strategies, Inc. trains and coaches IT professionals in corporations and professional services firms in basic consultative skills and behaviors. Through the use of its proprietary training programs such as *IT Consulting 101, IT Project Management 101,* and *Selling IT Services 101,* CSI helps technicians, engineers, and sales professionals become business advisors. Please visit CSI's website at www.consulting-strategies.com.

You can reach Rick at rickfman@consulting-strategies.com.

SYSTEM REQUIREMENTS

Windows PC
- 486 or Pentium processor-based personal computer
- Microsoft Windows 95 or Windows NT 3.51 or later
- Minimum RAM: 8 MB for Windows 95 and NT
- Available space on hard disk: 8 MB Windows 95 and NT
- 2X speed CD-ROM drive or faster
- Netscape 3.0 or higher browser or MS Internet Explorer 3.0 or higher

Macintosh
- Macintosh with a 68020 or higher processor or Power Macintosh
- Apple OS version 7.0 or later
- Minimum RAM: 12 MB for Macintosh
- Available space on hard disk: 6MB Macintosh
- 2X speed CD-ROM drive or faster
- Netscape 3.0 or higher browser or MS Internet Explorer 3.0 or higher

NOTE: This CD requires Netscape 3.0 or MS Internet Explorer 3.0 or higher. You can download these products using the links on the CD-ROM Help Page.

GETTING STARTED

Insert the CD-ROM into your drive. The CD-ROM will usually launch automatically. If it does not, click on the CD-ROM drive on your computer to launch. You will see an opening page. You can click on this page or wait for it to fade to the Copyright Page. After you click to agree to the terms of the Copyright Page, the Home Page will appear.

MOVING AROUND

Use the buttons at the left of each screen or the underlined text at the bottom of each screen to move among the menu pages. To view a document listed on one of the menu pages, simply click on the name of the document. To quit a document at any time, click the box at the upper right-hand corner of the screen.

Use the scrollbar at the right of the screen to scroll up and down each page.

To quit the CD-ROM, you can click the Quit option at the bottom of each menu page, hit Control-Q, or click the box at the upper right-hand corner of the screen.

TO DOWNLOAD DOCUMENTS

Open the document you wish to download. Under the File pulldown menu, choose Save As. Save the document onto your hard drive with a different name. It is important to use a different name, otherwise the document may remain a read-only file.

You can also click on your CD drive in Windows Explorer and select a document to copy it to your hard drive and rename it.

IN CASE OF TROUBLE

If you experience difficulty using the The IT Consultant CD-ROM, please follow these steps:

1. Make sure your hardware and systems configurations conform to the systems requirements noted under "Systems Requirements" above.

2. Review the installation procedure for your type of hardware and operating system. It is possible to reinstall the software if necessary.

3. You may call Jossey-Bass or Jossey-Bass/Pfeiffer Customer Service at (415) 433-1740 between the hours of 8 A.M. and 5 P.M. Pacific Time, and ask for Jossey-Bass CD-ROM Technical Support.

Please have the following information available:
- Type of computer and operating system
- Version of Windows or Mac OS being used
- Any error messages displayed
- Complete description of the problem.
- (It is best if you are sitting at your computer when making the call.)